THE PRIVATE IS POLITICAL

The Private Is Political

Identity and Democracy in the Age of Surveillance Capitalism

Ray Brescia

NEW YORK UNIVERSITY PRESS
New York, New York

NEW YORK UNIVERSITY PRESS
New York
www.nyupress.org

Library of Congress Cataloging-in-Publication Data
Names: Brescia, Ray, author.
Title: The private is political : identity and democracy in the age of surveillance capitalism /
Ray Brescia.
Description: New York, New York : New York University Press, 2025. |
Includes bibliographical references and index.
Identifiers: LCCN 2024007786 (print) | LCCN 2024007787 (ebook) |
ISBN 9781479832330 (hardback) | ISBN 9781479832347 (ebook) |
ISBN 9781479832392 (ebook other)
Subjects: LCSH: Electronic surveillance—Law and legislation | Computer networks—
Law and legislation. | Privacy, Right of—Political aspects. | Identity politics. |
Information technology—Social aspects. | Consumer behavior—Data processing. |
Consumer profiling—Data processing. | Democracy.
Classification: LCC K3264.C65 B74 2025 (print) | LCC K3264.C65 (ebook) |
DDC 343.09/99—dc23/eng/20240224
LC record available at https://lccn.loc.gov/2024007786
LC ebook record available at https://lccn.loc.gov/2024007787

This book is printed on acid-free paper, and its binding materials are chosen for strength
and durability. We strive to use environmentally responsible suppliers and materials to the
greatest extent possible in publishing our books.

Manufactured in the United States of America

10 9 8 7 6 5 4 3 2 1

Also available as an ebook

For Amy and Leo

CONTENTS

1

Political Privacy and the Integrity of Identity

Early in the digital age, before smartphones became personal appendages, techno-futurist Ray Kurzweil envisioned a new type of consciousness—"the singularity"—that would emerge as a product of the fusion of computers and human intellect.[1] While this prediction has not yet come to pass, in many ways the melding of the personal and the digital is well underway. Since the early 1990s, an array of new technologies has transformed the ways we live and the power of individuals to influence society and change the world. With the rise of the internet, mobile technologies, social media, and artificial intelligence, the ability of individuals, groups, movements, and political parties to effectuate change has never been greater. A video of the police killing of George Floyd in Minnesota, captured by a teenage bystander on her smartphone, goes viral, launching massive protests across the United States and even around the world. Creative leaders and organizations use online petitions and social media networks to combat human trafficking.[2] Groups can form overnight on social media platforms, seeking to address issues great and small, from global climate change to improving traffic safety in a local school zone. Images of human rights atrocities can circulate throughout the world, raising awareness and shining a spotlight on rogue states.[3] A mass shooter can livestream indiscriminate murder.[4] A machine gun operated from a thousand miles away can carry out an assassination.[5] An insurrection can organize itself on Facebook.[6] In the words of legal scholars Woodrow Hartzog and Neil Richards: "When the internet entered the public consciousness in the mid-1990s, it was touted as promising revolutionary empowerment of citizens and a new, more responsive democracy. Two decades later, we can see that some of those revolutionary promises were naïve at best."[7]

What is more, soon we are likely to see the widespread adoption of driverless cars; the proliferation of the Internet of Things, a global network of products connected to the internet and to each other; and the encroachment of generative artificial intelligence across all aspects of life. Records of our bodily functions will be digitized and medical treatment revolutionized. Computer servers throughout the world will contain a vast amount of biometric data about us. Our movements will be monitored, just as our steps are being tracked today. Strangers will know and artificial intelligence will track our heart rate, breathing, glucose levels, body temperature, and other biometric data in real time. Our state of being itself—our opinions, our moods, our fears—will fall within this digital system, a shadow, parallel world, like the "Upside Down" from the Netflix retro sci-fi thriller *Stranger Things*. It is in this world where blurry, spectral versions of us will take shape; yet the characteristics of our avatars may be a more accurate reflection of us than the image we project of ourselves in the real world.

While the existence of such a future state of affairs may be discomforting, in reality it is already with us in many respects. Companies are creating "data voodoo dolls," as one venture capitalist has called them,[8] which represent not just our online actions but also our thoughts: the information gleaned from the internet searches we conduct; the items we post and share with our friends; the online groups we join; the comments we make on social media; the medical symptoms about which we inquire; the information we seek regarding current events; our inquiries into efforts to make social change; the people with whom we may have intimate relations or even someone on whom we have the initial makings of a crush.[9] George Orwell's Big Brother had nothing on the surveillance state that currently exists.

This parallel universe paints a deeper and more disturbing picture than anything Orwell imagined. He described "Thoughtcrime" as "the essential crime that contains all others in itself."[10] The commission of such a crime occurred when one passed along a subversive message, wrote something critical of the state in a diary, or whispered secrets to a lover. Today's surveillance state monitors thoughts themselves as manifest in our digital actions: our movements; our fleeting ideas; and the whims we might express in internet searches, the things we watch, the networks of which we are a part. These are our associations: both with what and whom we associate and the things, people, and groups that are associated with us.

But it is not any government that operates in or maintains this shadow world. The digital Upside Down is a space run mostly by private entities: the companies that draw us into it and extract from us some of life's most intimate details. It is this information that populates this shadowy world. It also represents our very identity, with all of its complexity, messiness, shading, and depth.[11]

There are aspects of this identity we do not disclose to others or reveal to only a select few of our closest friends. We also can choose to publicize and make this identity manifest in important ways, by seeking out and associating with others to not just explore this identity but realize it. We search for others who share characteristics of this identity and make communities, both real and virtual, that reflect it. What is more, it is through this identity that we pursue political goals, large and small, and satisfy our innate desire for the individual and collective self-determination that is at the heart of the democratic project. This identity becomes a catalyst for communion and an engine for social change, as we *identify as* having certain characteristics or beliefs, we *identify with* others who share those beliefs, and we are *identified by* others as having those characteristics and beliefs when such information about us is apparent to or surmised by others.[12] Furthermore, the mere sharing of such personal information can create trust and develop bonds that can serve as lubricants for cooperation.[13]

Identity is not just a linchpin of our views of ourselves but is also a means to connect with others and a lever for communal and societal change.[14] It operates on two planes. It is internal, reflecting our subjective understanding of the self and our individual identity.[15] It is also external and physical, manifest and realized in our associations with others: the groups we join, the alliances we form, the movements we support. In turn, this identity becomes a catalyst for change as we harness, realize, and shape this identity and live it out in collaboration with others while directing it toward broader impact, whether in one's block or hometown or on a global scale.

Political science has long taken note of the role that identity plays in American politics[16] and the ways in which social movements have leveraged identity to shape life in the United States.[17] I am not talking about "identity politics" here, or at least the ways in which that term has been brandished in recent years as essentially a slur. Indeed, identity politics, when only white men could vote and served as the vehicle through which systems of oppression existed based on identity, played out every day in the United States for nearly a century. It continues through to this day in many respects, preserving existing hierarchies and subordinating classes of people based on an identity that is often ascribed to them. What I am talking about here is different, though at times related. "Identity" as I use it here reflects the ways in which many different identities can form who we are and those with whom we identify: one's status as a voter, as a firearms enthusiast or gun-control advocate, as an educator or medical professional, as someone who believes there should be universal daylight savings time, as someone who wants to express their identity as a woman. The list can go on and on. When these identities serve as a catalyst for change, collaboration, communion, and individual and collective self-determination, they can play out in the public arena, as we work with others of like minds—who share an identity—to work together toward a goal. While the "identity" that might be ascribed to someone using an identity-politics lens might also include an identity that one would embrace and leverage as a catalyst for change, this is not the only type of identity that can play out in social movement mobilization. Yes, one might be labeled a "liberal tree-hugger" by someone wishing to demean them; "environmental activist" might be the identity that individual might embrace. Realizing their activism becomes a part of their identity, however they might describe it.

Given the current communications landscape and the tools available for individuals to find one another, it is easier than ever to find people who share similar interests and identities, who may want the same things, and who will work collectively with others to achieve them. When, in the not-too-distant past, one might have had to hide an aspect of one's identity, never even knew what it meant to have such an identity, and never knew there might be people just like them, today it is easier to explore aspects of one's identity and possibly find someone or a community with which one might identify. These identities can become sources of strength, of self-realization, and can become a catalyst for change. And the technology exists now that makes this exploration easier than at any point in human history.

When Shannon Watts heard news of the school shooting at Sandy Hook Elementary in Connecticut in late 2012, she was folding laundry.

A former communications executive who had turned to raising her five children on a full-time basis, she did not consider herself an advocate or someone who could effectuate broad-based social change. Nevertheless, she decided she had to do something about rampant gun violence in the United States. She created a Facebook page, which was first titled "One Million Moms for Gun Control." With seventy-five friends on Facebook, she did not know how much of an impact her efforts would have. Slowly momentum began to build online.[18] Today, the group, which now goes by the name "Moms Demand Action," boasts almost 10 million supporters with chapters in every state. She considers herself an "accidental activist," someone who was not all that active (prior to starting this group, of course), not someone who ever imagined herself becoming a national leader for gun safety in the United States.[19] But through her grit and determination, and a major assist from social media, she found other individuals equally incensed about the spread of gun violence in the country. The connections she formed became the backbone of a national movement. It also changed her identity: she became a national advocate for gun control and has inspired millions to take their own action in their own communities for reform.

But this new capacity for identity formation and advocacy is not without its risks. New digital tools and a fragmented and fragmenting media landscape have increased not only the melding of identity and political mobilization[20] but also political polarization.[21] We see this across the political spectrum, from advocacy on behalf of the rights of trans people to efforts to forbid the teaching of certain issues in schools and the banning of books that are disfavored by conservative activists. Because of the new tools at our disposal, our digital activities are also deeply connected to identity formation as well as efforts to pursue collective self-determination in line with that identity. At the same time, virtually all information about such activities—and our identities—is subject to sale, use, and disclosure beyond the typical consumer's knowledge. But much of the way our information is handled and distributed is entirely legal. Indeed, what many might consider privacy violations have become fairly common. We are in, as Harvard's Shoshana Zuboff calls it, a period of Surveillance Capitalism, in which private companies mine our information and trade on it.[22] It is certainly no great cause for concern when information available about our thoughts and actions is accessed to advertise to us and tell us, as the Rolling Stones once lamented, how white our shirts can be.[23] But when that information is used to chill our political actions, stifle our ability to collaborate with others, or restrict our capacity to bring about social change—or when its use results in violence or oppression—we are way beyond selling consumer products. The ride-hailing company Uber has used information about its drivers to monitor their participation in political rallies.[24] The computer behemoth Apple limited its employees' use of the collaborative communication app Slack when it became apparent that they were using it to advocate for pay equity at the company.[25] A trove of internal documents and data from inside Facebook revealed that the company is aware of the many ways in which its product is being used to foment discord.[26] Such violations threaten not just our identities but also the functioning of democracy itself. They are even more pernicious because, by stifling civic engagement and social mobilization, they impact our ability to strengthen the legal regime that could protect against such intrusions upon our private information in the first place. With another nod to Orwell, while all privacy infractions are harmful, some infractions are more harmful than others.

The search for identity and for communion with others who share it has never been easier in all of human history. At the same time, our individual and collective identity is also under threat by a surveillance state like none that has ever existed before. This surveillance state can be weaponized, not just for profit but also to promote political ends, and undermine efforts to achieve individual and collective self-determination. When our digital self is endangered in these ways, so are our identities and our efforts to collaborate with others to create the world we wish to inhabit as we strive to realize the promise of democracy, which is individual self-determination multiplied. Indeed, the political ramifications of these threats are profound, and they are all around us, despite repeated instances where the system has been blinking red.

Political Privacy, Identity, and Democracy

The new technologies already among us and those that will emerge in the near future can bring the world together like never before and are likely to change life dramatically in the coming decades. But the very same technologies that provide the capacity for identity formation, communion, and change actually have within them the ability to curtail our power to impact the social arrangements themselves: our political activities; communal life; democratic institutions; and the laws that construct and constrain the entire human enterprise, including the laws that protect privacy. The ability to access the information harvested through these technologies threatens the private spheres within which critical identity-forming and social change–making functions take place. While all violations of privacy can have harmful effects on an individual, I will focus on a particular type of privacy here—what I call "political privacy"—to show not just how critical it is to human flourishing but also how, when we endanger it, we are endangering our ability to realize democracy and individual and collective self-determination.

This form of privacy, political privacy, is so important to us because our individual and collective identity is reflected in our choices and desires, our personal and political affiliations, the social activities in which we engage, and the social movements in which we participate. This identity plays a central role in realizing our individual and collective self-determination, the act of individual and collective meaning-making, the cultivation of social capital, the formation of societal trust, and efforts to bring about of social change that overcomes subordination. Central to the democratic process is the maintenance of what I call throughout this work the *"integrity of identity,"* defined here as the protection of our ability to preserve a private sphere for the pursuit, cultivation, and maintenance of the self.[27] In this new, hyperconnected world, that sphere includes a range of phenomena: the information we seek over digital platforms, the candidates for whom we vote, the political parties with which we associate, the groups through which we advocate for that social change, and the political arrangements we pursue. Our identity is not just a source of those choices but also a product of them as well. When we seek to change society, we must link with others to seek avenues for making such change, and when that identity is *shared*, it becomes a well-spring of collective action.[28] When that identity is *multiplied*, the connection between individual identity and collective identity becomes apparent. This connection is essential to mobilization, which occurs when one's personal identity is tied to that of a social movement and then takes on a collective identity in union with others.[29]

Protecting the integrity of this identity is no less important to democracy and the pursuit of self-determination than are freedom of speech, the sanctity of the vote, and the right to organize. In fact, protecting the integrity of identity is often a gateway to the achievement and maintenance of these other rights and is thus central to the functioning of democracy. This integrity of identity is protected mostly through the cluster of phenomena that has come to be known as the "right to privacy,"[30] but it is through a particular type of privacy—political privacy—where these broader notions of free speech, associational rights, the right of self-determination, and the ability to bring about social change are centered. While some legal scholarship addresses the role that privacy plays in promoting individual autonomy in democracies,[31] this book approaches the issue of political privacy from a somewhat different perspective. It brings a body of social movement scholarship to bear on the understanding of the role this form of privacy—as manifest in the integrity of individual and collective identity—plays in liberal democracies. Informed by this body of social movement scholarship, I will attempt to elevate the importance of the integrity of both individual and group identity as collective and public goods themselves—as products of, and which are manifest in, our associational ties. When these associational ties are threatened, democracy itself is in jeopardy. Indeed, because of the benefits this form of privacy brings, its protection is central to democratic society.

Political privacy is, by no means, the only kind of privacy that exists, nor is it the only one that matters. At the same time, its importance to the democratic project cannot be overstated. Privacy scholar Danielle Citron describes another kind of privacy: what she calls "sexual privacy,"[32] which "concerns the social norms governing the management of boundaries around intimate life," including "access to and information about" naked bodies, "sexual desires, fantasies, and thoughts"; and "communications related to . . . sex, sexuality, and gender."[33] Such privacy is critical to "the exercise of human agency and sexual autonomy," and it permits individuals, especially those from marginalized communities,[34] to "set the boundaries of their intimate lives."[35] For these reasons, for Citron, the protection of sexual privacy is an important component of a society that promotes individual human flourishing. What is more, with new, digital communications tools, and the ease with which they can be utilized to infringe upon sexual privacy, the threats to sexual privacy are real and exceedingly harmful. Citron also asserts that this form of privacy also has implications for politics in that individuals who fear that their intimate lives might be exposed should they enter electoral politics might refrain from doing so or might have to leave public life if they are subject to such exposure. This happened to U.S. Representative Katie Hill when naked images of her were released to the public, leading to her resign her position in Congress.[36] As Citron explains: "When victims of intimate privacy violations withdraw from online and offline activities, we are left with less diverse and less rich public conversations."[37] But the potential political ramifications of breaches of sexual privacy are second-order effects. When political privacy itself is breached, the impacts are more closely linked to democracy.

What is more, ensuring a degree of sexual privacy—especially in light of the risks to it posed by new technologies—serves as a way to *protect* marginalized communities. As such, we might consider it to be what political theorist Isaiah Berlin called a "negative" liberty or right, a *freedom from* intrusion.[38] The concept of political privacy goes further, however. We can certainly conceptualize it as a sphere that also deserves protection, where one should be free from interference. But it does more. It is what Berlin would also call a "positive" right: a *freedom to* achieve something. When one enjoys political privacy, one can realize their political identity. Similarly, when privacy is seen strictly as an individual right, as is more common in the context of sexual privacy, it can also undermine the ability of groups to build collective power by drawing the focus away from group interests and toward those of atomized individual actors.[39]

Political privacy also serves as an engine of democratic action, a springboard for association-building and the formation of social capital, a means of solving collective-action problems, and a centerpiece of democracy itself. What is more, this form of privacy is manifest in our associations—both those ways in which we realize our identity *in* those associations as well as how we identify *with* those with whom we associate. Thus, political privacy is deeply associational, more so than sexual privacy. In this way, privacy is, as described by legal scholar Salomé Viljoen, "relational" because a "basic purpose of data production as a commercial enterprise is to relate people to one another based on relevant shared population features."[40] As with sexual privacy, though, all forms of privacy are tied to the medium used to communicate, and the shape, scope, structure, use, and value of privacy all change and evolve as the media utilized to make these associational ties also change.

Moreover, our ability to communicate helps to shape with whom and how we cooperate as well as the reach and extent of the potential for cooperation. The limits of our ability to communicate with others and process information about a group of individuals appears hard-wired, a product of evolution that is, perhaps, still evolving. Early tribes and bands of hunters maintained discipline, recruited new members, and gave directions and orders in the field of battle or in pursuit of a mammoth through oral communications and hand gestures. As the research of Robin Dunbar and others has shown, the human brain at present is able to process information regarding about 150 people at a time: to develop relationships with them, foster trust, and understand whether they are good potential partners and mates.[41] Similarly, the ability to communicate commands and expressions of cooperation, when limited by the ability to communicate orally, probably corresponds to this number of people.

Yet the capacity to commit information to writing helped to convey guidance and messages to networks of supporters and recruits well beyond one's kin, immediate circle of friends, and allies. The printing press reduced the cost and difficulty of spreading such messages. The telegraph and telephone then made it possible to convey news of events to galvanize and activate supporters in real time, facilitating the instantaneous coordination of actions among advocacy groups. But such innovations in communications did not just facilitate improved coordination between ever-larger groups of people: they also catalyzed the emergence of new social movements, at least in the United States.

Indeed, over the course of American history, social movements have had a symbiotic relationship with the technology that makes communication and organizing possible. New social movements in the United States have often taken root at the same time as the introduction of a new means of communication.[42] The American revolutionary spirit emerged with the expansion of the printing press in the New World, helping to bind a new nation together and creating a nascent national identity.[43] When steam power then supercharged the printing press, it increased the output of these machines exponentially, strengthening the then-nascent Abolitionist Movement in the 1830s.[44] A decade later, the telegraph helped launch the Women's Movement, spreading word of the historic convention in Seneca Falls, New York, and encouraging others to convene and organize for women's rights and interests.[45] The Progressive Era came about in the wake of the invention and widespread adoption of the telephone and the construction of the transcontinental railroad; both helped progressive leaders communicate and travel throughout the country in the pursuit of sweeping legal and social reforms.[46] The Civil Rights Movement grew up with, and harnessed, the power of the television, creating opportunities to expose the vicious and brutal tactics utilized by Southern law enforcement and private vigilantes attempting to suppress community advocacy.[47]

As each new technology emerged on the scene, a new social movement embraced it and used it to advance its political ends. These connections are not merely coincidental; they are a product of more than new technologies introducing new ways of communicating and organizing. In the social change space, the introduction of a new mode of communicating seems to do more than merely change the way we communicate. As twentieth-century media theorist Marshall McLuhan argued, the medium "alter[s] our relations to one another and to ourselves."[48]

For millennia, one way this alteration of relations occurs when a new means of communication is introduced is that groups and movements often taken the shape of that new method of communication. When oral communication was the primary mode through which direction and inspiration could be shared, groups assumed a size and shape consistent with the reach of such local communication. In the United States— which had one of the more advanced postal systems in the world in the early nineteenth century, despite being a relatively new nation, and groups could correspond effectively with each other over the mails— new chapters of national organizations often formed wherever there was a new post office outpost.[49] Indeed, the American civic landscape was built upon the postal system's footprint. What is more, national groups with a grassroots base often mimicked not just the reach but also the very structure of the postal system: a large, nation-spanning network built upon local nodes.[50]

This basic organizational structure fostered an explosion of civic activity through what are sometimes referred to as "translocal groups"—

organizations with local chapters connected to hubs at the regional, state, and, ultimately, national levels.[51] This organizational form would last for roughly 200 years, from the colonial era through to the early 1970s, with groups as diverse as the Sons of Liberty, Shriners, the NAACP, and the Women's Christian Temperance Union all taking on this networked approach: local chapters connected to larger, nation-spanning networks.[52] Even during radio's emergence and the first few decades of television's existence, these technologies still assumed this shape. National broadcast networks were (and in many cases still are) connected to local affiliates, and their reach extended only as far as the power of their local signal. In the early 1970s, though, a new technology, the computerized mailing list, led to a transformation of social movements from translocal networks to groups with centralized leadership and professionalized staff—a membership on paper only, with no local base.[53] This new technology separated leaders from the traditional structure that groups had embraced since the founding of the republic: layers of grassroots groups embedded in a larger network.

The symbiotic relationship between technology and social movements means that such movements replicated the form of the latest communications technology available to them; as a result, technology has, in turn, helped to reshape the American civic landscape. In this way, in the words of McLuhan once again, the media become "extensions of ourselves," and the "personal and social consequences" of any media come about as they introduce a "new scale" into human endeavors.[54] No matter the technology, the shape of the social movement, or the movement's relative scale, however, advances in technology and individuals' use of that technology to organize and pursue social change also brought risk. Today, new technologies like generative artificial intelligence and quantum computing stand poised to supercharge all aspects of communications technologies in ways that are beneficial to humankind but, in others, that will likely prove destructive, completely shredding all semblance of digital privacy along the way and undermining the freedom to advance change.

But the history of all of these technologies and their incorporation into social movement advocacy also had another component to them. Each advance in the ability to communicate brought with it a new threat of surveillance and manipulation. A group's private communications could be subject to infiltration, exposing the group's members to real harm. Such surveillance could chill speech and subject group members to criticism, or worse, especially in disfavored or marginalized groups—that is, groups most in need of societal change. New technologies also have become the channels through which propaganda, "fake news," and efforts to shape public opinion spread. These technologies have mediated individuals' understanding of the world and even their sense of themselves.

Because of these phenomena, technological innovation brings new opportunities to change the social structure through social movement advocacy, but it also brings threats—and those threats diminish the ability to bring about change itself. What is more, the means of communication—and the integrity of group communications using such media—has often become a target of social movement advocacy itself as groups sought to ensure that they could communicate safely without fear of retribution. In other words, they have organized to secure political privacy itself, the essential freedom from which all other freedoms may emerge. Movement leaders over the course of American history have understood the symbiotic nature of this relationship among technology, privacy, and social change. Groups like the NAACP and the Southern Christian Leadership Conference harnessed the media to advance the cause of civil rights for the African American community. They would use the television and other forms of media to capture the brutal treatment of the protestors at Birmingham and Selma[55] and even used coded messages over the radio to coordinate demonstrations.[56] They also worked to preserve the integrity of their organizations for surveillance and intrusion. Some of the leading modern cases that protect the critical freedom of association emerged from the civil rights struggle,[57] even as the federal government routinely spied on Martin Luther King, Jr.[58]

Since before even the founding of the United States, social movement organizations have often made their ability to communicate effectively, safely, and free from intrusion if not the centerpiece of their efforts, then a critical component of them. One of the very first acts of the Continental Congress, before any fighting had occurred at Lexington and Concord, created a postal system free from oversight by Loyalist postmasters who could choose not to circulate rebel communications or, worse still, would open such communications, exposing activists to charges of treason.[59] In the early nineteenth century, the U.S. postal system spread throughout the United States and became a locus of community life. Fearing that the nation's citizens would become distracted from Sunday worship by activities at post offices when the mail came to town, and such distractions would undermine the collective identity of the nation as a god-fearing and pious one, a group known as Sabbatarians directed their efforts at shaping the functioning of this critical source of communication throughout the nation. It did so by advocating for the closure of post offices on Sundays, when, its members thought, communities should be engaged in religious worship, not occupying themselves with business affairs and social activities that often took place at the post office. Presbyterian minister Lyman Beecher, father of Harriet Beecher Stowe, proclaimed: "The present, undoubtedly, is the generation which is to decide the fate of this great empire, by deciding whether the Sabbath of God shall be preserved or blotted out."[60]

When the steam printing press gave the Abolitionist Movement a new technology that helped it distribute antislavery tracts throughout the Southern states, President Andrew Jackson sought the power to suppress the distribution of such literature,[61] and those printing presses and the individuals who operated them themselves often became the target of vandalism, violence, terror, and even death.[62] Today, as young people use social media sites like TikTok, efforts to rein in that service (or ban it), to place greater safeguards for minors, and to encourage stronger content moderation on social media generally have become the focus of advocacy campaigns, often waged on these social media platforms themselves. But, unlike in prior eras, a campaign to preserve political privacy over these new means of communication has not yet fully materialized, even as those technologies both offer social movements new means of organizing and agitating while also subjecting their members to greater and greater exposure. Still, as technology changes to create new ways of communicating and new forms of organization, the law must also change to preserve the capacities these new technologies offer to those who use them to bring about social change.[63]

New technologies make the search for one's political identity easier, more expansive, more affirming, and more liberating, but they also create a paradox: this search for identity and community is also one that, because of who has access to our online activities, is afforded few legal protections in most of the places where it occurs. Political privacy is generally protected from government intrusion because a relatively robust—or at least well-established—set of institutions and laws in the United States is supposed to guard its citizens from this type of intrusion by public actors. Under Surveillance Capitalism, however, the threat to these activities does not emanate, for the most part, from government. Indeed, while our individual and collective identities are subject to exposure, sale, distribution, and manipulation, much of this occurs outside the restrictions imposed on government actors. We might consider private actors that can infiltrate the integrity of identity Digital Pinkertons: private entities like those in years past that often surveilled and undermined fledgling unions and other social change organizations. Because of this, is the system that currently exists, which largely regulates public actors more than private ones, up to the task of protecting political privacy?

The Public and Private in Privacy Law

Because much of the private information in the Upside Down is under the control of private actors, the responsibility to safeguard it is governed mostly by what is known as "private law," the law that affects private actors, rather than public law, the law that constrains and guides the functions of government. (Think contracts rather than constitutions.) At the same time, the lines between public and private have become blurred, and governments can try to evade the restrictions imposed on them by seeking such information from the private entities that possess it.[64] When government actors circumvent public-law protections to obtain information protected only by the weaker private-law privacy regime, it is no less harmful than when government takes such action against us directly. Indeed, a violation of one's privacy is still meaningful regardless of the source. If what we might not tolerate from government is easily achieved because of the weaknesses in private law regarding our personal information, private-law protections of political privacy must keep pace with those found in public law. Whether there is what privacy scholars call "dignitary harm" due to violations of privacy,[65] like harm to one's reputation or a feeling that one is been disrespected,[66] or the intrusion upon one's private matters chills the actor from taking political action or from coordinating with others to advance social change, it probably does not matter whether the entity threatening one's private domain is a neighbor, the secret police, a local business, or a multinational corporation. Certainly, an intimidating visit from a government goon squad is far more dangerous than being the target of annoying email messages or cell-phone calls seeking to convince you to buy a product or extend your vehicle's warranty. Still, when a private entity can nudge you to join a radical group, pushes information to you on social media that foments violence, or sells your private information so that you could be the target of a financial scam, or worse, we are in dangerous territory. Privacy violations by private actors can be just as harmful and just as violative of the integrity of identity as those that emanate from government actors, even when a public official has no role in that violation. It is thus critical to protect the integrity of identity wherever it is threatened: in spaces governed by public law, but also those spaces where only private law applies.

Given the critical role that private digital platforms play in fostering the exploration, creation, and maintenance of individual and collective identity today,[67] and the growing role they are playing in social movement mobilization,[68] phenomena I will discuss in greater length in chapter 2, I argue here that the integrity of individual and collective identity deserves greater recognition and protection, especially in the digital space where such interests are exposed at present and where the law is less robust than in public-law settings. Democracy requires a high degree of protection for individual identity and political privacy, regardless of the source of the threat to that privacy.

Protecting Political Privacy and Preserving the Integrity of Identity

What I hope to show throughout this work is that the central political right—the right that makes all others possible—is privacy, and privacy of the political kind. Economist Paul Romer has defined "meta-ideas" as ideas that generate other ideas.[69] The preservation of the integrity of our identity is a "meta-right": a right that makes other rights possible.[70] The importance of the integrity of identity to democracy cannot be overstated. In subsequent chapters, I will explain how, in the United States at least, there is a fairly robust and long-running set of institutions, institutions that reach to the nation's constitutional firmament itself, that protects American citizens from intrusion into the sphere of political privacy and preserves the integrity of identity. That is, American public law goes far in protecting and preserving our political privacy. Once again, though, this generally restrains public actors. At the same time, in the digital Upside Down—that sphere of personal information amassed as a result of our activities in the digital realm—the threats to political privacy do not come primarily from those government actors. Yet, again, a threat to political privacy is no less troublesome if it comes from private rather than public actors. The fact that many of the threats to political privacy with respect to our digital existence emanate from private actors, and because the institutions that would protect privacy from nongovernmental actors are much weaker than those that constrain the government, enhanced protections for political privacy are necessary in the private-law context if we are to preserve the integrity of identity that is so central to the democratic project.

How should we protect this political privacy when private actors violate it? What are the best laws and settings for protecting political privacy in the private-law space? Are there legal protections, norms, practices, and actors that are better at protecting, or are in a better position to protect, political privacy than others?

Some believe that company self-regulation is sufficient to protect political privacy. Businesses operating in the digital space, the argument goes, should be free to act beyond the reach of regulators and legislators because those government officials do not understand the business models of these companies, and efforts to impose controls on the internet and mobile technologies will stifle competition and hinder innovation. There is something to this, as legislators are often at a loss to understand how such companies work. Famously, and displaying a staggering naivete, one member of the U.S. Congress as late as 2018 asked Facebook CEO Mark Zuckerberg how his company made money if it did not charge its customers for using its service; Zuckerberg gently told this legislator that the company sells advertising, indicating that its true customers are really the businesses that purchase information on the users of the product.[71]

At the same time, these companies have not proven capable of regulating themselves, often taking advantage of their customers and hiding behind complex provisions in end-user agreements that mean they are unaccountable to their users, especially around the sale and distribution of those users' private information. Companies also build into these agreements provisions that attempt to strip end users of the ability to go to court to challenge violations of their privacy by the companies. Contracts channel victims into industry-friendly fora that are difficult for private individuals to navigate, essentially immunizing the companies from liability. While the European Union and some U.S. states have stepped in to require companies to improve the disclosures surrounding their privacy practices, these laws do little in the way of improving the contracts the companies impose on their end users as the price of admission to the use of their products, and there does not seem to be enough political will to make significant changes that will protect privacy in a robust and meaningful way. Legal scholars regularly criticize the current state of privacy law. Woodrow Hertzog argues that it has become "ossified,"[72] and Ari Waldman has described the current system as a "house of cards."[73]

Even when legislators do step in to regulate the digital sphere, some would say that they can do more harm than good. As another legal scholar, Anupam Chander, has argued, government created Silicon Valley by, among other things, passage of the Communications Decency Act,[74] which provides internet and social media platforms with immunity for content that their users post over those platforms.[75] False and radicalizing information readily available on the internet and social media would not have a place there if we had robust mechanisms that required platforms to engage in more aggressive content moderation. Because of the immunity such platforms enjoy, there is little incentive for them to rid their sites of false, misleading, and violence-inducing information to make the internet and social media less harmful places. Issues of privacy are tied to this immunity because it is through the platforms' algorithms, based on personal information, that such content is pushed to us—a product of the identity-reflecting and identity-generating profiles those platforms maintain of us.[76]

As this book goes to print, the U.S. Congress continues to consider a national internet privacy law and explore whether and how to regulate artificial intelligence and even individual social media sites like Tik-Tok, and the United States Supreme Court has toyed with weakening the protections afforded through the Communications Decency Act. Some see the potential for federal oversight actually endangering efforts in the states to provide stronger protections to consumers, however. Indeed, through the process known as "federal preemption," if Congress regulates digital privacy in the United States and does not preserve the right of states to go beyond what federal law provides, that national legislation will displace more extensive efforts, providing companies with protection from stronger state oversight.[77] Thus, governments at different levels can work at cross-purposes when it comes to protecting political privacy.

One avenue for consumers to hold companies accountable for violations of their political privacy is through litigation, but, as I have already mentioned, many end-user agreements keep disputes between consumers and the companies that hold their personal data out of the courts. Although some lawsuits have had a degree of success in reining in some of the worst privacy abuses, even by private companies, the combination of private contracts and legislative immunity has proven a powerful barrier to robust judicial protection of political privacy, revealing how the functioning of markets, governments, and courts are deeply intertwined. It is thus difficult to move forward to protect digital privacy if these three settings fail to work together—or at least do not operate at cross-purposes—to produce effective protections for digital privacy.

Protecting the Integrity of Identity and Privacy

When it comes to ideas for regulating digital communications and protecting the integrity of identity, there is no shortage of recommendations. Some have argued that we should protect digital privacy as if it were a form of property.[78] Others assert that those managing digital privacy data act as fiduciaries in relation to those whose information they possess, meaning they must put the interests of the users ahead of their own interests.[79] Still others suggest that companies that possess information about consumers should have to pay those consumers to use those companies' digital platforms.[80] To date, these efforts have generated little in the way of actual policy innovation, however.

The approach I will introduce here provides not just a framework for protecting political privacy but also a methodology for generating actual change. It will also take an *institutional approach* to situating our understanding of the integrity of identity, how social change happens, and how to consider the locations where and methods by which we might protect political privacy. I have made several references to the term "institution" throughout this work already, and most readers would gloss over it, taking the term as a given. But think about what that term means for a moment and the ways in which we use it both in common conversation as well as in more theoretical discussions. It turns out that we use the term to mean many different things, yet it carries a certain weight. It tends to connote something more than the thing itself. Think of the United States Senate. It certainly is a governmental entity. But it is also an institution in the sense that it is has cultural importance. As a body, it retains a degree of respect from the broader community, both as an organization as a whole and for its individual members. Those members engage in certain habits and practices that are both passed down as cultural norms but are also written into the very rules by which the Senate operates. And it is a lawmaking body that follows proscribed guidelines and rules for making laws themselves. The Senate is thus a lawmaking body that holds a certain cultural position within society, follows written and unwritten rules for behavior, and follows those rules when it takes part in the passage of legislation. To put our understanding of the Senate in institutional terms then, using the term in its broadest sense, the Senate is an *institution* (an entity) that follows certain institutions (norms and rules) when it institutionalizes the institutional order (passes bills on their way to them becoming laws).

To return to the example of the Civil Rights Movement, groups like the NAACP, SCLC, and the Student Nonviolent Coordinating Committee were all institutions in their own right, both in their material and symbolic forms. They were symbolic in the sense that they stood for something and membership in the group conveyed that an individual embraced the cause. Each organization had a set of institutional practices, whether it was a top-down leadership style or one in which leaders of local chapters of these groups operated in a more bottom-up fashion. But even groups with charismatic (and, at times, incrementalist) leaders like Thurgood Marshall and Martin Luther King, Jr., had to, at times, respond to the grassroots demands for more immediate action and more aggressive reform.[81] What is more, these organizations (as institutions) engaged in efforts to reform what we might call the "institutional order" itself: the laws, norms, social and cultural practices, and mores that made up the broader Jim Crow system.

As I will explore in much greater detail in later chapters, institutions are organizations, the embedded practices of those organizations, and the legal and cultural structures that shape society. Certain types of organizations—social movements, large companies, prestigious universities, popular media outlets and social media sites, governmental bodies—hold greater institutional sway in society than others. They must also have a significant role to play in the institutionalization of norms into laws and other practices that guide behavior. They thus have both symbolic meaning and material form. They also have a profound relationship to our identity within modern mass culture and society: they shape who we are, and when we come together in institutions, we help to shape those institutions themselves. They are thus engines and products of identity. And how we utilize institutions to make legal change—with law being an institution itself—we help transform society itself. This institutional view on identity, privacy, and social change that I will use throughout this work will help lead to recommendations about what sorts of legal and regulatory innovations are needed to preserve the integrity of identity. It will also offer a vision for how to bring about that change and yields insights into social change itself.

As for my prescriptions for a new approach that might protect political privacy, first I recommend the adoption of a muscular disclosure regime that has real teeth to it—not a weak one that allows companies to bury their consumers in disclosures so that those consumers are unlikely to read the fine print of end-user agreements. Such a disclosure regime would include a number of protections: it would require clear information to consumers along a range of key metrics around the maintenance of personal information, the extent that information is shared, whether the company agrees to serve as a fiduciary toward the end user, clear guidance on the use of artificial intelligence in the company's practices, and the extent to which the consumer can sue the company in court when that consumer's privacy has been breached. In proposing such a regime, I will borrow, in part, from the world of property law, where land-use restrictions, called "zoning ordinances," determine the ways in which property owners can use their land. Unlike zoning laws in the physical world, in the

Upside Down the law will not dictate what a company can do with the private information of its users. It will identify the different types of privacy and consumer protections that a company can provide its users, and then the company will have to be clear and concise about what set of protections guarantees its customers. Throughout this work, I will develop the basis for this "digital zoning," an approach that attempts to blend the best of different policy regimes and offers a robust, flexible system that puts consumers in the driver's seat so they may ensure that their personal information, and the integrity of their identity, are preserved. This approach will also harness the best features of different institutional systems—like the private sector, the legislative process, and the courts—and put them to work in a collaborative fashion to protect political privacy. But what I will also attempt to do is to provide an approach, informed by some of what I think are some of the best theories about how social change occurs, that might help turn these ideas into actual policy.

Plan of the Book

To build the case for such a regime, this work proceeds as follows. In chapter 2, I explore the ways that technological change has advanced the search for identity, community, and social change over the course of American history and show that these phenomena occur within and through institutions, broadly defined. In chapter 3, I trace the ways that privacy law has attempted to keep pace with these technological changes. In chapter 4, I delve deeper into the disciplines of institutional theory to bring an institutional lens to the problem of protecting political privacy. I explore the different ways in which the laws, norms, constitutional protections, and practices—that is, the institutions—surrounding political privacy in private-law contexts essentially provide immunity to those companies that have access to our digital selves. This immunity creates a form of moral hazard in which those same companies are largely free from oversight and responsibility when they violate the integrity of identity. I will show, once again using an institutional framework, that in the private-law space we have created what political economists Daron Acemoglu and James Robinson call an "extractive" system rather than an inclusive one: that is, the institutions that protect (or do not protect) political privacy in private-law settings foster predatory rather than protective conduct.[82] Since economic historians tell us that extractive institutions are unsustainable and can, in turn, undermine our democratic institutions, the current approach to protecting political privacy poses great risks to the long-term viability of democratic society itself.[83] This discussion is grounded in an institutional perspective on political privacy and will lead to an analysis of the proper set of institutions that might protect this form of privacy.

As part of that analysis, I will also assess the extent to which a comparative institutional approach offers the tools for doing so effectively. For this element of the analysis, I will seek to build on the work of legal scholar Neil Komesar. In his own work, he would refine the discipline of Comparative Institutional Analysis, first introduced by economist Ronald Coase. That approach attempts to identify the appropriate institutional setting—which Komesar defined as either the market, the political process, or the courts—in which to achieve a particular policy goal.[84] Komesar urged policymakers to analyze problems using this comparative institutional lens, one that would help identify the appropriate system for achieving a desired goal. But a comparative institutional perspective on protecting political privacy, one that seeks to identify a system in which to locate such protections, fails to come to grips with the reality of how our system of protecting political privacy in private-law contexts has become warped such that there is not a single system in which to achieve the desired policy goal. Each system, as it currently operates, appears to impose negative restraints on the others, meaning efforts within one setting can quickly become undone by efforts in another. Indeed, in chapter 5, I will look at how the free market, lawmakers, and the courts have not only failed to protect political privacy but also often work at cross-purposes, weakening the ability of each other to rein in identity-violating behavior. Because of this fact, I will strive to take a holistic approach, one that looks not only at whether one arena should be the sole locus of privacy-protecting measures but also the ways in which these different arenas should support and work collaboratively to ensure the integrity of identity.

In chapter 6, with an appreciation for the interdependent nature of the institutions that affect the integrity of identity, I propose a series of reforms that draw from the institutional strengths of the market, government, and the courts to achieve robust protections for political privacy that can preserve the integrity of identity in both public- and private-law contexts. These reforms will draw out some of the best features of these institutional settings to create a holistic and integrated system for the protection of digital privacy.

Chapter 7 then presents a theory of social change that is catalyzed through an institutional perspective. This chapter will offer insights into how social change can occur on an institutional level as it relates to privacy, but it also speaks to larger questions of change: institutional change. It strives to offer advocates a methodology and approach for achieving meaningful social change designed to preserve political privacy in private-law contexts, but it also serves as a reflection of social change generally when seen as institutional change. I introduce the concept of Institutional Convergence, an approach to legal, cultural, and policy reform that builds on past works by such legal scholars as the late Derrick Bell, but I also look to move beyond it, to offer a richer vision of social change, one not just informed by the institutional perspective that I embrace here but also one that catalyzes an institutional perspective on social movements and the change they wish to advance. As a result, I offer not just a framework for protecting political privacy as set forth in chapter 6 but also a methodology for bringing it into existence, one that, I hope, can inform social change in this context and in others as well.

Given the critical role that the integrity of identity plays in the achievement of personal self-realization, as well as individual and collective self-determination, our institutions, laws, and norms must offer robust protections for our private actions and engagements, even our thoughts, as they are manifest in the digital and analog worlds. A recognition of the severe threats to political privacy that lurk in the digital Upside Down is necessary to understand that preserving the integrity of identity is an essential feature of a functioning democracy. This work is an attempt to explore the ways that our laws, institutions, and norms can catch up to new technologies, with all of their capacities as well as the threats that lurk within them, to ensure that we can preserve the integrity of identity in the digital age and advance and enrich the pursuit of democracy, meaningful social change, and, ultimately, human flourishing.

What I hope to offer my intended audience—advocates, would-be advocates, policymakers, legislators, and scholars—is a new way of looking at privacy, one that recognizes its deep connection to individual and collective self-determination and the extent to which this form of privacy—political privacy—is deeply embedded within an institutional framework. Furthermore, utilizing this view, this book also strives to offer a way to utilize an institutional approach not just to protect political privacy but also to bring about the social change necessary to adopt the system I propose here for doing so.

2

Political Privacy and Institutions

In the months following the U.S. presidential election of 2016, news broke that a U.K.-based company, Cambridge Analytica, gained access to the private Facebook pages of nearly ninety million Americans.[1] The company claimed it had created digital versions of American voters along a number of key characteristics based on their social media usage and activities. It mined the users' private information that made up aspects of their identities and recast this information to create profiles of them. It then used this information to target them for content created to help Donald Trump eke out a victory in an election he would lose by several million votes but still win based on the idiosyncratic nature of the American electoral college.[2]

Microsoft's Brad Smith has called the Cambridge Analytica scandal privacy's "Three Mile Island,"[3] believing that attention to the scandal would lead to a dramatic change in the legal infrastructure that protects digital privacy. While Cambridge Analytica's actual impact on the results of the election remains unclear to this day, is it fair to compare this scandal to a nuclear disaster that transformed the legal regime around nuclear power and has kept residents of the United States safe from accidents at nuclear power plants for generations?

In the spring of 1979, the reactor core of the nuclear power plant in Three Mile Island, Pennsylvania, malfunctioned, releasing radioactive material into the atmosphere and spreading it throughout the communities surrounding the plant. The public health impacts of this disaster were, for the most part, slight. In contrast, the political fallout was substantial. Indeed, lawmakers and regulators increased their oversight of companies generating nuclear power and those that might want to do so in the future. This increased attention translated into stricter laws and more complex—some would say burdensome—regulations that caused the cost of generating nuclear power to skyrocket. For more than thirty years after the Three Mile Island incident, not a single nuclear reactor was approved for construction by the U.S. Nuclear Regulatory Commission. At the same time, the United States has not faced a similar nuclear disaster in four decades. Unlike in the wake of the Three Mile Island incident, however, the legal regime in the United States that is supposed to protect the personal information of hundreds of millions of individuals who utilize mobile technologies and the internet has not changed considerably since the scope of the Cambridge Analytica scandal came to light. That information remains mostly exposed to sale to third parties.

Other, more recent examples reveal that such digital surveillance and abuse only continues, practically unabated. In the summer of 2021, an investigation by a consortium of media outlets and human rights groups exposed the fact that the technology of a private security firm, the NSO Group, may have penetrated the cell phones of thousands of journalists, government leaders, and human rights activists and could have tracked their whereabouts and their communications.[4] The attorney general of the state of Tennessee has sought and obtained the private medical records of transgender individuals who received gender-affirming care from the privately run Vanderbilt University Medical Center.[5] In this same area, a private antiabortion group in Wisconsin obtained the geolocation data from private cell phones to track individuals who had sought abortion services and used such information to send targeted messages to them.[6] The state of Texas has a so-called bounty law that enables private citizens to file actions against individuals who have obtained reproductive care, and individuals who might be the target of such lawsuits have attempted to remove the private health information from their cell phones, messaging apps, and certain websites out of fear that unwanted access to such information might subject them to private lawsuits by those seeking to cash in on the bounty provided under state law.[7] This sort of surveillance will likely result in those seeking such care facing unwanted and aggressive intrusion into their personal lives by the state and possibly private actors; it is also likely that fear that such information might come to light will also discourage individuals from seeking such care in the first place.

In addition, in the late spring and summer of 2020, a private company purchased digital location data on protestors participating in demonstrations regarding police violence; the company published that information, including information related to the gender and ethnicity of the protestors.[8] In yet another example, embarrassing information surfaced about the use of "hookup" apps by high-profile, ordained members of the Roman Catholic Church in the United States; the apps were mostly popular with individuals looking for discrete sexual encounters with people of the same sex.[9] It has also come to light that pharmacies are also routinely sharing information with law enforcement officials, even without those officials obtaining a warrant, covering such details as medications and treatments the pharmacies' customers have received.[10] There is also a direct line between information shared on Facebook and abuse and violence, particularly that which seeks to attack people for their identity.[11]

These intrusions strike at the heart of identity-forming actions, but they also can impact democracy itself, whether it is in fledgling democracies across the globe or in one of the world's oldest democracies, the United States. Indeed, in the leadup to the events in Washington, D.C., on January 6, 2021, when a violent mob stormed the U.S. Capitol, it was reported that at least some portion of the individuals who participated in the rally were members of groups that formed through Facebook.[12] The platform's algorithms often tapped into these individuals' searches, posts, and reading histories to encourage them to join such groups and attend events as a way to enhance and sustain engagement with the site because greater engagement means higher ad revenue for the company.[13] Similarly, throughout the world, political leaders and their backers are using Facebook and other apps to encourage mob violence. Such efforts typically tap into—and divide—different identities, often with a distinct ethnic, racial, or religious cast to them.[14] Even efforts to lower the outrage communicated over social media have backfired, making users engage in more acrimonious dialogue, not less.[15] As research consistently shows, social media and online communications thrive on pushing users toward more outrageous and radicalizing content, which has personal and political ramifications, transforming identities in deep and powerful ways.[16]

Other examples from the 2016 U.S. elections underscore the ways identity can be weaponized in efforts to attempt to catalyze, or impede, social change. In the spring of 2016, Russian operatives allegedly organized opposing rallies designed to take place at the same location and at the same time. As a U.S. Senate Intelligence Committee report found, a Facebook group with the name "Heart of Texas," which was actually operated out of St. Petersburg, Russia, called for a rally to take place at noon on May 21, 2016, in front of the Islamic Da'wah Center in Houston. The purported goal of the rally: "Stop Islamization of Texas." The Facebook page of "Heart of Texas" eventually attracted over 250,000 followers. Another Russia-based Facebook group, United Muslims of America, organized a second rally to occur at the same time and the same place. This fictional group's page, which still attracted over 325,000 followers, planned the rally to, as it claimed, "Save Islamic Knowledge." The report concluded that individual accounts linked to both groups, probably Russian internet trolls, attempted to "exploit the country's most divisive fault lines."[17] Similar efforts targeted African Americans and individuals and groups associated with the Black Lives Matter movement, often promoting messages designed to discourage African Americans from voting for Hillary Clinton—mostly by suggesting they should not vote at all.[18]

What each of these phenomena reveals is that, first, the actions we take in the digital sphere are simultaneously a product of and an engine for individual identity formation. We identify with different individuals, personal traits and characteristics, groups, identities, political parties, even products. We then become someone who is identified by those associations, regardless of whether we like it or not and whether we think others can and do know about those associations. That identification also occurs whether or not those associations are an accurate depiction of who we are or, more important, how we would like to be seen. As sociologist Erving Goffman explained at the end of the 1950s, our individual identities in relation to others—how we wish to be perceived and how others perceive us—involve, in his words, "two radically different kinds" of phenomena: how one expresses oneself (what he described as the expression one "gives"), and how one is perceived (what one "gives off").[19]

For millennia, those identities were sometimes chosen by us, and we may have been proud to embrace them; at the same time, they were often ascribed to us, as members of a particular race, class, or gender. At least some of these characteristics might have been hidden from view, or perhaps people successfully "passed" as something they were not. Now, to the extent one might make such determinations about us through our digital activity—our searches, our private messages, the online groups of which we are a part—that information is often up for sale and is fairly easily accessed by the private companies that provide the platforms where that activity takes place. Additionally, individuals, groups, corporations, social movements, and nations are tapping into our identities to agitate and inflame and to bend people toward particular political ends. This access to our actions and presence in the digital world—and, in turn, our identity—is occurring without our consent and in the pursuit of goals we might not share.[20]

These processes of identity formation and the social mobilizations they might catalyze (or thwart) are often tied up with the technologies at our disposal that facilitate both. We saw in chapter 1 how communications technologies have shaped social movements and continue to do so as we have moved into the digital age and as we enter the age of artificial intelligence. While nuclear technology is not a communications technology, the advent of the atomic age had many fearing its potential destructive power but also holding out hope that its innovation could provide inexpensive, abundant, and clean energy; more leisure time; and a world free from wars. Today, new technologies have been touted as a means to the creation of a global community, one graced by greater understanding and peaceful coexistence, a product of enriched connection and deeper mutual respect. These technologies also capture, and can expose, the most intimate aspects of our lives. The promise that technology can help us live fuller and more complete lives may actually lead to an existence that is cramped and constrained, limiting our abilities and our capacities. If we fear retribution or recrimination based on information that might be associated with us, especially our membership in disfavored and marginalized groups, it might chill our inquiries and outreach to those within those groups with whom we might collaborate to bring about positive social change. Today we have new opportunities to discover more about ourselves and others. We can seek to connect with and form associations with those who are both like us and are like who we want to become. We can also align and associate ourselves with others in ways that can shape society so that it serves as a better reflection of the vision we have for ourselves and the communities and nations in which we live. This power and capacity to associate with others has never been stronger; it has also never been in such jeopardy.

In this chapter, I explore the role that identity plays in democracy and the ways in which such identity often becomes encoded onto the institutions of society and the social movements we join. In turn, social movements often leverage that identity to change the institutional order, whether that order comprises informal norms and practices or formal laws, organizations, and government structures. Often that institutional order is made up of a web of informal and formal elements. What is more, I argue that privacy itself is an institution in the broadest sense of that term. Its preservation or destruction may determine the potential success of a social movement. In addition, changing the institutional order surrounding privacy presents unique challenges, ones that I begin to explore in this chapter.

To lead off this discussion, I start with notions of identity in democratic thought, which are deeply intertwined with different visions of the self. I then explain how this concept of identity becomes a critical driver of social movement mobilization, which consists of any effort to change what I call the "institutional order": the informal and formal web of norms, habits, practices, laws, organizations, social movements, and public structures that give focus, shape, and meaning to our lives. It is to these ideas that I now turn.

The Self, Autonomy, and Democracy

At the center of liberal democracies is the notion, as the eighteenth-century German philosopher Immanual Kant said, that the individual must not be a means to an end but an end in him- or herself.[21] That principle has informed democratic thought for centuries, but we can trace the origin of democracy back to the Greek city-states, and it is there that the notion of democracy (rule by the people) became coupled with autonomy (the idea of individuals and communities being able to rule themselves and not be subject to some other power).[22] As legal scholar Robert Post argues: "[D]emocracy attempts to reconcile individual autonomy with collective self-determination by subordinating governmental decision-making to communicative processes sufficient to instill in citizens a sense of participation, legitimacy, and identification."[23] The centerpiece of a liberal democracy is the idea of individual and collective self-determination. Self-determination has many components, and it includes a degree of freedom, and a range of freedoms, including the freedom to make choices, to decide how to act, what to believe, and even what information to consider or disregard when making such choices.[24] This autonomy always has a degree of theoretical equality to it, the notion that one individual should not be more autonomous than any other, or, in the classic formulation, that the right to swing one's arms ends at your nose.[25] This also means that every individual should have the equal right to take part in decisions affecting the policies and laws that govern society and that the individual will respect the laws and rules of the community when the community respects the individual's equal worth and dignity.[26] This is operationalized, as the political theorist Philip Pettit argues, in democracy itself, which is "a set of rules under which government is selected and operates—whereby the governed people enjoy control over the governing authorities."[27] In turn, self-determination requires a degree of decision-making autonomy, and decision-making autonomy leads to self-determination when tied to critical life and societal choices. What is more, autonomy means "being or doing what one freely, independently, and authentically chooses to be or do."[28]

But how free—how autonomous—are we when we set out to make the choices that are so critical to and reflect self-determination? How free should we be? Do our prior choices and our life situations cloud our decision-making and hamper our ability to make autonomous choices, choices that we might make differently with different information, with different life experiences? American political philosopher John Rawls believed that we are truly autonomous when we act through our "rational" self, a self that is unencumbered by experience, preferences, backgrounds, or attachments. For Rawls, the ideal political system is one chosen by the rational self behind what he called the "veil of ignorance." If I did not know my race, gender, economic status, or other characteristics, I would create a system that was as fair as possible to everyone, simply because I have no knowledge of where I would fall within that society once the veil of ignorance is lifted.[29] In the Rawlsian view, the truly autonomous self is one that is free from prior attachments or commitments, and that freedom creates a space to decide and act that is not biased by that individual's characteristics or tilted toward favoring one group over another.[30] For Rawls's critics, however, those attachments make us who we are. As Michael Sandel would argue, our status as "members of this family or community or nation or people" is "inseparable from understanding ourselves as the particular persons we are."[31]

What, then, is true individual autonomy? As philosopher Kwame Anthony Appiah asks: "Just how autonomous do you have to be to have true autonomy?"[32] Philosopher Thomas May argues that we say that a person has autonomy when "she does not simply react to her environment and other influences[] but actively shapes her behavior in the context of them."[33] Political philosopher Gerald Dworkin argues that autonomy "is not merely an evaluative or reflective notion[] but includes as well some ability both to alter one's preferences and to make them effective in one's actions and, indeed, to make them effective because one has reflected upon them and adopted them as one's own."[34] This cannot happen in a sort of Rawlsian vacuum. This exploration will always be inflected in a way by accidents of history, experiences, and emotions; in the end, one's identity is both a product as well as a reflection of these attributes.[35]

Whether or not our attachments hinder our judgment, or are what make us human, what is essential for a just, democratic society is that it creates the conditions in which individuals have the capacity to choose those attachments and to change them should they wish to do so. Economist Amartya Sen asserts that the capacity for, and the conditions necessary to, change are together central to an understanding of human existence that enables us to lead complete lives. For Sen, true autonomy consists of "being free to determine what we want, what we value[,] and ultimately what we decide to choose."[36] There is an "opportunity aspect of freedom" that is linked to what Sen calls our "capabilities," that is to say, "the freedom a person actually has to do this or be that—things that he or she may value doing or being."[37] Sen's view involves processes and opportunities: the processes that "allow freedom of actions and decisions," and the opportunities "people have for achieving what they minimally would like to have."[38] Exercising these capabilities to make choices about what individuals may want in their lives comes through "scrutiny and critical assessment," but it is not a solitary affair performed by "secluded individuals." For Sen, it is a public act, carried out through public discussion and deliberation that "can lead to a better understanding of the role, reach[,] and significance" of choices an individual or community might make in the ordering of society.[39] Indeed, we *can* change both our selves and the world around us, especially when we align and associate with others who share the same or similar goals. Psychologist Albert Bandura described the concept of individual and collective self-efficacy as the feeling of independence and ability to change the surrounding environment.[40] What is more, making changes that matter are those that occur beyond the power of any one individual to bring about. Indeed, our capacity for such change is always tied to our ability to collaborate *with others*, and it is through such collaborations that we, in a way, discover our selves, the people we want to be, and the world in which we want to live.

Identity, Self-Determination, and Collective Mobilization

While this individual capacity to change one's associations is essential to human flourishing, historian Yuval Noah Harari goes one step further: he argues that this capacity for change *through cooperation with others* is what may truly make us human and differentiates us from other species.[41] Certainly small bands of primates, the bees in a hive, or a mob of meerkats all appear to coordinate their actions to a certain extent, but, to date, none has created the nation-state, split the atom, sparked a global cultural sensation, or created religions that have spanned millennia. More than mere *attachments*, true individual autonomy in a democracy—the realization of the society in which we want to live—is a critical, and uniquely human, capacity, one that is made manifest through our associational *commitments*.[42] Moral philosopher Martha Nussbaum, building on Sen's work, lists the concept of "Affiliation" as one of the ten "Central Capabilities" required of a "life worthy of human dignity." This involves "[b]eing able to live with and toward others, to recognize and show concern for other human beings, to engage in various forms of social interaction."[43]

We realize this "capability" when we strive to convert an individual identity into a collective identity.[44] A collective identity is the "shared definition of a group that derives from members' common interests, experiences, and solidarity."[45] Sociologist Steven Buechler argues that "the most central process" in many social movements "is the social construction of a collective identity that is symbolically meaningful to participants."[46] Similarly, as sociologists Hank Johnston, Enrique Laraña, and Joseph R. Gusfield have explained, "the collective search for identity is a central aspect of movement formation."[47] Indeed, collective identities become "essential outcomes of the mobilization process and crucial prerequisites to movement success."[48]

The late sociologist Alberto Melucci argued that collective identity involves "formulating cognitive frameworks concerning the ends, means, and field of action"; "activating relationships between the actors, who interact, communicate, influence each other, negotiate, and make decisions"; and "making emotional investments, which enable individuals to recognize themselves."[49] One channel through which this collective identity helps a group to see the world is a function of a process called "grievance interpretation": the assessment of the injustices present in society.[50] Identity thus becomes a prism that refracts that grievance; in turn, that identity—as an individual or group that is aggrieved—serves as a catalyst for change.[51]

According to social movement scholars Debra Friedman and Doug McAdam, collective identity becomes "a shorthand designation announcing a status—a set of attitudes, commitments, and rules for behavior—that those who assume the identity can be expected to subscribe to."[52] This identity is both "a public pronouncement of status" and an individual's "announcement of affiliation, of connection with others."[53] For Friedman and McAdam, "[t]o partake of a collective identity is to reconstitute the individual self around a new and valued identity."[54] Any collective identity a group of individuals shares precedes any decisions about what actions the group might take or the change it might want to pursue.[55] Bruce Fireman and William Gamson explain the connection between identity, mobilization, and organization as follows: "Solidarity is rooted in the configuration of relationships linking the members of a group to one another." They add that "[p]eople may be linked together in a number of ways that generate a sense of common identity, shared fate, and general commitment to defend the group."[56] As just one example of this phenomenon, when sociologists Verta Taylor and Nancy Whittier studied the functioning of the Lesbian Feminist Movement in the United States, they found that identity and collective identity were central components of that movement's ability to attract, engage, and mobilize activists.[57]

For sociologist Sidney Tarrow, social movements, to succeed, must leverage feelings of solidarity and identity.[58] Indeed, identities become powerful engines of mobilization, but they must be harnessed and channeled into action: individuals must connect their analysis to their personal identity but also "commit themselves and the resources they control to some kind of collective actor—an organization or advocacy network."[59] Similarly, Melucci argues that individual identities translate into movement identities "through negotiation among various groups," and it is through this negotiation that a collective identity emerges. What is more, within this collective identity, "the orientations and constraints of action are defined and redefined within the solidarity networks that link individuals together in their daily lives."[60]

Realizing the "capability" of cooperation, as Sen and Nussbaum describe it, Americans have long collaborated with others to bring about the societal arrangements that best reflect their political preferences and choices. And just as this capacity for cooperation is what may make us human, the history of community engagement and social movement mobilization might just make Americans, well, American. Whether it was the revolutionaries who helped free the colonies from colonial rule; the small, local associations praised by Alexis de Tocqueville in a new nation;[61] the great social movements of the nineteenth century;[62] the "nation of joiners" described by Arthur Schlesinger;[63] the movements of the second half of the twentieth century, like the civil rights, women's rights, environmental, and those fighting for the LGBTQIA+ community; or the Movement for Black Lives today: the United States has been shaped by social movements since before its founding, and social movements will continue to play a central role moving forward, especially in preserving and defending democracy and the rule of law, to protect its democratic future.

But how are we to preserve such a future? And to what extent is that future dependent on protecting political privacy? What are the norms, laws, rules, and arrangements that can help ensure such privacy is protected so that individuals can realize autonomy and self-determination, both as individuals and collectives? How can such autonomy catalyze social change? These questions are central to this book, and I try to answer them in remaining chapters. At the center of these questions are a range of concepts—*institutional* concepts. As I show just below, an institutional view on questions of identity, democracy, social movements, and privacy is critical to understanding not just the importance of the integrity of identity but also the means of protecting it. Developing such a sense of how institutions work will help inform a range of strategic decisions designed to preserve political privacy. Since my focus in this book is to explore exactly this type of strategic decision-making that might serve to protect the integrity of identity, in the next section I try to engage in a degree of definitional level-setting around institutions that, I hope, will inform the reader throughout the remainder of this work.

Understanding Institutions and Their Role in Society

Issues of identity, social mobilization, and technology are all tied up in larger societal structures and concepts: race and ethnicity, religious affiliations, gender, gender identity, sexual orientation, and so on. These concepts, in turn, are encoded onto our *associations*, formal and informal, symbolic and material—that is, the groups we join, the beliefs we espouse, the characteristics we embrace, and those characteristics that are ascribed to us. These associations take on larger meanings for us, and they help us to make sense of, and allow us to move in, the larger world. They are all part of a larger system of interconnected concepts, practices, and entities that shape who we are and, to the extent we are able, that we can also help to shape. They are, in a word, institutions, and we become a part of them and they become a part of us. Indeed, institutions "transcend[] individuals to involve groups of individuals in some sort of patterned interactions that are predictable, based upon specified relationships among the actors."[64] Institutions are important in our lives and become woven into the fabric of society. They are sometimes seen as a set of "social factors" that produces consistent behavior.[65] What is more, once institutionalized, a belief, practice, habit, norm, entity, or relationship becomes harder—but not impossible—to change. As sociologist Lynne Zucker has argued, institutionalization results in acts and practices having a "more or less taken-for-granted" aspect to them.[66] When something is institutionalized, it is transmitted and maintained within a culture and is resistant to change.[67] Once chosen (or imposed), institutions can create a sort of dependency, setting a society down a particular path from which it can become more difficult to diverge. At the same time, individuals are always shaped by institutions, but they can also work collectively, in institutions, to shape the larger institutional order as well. In addition, privacy is itself an institution: it has both practical and symbolic functions because its protection has significant dignitary value.

An important component of institutions and institutional practices are the technologies that facilitate the development, strengthening, or weakening of other institutions. What is more, like with privacy, technologies can become institutions themselves. The process of institutionalization is often bound up with the different means of collaborating and communicating, whether that consists of traditional forms of speech or newer forms of communication brought on by advances in technology. As we enter a world dominated by generative artificial intelligence, the institutional order is likely to change, and not necessarily for the better. In such a future, the ability to seek out, leverage, manipulate, and inundate individuals with information that will try to sway their actions, chill their speech, incite them to engage in harmful ways, or cause them to disengage such that their inaction is actually against their interests is nearly limitless. Before going much further in this exploration of the role institutions play in society, and their relationship to privacy, it is helpful to consider how institutions are defined, no only in common usage but also in the disciplines from which I will draw for the analysis to which the remainder of this book is dedicated. Since I focus not only on how institutions work but also on how they evolve and are changed, the following discussion will provide a framework and a vocabulary for much of the discussion that follows.

Defining Institutions

Different theorists from across the disciplinary spectrum define institutions in somewhat different terms. Webster's defines an institution as "an established organization" *or* "a significant practice, relationship, or organization in a society or culture" (using "the institution of marriage" as an example).[68] We see these aspects of the popular definition emerge within different scholarly disciplines that engage in institutional analysis, even if there is little cross-disciplinary work when it comes to such analysis.

For starters, in economics, institutions are sometimes characterized as established norms, rules, and practices within society, and they have profound impacts on how societies operate and change.[69] As Douglass North, one of the leading theorists of the New Institutional Economics school, would assert:

Institutions are the rules of the game in a society, or, more formally, are the humanly devised constraints that shape human interaction. In consequence, they structure incentives in human exchange, whether political, social, or economic. Institutional change shapes the way societies evolve through time and hence is the key to understanding historical change.[70]

In addition, an institutional view of society has long penetrated the social sciences[71] and has emerged as an important strain of legal and economic thought. This is seen most often in the search for effective settings in which to advance policy change.[72] Indeed, a broad approach to the definition of institutions is consistent with evolving thought in social movement scholarship. Tracking the different aspects of the formal definition of institutions described earlier, many social movement scholars recognize that institutions exist in two different ways: in the material sense and the symbolic. As Roger Friedland and Robert Alford argue: "The central institutions of contemporary Western societies—capitalism, family, bureaucratic state, democracy, and Christianity—are simultaneously symbolic systems and material practices."[73] As symbolic systems they possess "nonobservable, absolute, transrational referents," but they also have a material side: they are "observable social relations" that "concretize" the symbolic.[74] The material side—the "concrete social relations"[75] like grassroots groups or nation-spanning networks—become the channels through which "individuals and organizations strive to achieve their ends."[76] In addition, "they also make life meaningful and reproduce those symbolic systems."[77] As a result, the social relations that emerge as institutions "always have both instrumental and ritual content."[78] Taking this view, institutions are not only symbolic because they are beliefs, norms, and practices but also emerge in the world in material structures and entities, forms that embed the symbolic in human networks and organizations.[79] And the more they become institutionalized, the more important they are in our lives and the harder they are to change.

Whether it is in economics, political science, or social science, and regardless of whether one embraces either the "institutions-as-rules" or the "institutions-as-norms-and-organizations" approach, institutions matter, and as political economists Daron Acemoglu and James Robinson show, the choice of effective institutions, like preservation of the rule of law, help to determine the long-term economic and political health of nations.[80] What is more, they differentiate between effective institutions and ineffective ones, considering the former "inclusive" institutions and the latter "extractive." Inclusive institutions "allow and encourage participation by the great mass of people in economic activities that make best use of their talents and skills and enable individuals to make the choices they wish."[81] Extractive institutions favor elites and further their interests at the expense of the wider community.[82] I will return to the inclusive/extractive framework in subsequent discussions. But what is the relationship between institutions and social change? And how do these concepts relate to questions of privacy, particularly political privacy? I explore these questions next.

Social Change: A Multidimensional, Institutional Framework

In his work *How Change Happens*,[83] legal scholar Cass Sunstein argues that social change occurs when norm entrepreneurs create "norm cascades": phenomena in which individual norm change becomes group norm change, which in turn becomes societal change.[84] But those norms first evolve and shift within small groups through what Sunstein calls "enclave deliberation."[85] Social change spreads between different enclaves when an idea or demand, conceived in one enclave, is introduced to other, similar enclaves. Once the new idea is embraced by a new enclave, those enclaves merge, in a sense, and begin to form a movement. We see in this approach the broad view of institutions and the many forms they can take in the social change context: norms emerge within material institutions and then have broader effects within organizations and then through a network of organizations, like an electrical current pulsing, house-to-house, through a community. For example, the Women's Suffrage Movement in the United states operated through networked organizations to advance dramatic change to the institutional order, transforming the very nature of American democracy.[86]

But what is the connection between these institutions-as-norms and institutions-as-organizations, on the one hand, and identity on the other? And how do they relate to privacy? Much of the effort around the development of norms within enclaves materializes where groups *focus on* identity explicitly and where supporters *identify with* either the movement itself or the cause it promotes.[87] Some may dismiss the role of identity in mobilization for social change as "identity politics," in which such identities might take the form of a personal characteristic or trait.[88] But, in reality, every act of collaboration with others in pursuit of social change is a statement about identity: a person can be someone who cares about the environment or someone who wants to reduce traffic deaths. These are identities we espouse, communicate to the world, and leverage to bring about social change. Taking the broad view of institutions, efforts at social change interact with the institutional perspective in several critical ways. Identity is a symbolic idea and serves as a prism through which individuals see themselves and the world. That idea is embedded—that is, institutionalized—in the organizations, formal and informal, that individuals join to help realize social change. The norms and practices carried out by those organizations and the form those organizations take—that is, the institutional practices within them and the structures they utilize—can often mean the difference between success and failure of the movement. Social capital and trust, as found within our institutional networks, are essential ingredients of social change and the process of solving collective-action problems, those thorny social challenges that we must solve collectively precisely where cooperation is difficult. All of these efforts are designed to have institutional effects: they are designed to change the broader institutions of society. Finally, privacy is a critical component of each of these elements: without it, it is nearly impossible for any group to engage in any sort of activity designed to change the institutional order. I now discuss each of these phenomena, and how they interact, in turn.

Identity Is Institutionalized in Social Movement Organizations

Historically, the search for personal and collective identity has been made manifest in groups: tribes, political parties, parent–teacher associations, tenant groups, block associations, the Committees of Correspondence during the American Revolution, temperance associations, Elks clubs—the list goes on and on.[89] We form groups to find a place where we can realize our identity. We thus encode the symbolic onto the material. As Marshall Ganz found in his study of the farmworker movement in California, joining a group can proclaim an identity and demonstrates that we are the type of person who joins a particular group. There, two unions were competing for farmworkers' support. One of the unions—the National Farm Worker Association—was more aggressive in its advocacy and took a more contentious stance toward growers. The other, the Teamsters, was more conciliatory. Choosing one union over the other expressed which camp a worker might be in and sent a message to other workers and the world of which approach they wanted to take toward their employers.[90] In many ways, our identities are mixed in with our associations, and our associations make our identities. In turn, both become the breeding ground for social change.

As sociologist William Gamson explains, a collective identity, as realized in these groups, represents the symbolic made material. It is "central in understanding people's willingness to invest emotionally in the fate of some emergent collective entity and to take personal risks on its behalf." It also "has consequences for how people understand the sociocultural system they are attempting to change and which strategies and organizational forms they will see as appropriate."[91] Success comes to those groups that integrate this personal and collective identity because they "have an easier time doing what it takes to launch many kinds of collective action."[92] The relationship between identity and organization reflects the symbolic and material elements of our understanding of institutions. It is through this melding of the symbolic and material that organizations, in turn, catalyze a change in the broader institutional order: the norms, rules, mores, and organizational structures and practices that dominate our lives.

Organizations Are Essential to Social Movement Success

Social movements are not just collections of individuals. They are organized, sometimes in coalitions, and sometimes in large masses of individuals practicing some sort of internal logic. Regardless of the shape and size (although, as I will show just below, the shape and size of an organization can impact its ability to function well), social movement organizations have always been essential to social movement success. Many social movements seek to generate what its leaders and members see as collective goods, and those goods are not just the identity-realizing benefits of such activity but also the change to the larger societal order that movement seeks.[93] Those broader goods are shared throughout society as what are known as "public goods."[94] The Civil Rights Movement of the mid-twentieth century certainly benefited the African American community, but it also improved the reputation of the United States in the arena of geopolitics.[95] It inspired other movements, like the gay rights and feminist movements.[96] While some feared there would be a backlash from the campaign for marriage equality in more recent years, that effort has enriched all communities, and the fears of what societal harms the recognition of marriage equality might bring about as described by its opponents have proven baseless at best.[97] The success of many of these movements has often centered around their ability to catalyze identity itself.[98] Those who support such movements satisfy their search for identity through their activity within formal and informal groups. They then realize that identity and achieve other benefits through such work, which is carried out in association with others. What they achieve, these identity-realizing actions and their material or political benefits, are the collective goods generated by that effort.[99]

Internal Institutional Structures and Practices Also Matter for Social Movement Success

All of this sounds well and good, but any social movement that seeks to produce such goods also faces a dilemma: how to hold the group together so that it realizes those benefits. The simple view of how social movements might change society is that the larger the group, the more powerful it will be. In other words, at least in theory, one would think that there is an apparent strength in numbers and that group size determines social movement success. But in the mid-1960s, economist and political scientist Mancur Olson would challenge this view and popularize the notion of the so-called free-rider problem.[100] For Olson, the larger the group, the greater the likelihood that individuals within the group would consider it more advantageous to them to shirk their own responsibilities, letting others do the work. The shirkers could still benefit from the labor of others while expending no energy themselves. Of course, this can and will create a vicious cycle. As conscientious members of the group see that others are benefiting from the labor of active members, while those others do little themselves, it can be dispiriting and lead to the collapse of the group effort.[101] What Olson was pointing to was what has come to be known as the "problem of collective action," and situations where this phenomenon can occur are considered collective-action problems themselves. As legal scholar Robert Hockett explains, "the hallmark of a collective action problem is its tending to aggregate multiple individually rational decisions, absent coordination, into a collectively irrational outcome—an outcome that is ultimately suboptimal for each individual agent."[102]

How do groups overcome collective-action problems? Economist Elinor Ostrom studied such collective-action dilemmas, usually situations in which communities had to manage a common-pool resource, like a forest, a community irrigation system, or a fishery, to note that communities that managed such resources well tended to follow norms and rules—what she called institutions—that led to greater cooperation. These included participation in the rulemaking process itself by those affected by those rules, monitoring of compliance, and graduated sanctions that increased the punishments for infractions of those rules given the severity or frequency of the infraction.[103] Both Olson and Ostrom also believed that one could create institutional structures that fostered greater cooperation, creating smaller groups within a larger network of organizations, where individual compliance could be more closely monitored.[104] And it is just these types of organizations, what are sometimes referred to as "translocal networks" (described in chapter 1), that represented the organizational form of many social movement organizations until the early 1970s in the United States, when new communications technologies enabled a different kind of social movement organizing. The focus of this new type of organizational form was much more top-down than bottom-up in its decision-making and leadership style, often eschewing notions of local control and local engagement for professionalized leadership that has been all-too-often disconnected from grassroots efforts.[105]

While social movement organizations often strive to change the institutional order that exists outside of that group (a concept I will return to just below), and the institutional structure of an organization can help it realize such efforts, certain practices *within* organizations are more likely to lead to them having greater extra-organizational effects: those internal practices will lead to greater success in bringing about social change that is external to the group itself. There are certainly organizations and entities that operate in a nondemocratic way, based on the charismatic leader model. As those groups grow in size, as Olson posited, it is harder to engage individual members of the group in meaningful ways; such a model is more likely to lead to the problem of the free rider. Groups made up of smaller component parts that are connected to a larger network, wherein individuals participate in decision-making, encourage local rule-setting, and engage in face-to-face encounters with each other so that they develop feelings of trust toward each other, are more likely to sustain their members' participation, and the group's potency, over the long run. For example, the groups that made up the Civil Rights Movement in the 1950s and 1960s were often structured as a network, with local chapters forming as nodes in larger, nation-spanning bodies.[106] While there were certainly charismatic national leaders trying to set policy and strategy for the movement, there were also local activists who sometimes pushed those national leaders to take more aggressive action than they might have chosen otherwise, as in Birmingham in 1962 and Selma in 1965, when local organizers led the way in more creative, more local campaigns that would ultimately draw national leaders in for support and not the other way around.[107] Organizations that function in this way, with local engagement that is spurred by national leaders but also catalyzes them toward more ambitious tactics and goals, that have intra-institutional practices that encourage that participation and creativity, are those more likely to generate more successful outcomes.[108] For such groups, internal institutional norms and practices are often the difference between success and failure in terms of a group's ability to generate extra-institutional effects—that is, a change to society's norms, practices, rules, social relations, and structures. As social movement scholars Elizabeth Clemens and James Cook explain: "[O]ne of the core insights of institutional theory is that institutions constitute actors" and that "different kinds of institutional orders constitute different kinds of actors and different patterns of ties among them."[109] In the end, participatory, inclusive institutional practices within an organization foster trust and trustworthiness. Such practices aid the creation of, as well as the benefits to be drawn from, what has come to be known as "social capital," a concept tied closely to notions of trust, which is, itself, an essential ingredient to group success.

Social Capital and Trust Are Realized in Institutional Settings

Though introduced in the early twentieth century,[110] the concept of social capital was popularized by Harvard political scientist Robet Putnam through his landmark work *Bowling Alone: The Collapse and Revival of American Community*.[111] For Putnam, social capital consists of those "features of social organizations, such as trust, norms, and networks, that can improve the efficiency of society by facilitating coordinated actions."[112] This resource helps communities work collectively to solve problems by overcoming some of the dilemmas of social action.[113] As Putnam explains:

> When economic and political negotiation is embedded in dense networks of social interaction, incentives for opportunism are reduced. At the same time, networks of civic engagement embody past success at collaboration, which can serve as a cultural template for future collaboration. Finally, dense networks of interaction probably broaden the participants' sense of self, developing the "I" into the "we," or enhancing the participants' "taste" for collective benefits.[114]

The centerpiece of social capital is trust, and social capital can be considered a type of "networked trust" because one does not possess social capital in the absence of others.[115] Social capital is embedded in networks of individuals, and the extent of the trusting relationship among those individuals probably charts out the outer boundaries of the social capital those individuals enjoy. Members of the network activate that trust to solve collective-action problems, including networks that are designed to bring about social change. Networks where social capital is high will have greater success at coordinating to solve such problems, and the problems they work to solve are often related to the institutional order itself. Indeed, social movements that strive to bring about social change often do so by targeting institutional change, a change to the laws or even the social norms that shape society. The trust that is an essential element of the practices of the social movement is more than just trust, however. It is *networked* trust. It is thus institutionalized and encoded onto our associations and manifest as something more than trust; it is social capital.

Often, this kind of trust, this networked trust, not only becomes the building block for social movements but also helps to sustain them.[116] Outreach to and organizing within a preexisting trust network is easier because of the relationships one has with others already in the network.[117] Individuals can spur others to action more easily in networks within which one has personal relationships. This was evident in the rise of the Civil Rights Movement as it emerged from a vast network of African American churches.[118] Similarly, the Women's Movement in the 1960s also arose from preexisting community networks of which would-be members were already a part.[119]

In addition, the density and richness of one's trusting connections within and across organizations can often determine the success of mobilization efforts.[120] In a landmark study of civil rights advocates engaged in Freedom Summer activities, the individuals who joined and remained active in the movement's efforts were those who had preexisting relationships with others already engaged with the campaign. Indeed, these connections were more important than ideology in ensuring an individual had staying power within the movement.[121] Similar findings about the importance of preexisting relationships for social movement mobilization were found in a study of college student activism: again, such relationships were more important than ideology to such efforts.[122] Existing social capital is at the center of these relationships; when we already have it, it is easier to activate it, build on it, and leverage it to strengthen a movement. It is another essential ingredient for social movement success because it is also baked in to our associational attachments as realized in groups and the practices by which those groups function. In other words, social capital is, like so many other concepts discussed here, institutionalized.

Social Movements Seek to Change the Institutional Order

Social movements often seek to change the institutions of society: that is, they strive to alter the very norms, laws, rules, and structures that govern, restrain, channel, and permeate communal life. Social movements are typically organized to bring about social change, but that social change often has an institutional cast. It is institutional change that such movements seek, when we recognize that institutions are both concepts and organizations. Thus, it is the richness of the associations of which we are members that helps give both our identities, and democracy, a degree of meaning and becomes a catalyst for change. Such change is, for these reasons, institutionalized. It is reflected in our associational commitments, the practices and structures carried out where those commitments are realized, and the ultimate change those associations pursue. Thus, in the end, social movements strive to change the institutional order in which their members live, rounding out this institutional element of social change, but it is not the last of these elements, as I will discuss in the next section.

A focus on identity; institutional forms and practices; the ways social organizations solve collective-action problems; and the efforts they undertake to change the institutional order itself: these all reflect the critical role of institutions, broadly defined. And the identities realized through them help to provide a lens through which to view social movements, the change they seek, and any successes they may accomplish.[123] Throughout the remainder of this book, I will explore the concept of social change as institutional change and how social movements can catalyze such change through a sensitivity to and an understanding of not just the idea of institutions and the process of institutionalization but also how institutions change. Again, I hope to offer a vocabulary and framework for creating meaningful social change. But there is one more element of this success, one more institution, that deserves mentioning, and its role in social movement success cannot be overstated: that is the institution of privacy itself.

The Role Privacy Plays in Reform of the Institutional Order

As I hope to have established by now, institutions have both symbolic and material forms. The idea of privacy, especially political privacy, exhibits these two forms. Privacy consists of a belief. It is also a practice that individuals will adhere to or violate. And it is a norm that is embedded in rules and laws that protect it. Believing that one has some degree of protection over one's thoughts and behaviors has real value to the individual and promotes that individual's dignity.[124] When we communicate with others through different types of media or in other ways, whether it is gossiping, sharing secrets, or plotting strategy, we might have some expectation of privacy, and that expectation, itself, is what prompts one to share such information in the first place. That expectation of privacy thus has both symbolic and instrumental value, and it is encoded—or institutionalized—into habits, practices, and networks.

What is more, as introduced in chapter 1, we often see the protection of privacy as what political philosophers consider a negative right—a *freedom from* intrusion. Viewing political privacy through the lens of social movement theory, we must think of political privacy in more robust terms: as a positive right—a *freedom to* achieve our desired political ends.[125] When observed in this light, it is easy to see that political privacy is central to a functioning democracy. It is also under serious threat in the digital age. Companies, large and small, possess information central to the identity of those individuals who utilize their services. Only a relatively weak set of legal institutions stands in the way, if those institutions offer any resistance at all, to those companies sharing such information in ways that undermine the integrity of identity, what should be a protected sphere of personal interests, desires, affiliations, and even our beliefs. What is more, because of the weaknesses of these institutions, at present, many Americans feel powerless to change this situation,[126] which undermines feelings of efficacy and trust and threatens individual and collective self-determination: the sense that we can change the systems that affect our lives.

* * *

The relationship among self-determination, identity formation, democracy, social movements, and technology reveals, if anything, that these concepts are deeply intertwined. Think back to some of the examples described in the opening pages of this chapter: the dueling demonstrations created by a meddling, foreign group; the Cambridge Analytica scandal; the surveillance and exposure of private, even intimate, acts. The institutional aspects of our identities are reflected in our activities online as well as in the real world. We reflect them and carry them out in actions, large and small, individually but mostly through our associational attachments. They are also encoded onto the institutional DNA of the United States itself.

But the ability to realize at least some of these critical symbolic institutions—individual autonomy, identity, collective self-termination, and democracy—is dependent on the functioning of other, more material institutions—most notably, social movements and social movement organizations. In turn, these are all connected on an existential level to the ability to act autonomously in a political sphere that is free from improper influence and penetration. Put simply, these institutions, to survive and thrive, require political privacy.

So, how might we work to protect political privacy in the present moment? How do we do so in light of present technologies and those that will emerge in the future? What impact does the preservation of privacy have on the institutional order and the ability of individuals to change that order? What is more, to look at privacy as an institution, is it an institution that needs to change from its current form to provide the protection necessary to preserve or change an institutional order so that it defends the integrity of identity, that sphere of rights we might consider our political privacy? Is privacy in its present form, as a set of institutional practices, up to the task of protecting the integrity of identity in the digital age? Chapter 3 explores this question and provides an overview of the emergence and development of the institutional framework in which we protect—or do not protect—privacy, with a particular emphasis on political privacy.

3

Political Privacy, Trust, and Technology

When individuals fear that their private communications might not be private, they are less likely to engage in such communications: their speech and any activities that flow from such speech become chilled. In the political realm, and in the digital age, individuals who might hesitate to utilize digital tools to find other like-minded people and connect with them to advance social change will thus have such identity-advancing activities curtailed, meaning they will not bring about the collective goods that would otherwise flow from authentic collective action.[1] These are real harms, particularly when an entity with access to this information could reveal it and embarrass a group's members or subject them to ridicule or violence.[2] Such disclosures could also chill identity-forming actions. If we fear disclosure of our online activities, we might not seek out and explore identities that are more in line with our authentic self or look to associate with like-minded people to advance social change. What is worse, when we share certain information about ourselves, we may invite manipulation by social media algorithms that lead us to espouse beliefs and take actions inconsistent with those we might embrace without such manipulation.[3] But is the current state of affairs with respect to digital privacy unprecedented? As I explore in this chapter, it is not. We have faced situations before where the laws and norms around new technologies had to catch up to those technologies to ensure their communications-enhancing qualities were not undermined by the risk that private communications might not remain private through the use of those technologies. What is more, as the following discussion shows, advances in the law of privacy emerged largely from an interest in and the desire to protect and preserve a particular kind of privacy: political privacy. And it was the central role that political privacy plays in democracy that often became the impetus for advocates to press for such advances.

Technology Outpacing the Law

Throughout the course of American history, the law of privacy, to protect the privacy of groups that utilized any new technology, had to keep pace with that advance. But technological change has often outrun the law's ability to preserve political privacy, at least at first. When the law tried to catch up, it often meant a significant sea change in the protection of political privacy. Indeed, the connection between a new technology and the need to protect the privacy of those who would use it has created key inflection points in American law and jurisprudence.

In colonial times, an emerging revolutionary sentiment formed against British writs of assistance: orders from executive officials to search homes, sometimes for materials critical of government authorities. In England, courts had found such searches contrary to the British understanding of liberty, including in one case, *Wilkes v. Wood* (1763), in which a member of Parliament had his personal papers ransacked by government officials looking for evidence of sedition.[4] When the British government began introducing this authority in the American colonies in the 1760s, the colonists' opposition to these writs in the courts spurred John Adams to claim as follows: "Then and there the child Independence was born."[5]

The legal resistance to these types of writs would have a profound impact on the American law of privacy. The English courts' decisions on cases regarding the writs, including in *Wilkes*, were well known in the American consciousness and would inform the Framers' adoption and understanding of the Fourth Amendment, which protects against warrantless invasions by government of our private spaces and information. As legal scholar Akhil Reed Amar has argued, the *Wilkes* case "was probably the most famous case in late eighteenth-century America, period."[6] The Fourth Amendment is, in many ways, the starting point for our general understanding of privacy. And, since the Fourth Amendment emerged from a desire to protect dissidents' political views, we can see that the very seeds of our sense of privacy generally emerged from a desire to protect a particular type of privacy: political privacy.

But political privacy was not just a more general starting point for the law of privacy. Advances in technology and concerns over privacy— especially political privacy—are commonplace throughout American history. Soon after the emergence of revolutionary sentiment in the early 1770s, when the Continental Congress began to meet, one of its first official acts was the creation of a new postal system. The one operating in the colonies at the time was overseen by British officials who could inspect rebel tracts and correspondence, threatening the security of the communications and the freedom of those who sent them.[7]

After the revolution, the U.S. Constitution placed the power to create a postal system in the hands of the legislative branch. Pursuant to this power, Congress passed the Postal Act of 1792, which not only authorized the expansion of the postal system and set favorable postage rates but also ensured the privacy of letters sent through the system.[8] In the 1830s, when the Abolitionist Movement was gaining traction and followers, a new steam-powered printing press was introduced that increased efficiency and productivity and considerably lowered the cost of publishing political tracts. President Andrew Jackson then argued that there should be a ban on abolitionist communications sent through the mail that might spark a slave revolt.[9]

Later in the nineteenth century, in response to the introduction of still photography and the fear that such photography might lead to journalists capturing private moments and publicizing them, future Supreme Court Justice Louis Brandeis and his coauthor, prominent Boston lawyer Samuel Warren, published an influential article in the *Harvard Law Review* that laid out the theoretical basis for the contemporary right to privacy.[10] Warren and Brandeis argued that recognition of this right to privacy was necessary because one's very personhood was under threat due to the emergence of new technologies.[11] Sounding Orwellian before Orwell, they asserted: "Instantaneous photographs and news[]paper enterprise have invaded the sacred precincts of private and domestic life; and numerous mechanical devices threaten to make good the prediction that 'what is whispered in the closet shall be proclaimed from the house-tops.'"[12] These technologies threatened to make life less meaningful and more coarse by subjecting individuals "to mental pain and distress, far greater than could be inflicted by mere bodily injury."[13] Moreover, Brandeis and Warren feared this intrusion into the private lives of individuals could have a pernicious effect on politics: "Peculiarities of manner and person, which in the ordinary individual should be free from comment, may acquire a public importance, if found in a candidate for political office."[14]

They also argued that this right should protect those concepts I have described to this point as making up one's identity, which they would call "personality": "[T]he protection afforded to thoughts, sentiments, and emotions, expressed through the medium of writing or of the arts, so far as it consists in preventing publication, is merely an instance of the enforcement of the more general right of the individual to be let alone." For Warren and Brandeis, the right to be free from intrusion on these interests "is like the right not to be assaulted or beaten, the right not to be imprisoned, the right not to be maliciously prosecuted, the right not to be defamed." It is because with all of these rights the interest that is threatened is "an inviolate personality."[15]

Not only would they describe the right to privacy as protecting this personality; they explicitly talked about violations of privacy in private-law terms. That is, most of their discussion revolved around establishing a tort—a private cause of action typically brought against nongovernmental actors—that would protect the right to privacy. And, over the years, their framework has led to the development of a body of private-law protections against violations of privacy carried out by nongovernmental actors.[16] While Warren and Brandeis spoke of the right to privacy as a private-law concern, and the basic framework they laid out eventually made it into the sphere of private-law protections for privacy, those protections have proven somewhat elusive and are easily sidestepped by companies operating in the digital sphere, as I will explore further in chapter 4. At the same time, the development of public-law protections for both privacy and associational rights, with both centering on notions of identity, has been fairly robust, as I will show in the next section.

The Right to Privacy in Public-Law Contexts

Since the late 1950s, U.S. Supreme Court jurisprudence has coalesced around the notion that Americans possess a constitutional right to be free from intrusion into our private spheres, including our associational relationships. The Court has drawn from different legal strands to weave together a bundle of rights that includes privacy rights, free speech rights, and protections for associational interests and relationships. In *NAACP v. State of Alabama*[17] and *NAACP v. Button*,[18] the Court protected the rights of individuals to join civil society groups and to come together in social movements to make social change.[19] In *NAACP v. Alabama*, the state government of Alabama had sought membership lists of the NAACP's local chapters in the state. The group correctly feared, given the climate of intimidation in the Jim Crow South at the time, that revealing its members to the state would have a chilling effect or worse. It would not just lead to individual members leaving the group or not joining it in the first place; it would likely also lead to violence and threats against those who remained. The Supreme Court found that Alabama's efforts violated the freedom of association protected by the First Amendment and recognized the right of the NAACP to preserve its members' anonymity.[20] In its opinion in the *Alabama* case, the Supreme Court held as follows:

> Effective advocacy of both public and private points of view, particularly controversial ones, is undeniably enhanced by group association, as this Court has more than once recognized by remarking upon the close nexus between the freedoms of speech and assembly. It is beyond debate that freedom to engage in association for the advancement of beliefs and ideas is an inseparable aspect of the "liberty" assured by the Due Process Clause of the Fourteenth Amendment, which embraces freedom of speech. Of course, it is immaterial whether the beliefs sought to be advanced by association pertain to political, economic, religious or cultural matters, and state action which may have the effect of curtailing the freedom to associate is subject to the closest scrutiny.[21]

Similarly, in *NAACP v. Button*, the Court considered whether activities of the NAACP, like bringing litigation to advance civil rights, was in furtherance of associational and other protected rights. It concluded that "there is no longer any doubt that the First and Fourteenth Amendments protect certain forms of orderly group activity,"[22] including "the right 'to engage in association for the advancement of beliefs and ideas,'"[23] as well as "the efforts of a union official to organize workers."[24] In upholding the rights of the NAACP to engage in legal advocacy, the Court stressed the importance of "minority, dissident groups"[25] to contribute to shaping society:

[T]he litigation [the NAACP] assists, while serving to vindicate the legal rights of members of the American Negro community, at the same time and perhaps more importantly, makes possible the distinctive contribution of a minority group to the ideas and beliefs of our society. For such a group, association for litigation may be the most effective form of political association.[26]

The Court's jurisprudence regarding the freedom of association and related rights often focuses on the rights of dissident, outsider voices. Even in the dated language of 1943, in *Martin v. City of Struthers*, the Court recognized the importance of protecting dissenting voices when striking down a law banning door-to-door canvassing:

[A]s every person acquainted with political life knows, door to door campaigning is one of the most accepted techniques of seeking popular support, while the circulation of nominating papers would be greatly handicapped if they could not be taken to the citizens in their homes. Door to door distribution of circulars is essential to the poorly financed causes of little people.[27]

On the heels of the Court recognizing the freedom of association explicitly, in *Griswold v. Connecticut*[28]—a 1965 case involving, in part, the freedom of association as an element of the larger right to privacy— the Court relied on its previous decision in *NAACP v. Alabama* to consider associational rights and held that the "right of 'association,' like the right of belief, is more than the right to attend a meeting."[29] The Court acknowledged that the right "includes the right to express one's attitudes or philosophies by membership in a group or by affiliation with it or by other lawful means."[30] This type of association "is a form of expression of opinion; and while it is not expressly included in the First Amendment its existence is necessary in making the express guarantees fully meaningful."[31] Turning to the question posed in *Griswold*— whether the Constitution protected access to contraceptives for married couples—the Court held that the challenged law banning such access "operate[d] directly on an intimate relation of husband and wife and their physician's role in one aspect of that relation."[32] In this way, the Court considered the relations between the married couple as a unit, as well as their relations—their associations and dealings—with their physician, when assessing whether to recognize a right to privacy. The Court in *Griswold* found that "the First Amendment has a penumbra where privacy is protected from governmental intrusion."[33] The Court concluded that the First, Third, Fourth, Fifth, and Ninth Amendments, as interpreted by the Court in decisions over the years and read together, create "zones of privacy"[34] and "bear witness that the right of privacy . . . is a legitimate one."[35]

In the decades since *Griswold*, the Court has extended the right to privacy to protect a range of intimate relations and choices, including the right to terminate a pregnancy (since rejected, as I describe below) and the right of individuals of the same sex to marry, often recognizing the identity-affecting aspect of many of these choices. In *Planned Parenthood of Southeastern Pennsylvania v. Casey*,[36] a majority of the Justices on the Court concluded that decisions affecting marriage and procreation "involv[e] the most intimate and personal choices a person may make in a lifetime, choices central to personal dignity and autonomy, [and] are central to the liberty protected by the Fourteenth Amendment."[37] Such liberty includes "the right to define one's own concept of existence, of meaning, of the universe, and of the mystery of human life."[38] If such matters were "formed under compulsion of the State," the Court wrote, they "could not define the attributes of personhood."[39] Justice Stevens, in a concurring opinion in *Casey*, wrote that the "decisional autonomy" protected by the right to privacy "must limit the State's power to inject into a woman's most personal deliberations its own views of what is best."[40] Similarly, Justice Blackmun's concurrence argued that the Court's decisions on the right to privacy "embody the principle that personal decisions that profoundly affect bodily integrity, identity, and destiny should be largely beyond the reach of government."[41]

More recently, in *Obergefell v. Hodges*,[42] the Court struck down state laws prohibiting same-sex marriage. There, the Court made explicit the connection between identity and the substantive rights protected in the Constitution when it held that the liberty interest protected by the Constitution "includes certain specific rights that allow persons, within a lawful realm, to define and express their identity."[43] In *Obergefell*, the identity-based interest was the right to "marry [] someone of the same sex and having their marriages deemed lawful on the same terms and conditions as marriages between persons of the opposite sex."[44] The Court concluded that "the right to marry is a fundamental right inherent in the liberty of the person, and under the Due Process and Equal Protection Clauses of the Fourteenth Amendment, couples of the same sex may not be deprived of that right and that liberty."[45] Protected in this way, the government cannot suppress such "identity-constitutive" conduct undertaken by the LGBTQIA+ community.[46] This echoes the argument of legal scholar Kenneth Karst, who wrote in 1980:

> An intimate association may influence a person's self-definition not only by what it says to him but also by what it says (or what he thinks it says) to others. . . . Transient or enduring, chosen or not, our intimate associations profoundly affect our personalities and our senses of self. When they are chosen, they take on expressive dimensions as statements defining ourselves.[47]

Once again, as in this line of cases from *NAACP v. Alabama* through *Griswold* and *Obergefell*, the individual's identity was, in many ways, associational.[48] Whether it was the freedom to associate to affect political change, to make decisions within marriage and in consultation with one's doctor, or to marry, the right to privacy in public-law contexts is, nevertheless, deeply intertwined with personal decisions and those made in concert with others. This cluster of privacy rights creates a space in which the individual has the ability to make identity-forming decisions about how to lead one's life such as whether to use and how to gain access to contraceptives,[49] how to think,[50] whom to marry,[51] and what information to access to educate oneself so as to form one's identity through that education.[52] While the Supreme Court's recent abortion jurisprudence scales back one of these aspects of the right to privacy considerably,[53] and at least one Justice has questioned the state of other, similar protections,[54] the core associational and identity-forming components of the right to privacy remain in place, at least for now. That they are under threat from the judiciary makes the need for a comprehensive approach to privacy even more essential, as this book argues in later chapters.

Still, it is difficult to disentangle the freedoms of privacy, free speech, and association, among others, from notions of identity in the Court's holdings. First and foremost, the right to privacy acts as a negative right—it creates a space from not only intrusion but also broader disclosure.[55] But it is also a positive right, a freedom to do many things: not just to make certain critical decisions about how to form one's identity but also how to associate, organize, collaborate, and work together to advance social change. It thus has external qualities, creating a space in which individuals can associate with others who have similar interests and identities and wish to advance collective ends. There is indeed another interest, one that flows from the other interests inherent in this right: the interest in connecting groups with other groups to pursue common interests collectively to realize the identities and interests that members in a movement might share,[56] which is a component of Nussbaum's concept of "affiliation" described in chapter 2.[57] Preserving the channels of dissent for such collectives is also critical to the maintenance of liberty and autonomy. As legal scholar Laurence Tribe explains: "Our system of ordered liberty values individual autonomy, and, any regime that would value individuals must at least tolerate—if not celebrate—diversity among the myriad personalities who breathe life into the abstractions we call liberty and community."[58]

This fairly robust cluster of rights protects individuals and groups from intrusion only by government actors, however, and, in recent jurisprudence, the Supreme Court has gone so far as to limit the use of new technologies in unwarranted surveillance and has also made it more difficult for government entities to obtain information from third parties.[59] But the full scope of public-law protections does not extend in equal measure when private actors curtail our privacy interests. It is one of the reasons why, time and again, when individuals complain that companies like X (formerly Twitter) or Facebook are infringing on their First Amendment rights, such an argument is completely unavailing: the provisions of the First Amendment simply do not apply to rein in the conduct of private actors, like social media companies, who may want to restrict speech on their platforms. At the same time, action by legislators and courts can, within limits, protect privacy interests in private-law contexts. But such institutions have often struggled to keep pace with changes in technology that might infringe upon the right to privacy in private-law contexts.

Advancing the Right to Privacy in Private-Law Contexts

One of the primary concerns of Warren and Brandeis was that the law preserving privacy was not keeping pace with advances in technology. Indeed, even as the new communications technologies of the late nineteenth and early twentieth centuries entered the public sphere, the law struggled to keep up. Throughout the twentieth century and into the early part of the twenty-first, the U.S. Congress and the federal courts have explored ways to extend privacy protections to new technologies. With the passage of the Communications Act of 1934[60] and what has come to be known as the Wiretap Act,[61] which was later modified by the Electronics Communications Privacy Act,[62] Congress attempted to protect the privacy of telephonic communications.[63] The courts have also tried to ensure that the law keeps up with technology, as even Justice Scalia—who often mocked the notion that the Constitution is mutable and should change with the times—recognized that traditional notions of privacy and the protections afforded through the Fourth Amendment needed to adapt to changes in technology, including innovations the Framers probably could have never imagined, like global-positioning technology. Indeed, he authored the Supreme Court's decision in *United States v. Jones*, which extended such protections to that technology.[64] If the interest in preserving the integrity of identity is to mean anything, it not only has to evolve to meet the challenge of new technologies but also must adapt to the threats those new technologies pose and the actors who wield them, whether they are public *or* private. Furthermore, when innovation, privacy, social movements, and politics come together, the law needs to adapt to the changes in technology that introduce new ways of communicating and empower new actors to use those technologies to advance social change. It also must ensure that the technology will not enable surveillance that threatens the integrity of identity, which is a critical driver of social change itself. When such phenomena coalesce, it often creates critical inflection points in the law, and we are in such an inflection point today.

New technologies offer incredible opportunities to find others who share our worldviews and who wish to collaborate with us to effectuate change. But those very same technologies are subject—and, as a result, subject us—to surveillance and manipulation. In prior eras, new technologies required new approaches to privacy protections. Today, our technology has gotten out in front of the laws, regulations, and norms that are supposed to protect our privacy. In an inflection point such as this, a new legal regime is necessary to protect and preserve the most fundamental of human rights: the freedom of association and all that comes with it. That freedom starts with the maintenance of the integrity of identity.

While new communications technologies create what I have called "Social Innovation Moments"—times when the introduction of a new mode of communication seems to have sparked the emergence of a new social movement[65]—they also raise the stakes for such social movements and democracy in general. When the law protecting the use of these technologies fails to preserve the privacy of those who would use it, the law must change. Given the centrality of political privacy to political change, though, threats to such privacy inhibit the ability to change the law itself. Making threats to the integrity of identity even more pernicious, when private actors have access to our most intimate information, it chills our ability to bring about social change generally; it also inhibits our ability to change the very laws that govern digital privacy and stand a chance of reining in the captains of surveillance capitalism.

Today, the search for identity is playing out in the digital world. Indeed, as legal scholar Julie Cohen argues: "In the networked information society," the "practice of citizenship" is "mediated by search engines, social networking platforms, and content formats."[66] For this reason, it is imperative that we protect these new forms of communication, especially where they are used to promote the search for individual and collective self-determination. That search, in turn, serves as a critical aspect of life in, and a central driver of, a truly democratic society.

What are the types of laws, rules, and norms that might preserve or threaten this form of privacy? As discussed above, on the public-law side, there is a fairly robust set of institutions in place that protect this form of political privacy from intrusion by government actors. The nature of these institutions is such that they are largely effective in protecting such critical rights in representative democracies. Comparing public-law protection of political privacy in representative democracies with protections in more repressive regimes like North Korea, the People's Republic of China, Russia, or even Turkey is like night and day. But private actors' access to our personal information in the United States looks a lot like government actors' access in those repressive regimes. And, institutional protections are far less robust in private-law settings, even in representative democracies, than in public-law settings in those democracies, especially in the United States. As I hope to show next, a metaphor from game theory places in high relief the dangers of the failure of private-law institutions to protect the integrity of identity and the ramifications that failure has for social movements and individual and collective self-determination.

Addressing the Tragedy of the Digital Privacy Commons

Central to the pursuit of individual and collective self-determination is the need for the protection of privacy interests that preserve the integrity of identity. Collective efforts are difficult enough without the fear that a group's communications will be subject to infiltration, leading to reprisals against members of groups that might be disfavored in society. Fear of such reprisal will likely have a chilling effect, not just preventing action from taking place but also leading to defections from a threatened group or prospective members not joining the group in the first place. When individuals in a group set out to advance some form of social change, they not only must face the challenge of seeking that change but also must overcome the dilemmas inherent in any collective effort.[67] Such challenges often lead to what are considered collective-action problems, where members of a group "find it difficult to coordinate their actions to secure their group interest."[68] One phenomenon plaguing group efforts is the free-rider problem described in chapter 2, where an individual member of a group may rely on the good will and actions of others in the group, hoping to benefit from group activities and labor without much exertion on their own part. If enough members choose the free-rider approach, the group collapses.[69] Garrett Hardin famously described this phenomenon as the "tragedy of the commons": where individual, wealth-maximizing activity undermines the collective and long-term interests of the group.[70]

In the privacy context, another legal scholar, Dennis Hirsch, has labeled abuses of digital privacy the "tragedy of the trust commons."[71] Such abuses by private companies in possession of our private and personal data will lead to less trust in these actors, discouraging users from engaging in the digital sphere. While this may be a "tragedy" for the private companies that might lose market share, I believe the harms from the breaches of privacy in the digital world are far more dangerous. When companies harvest and sell our personal information, they internalize all the benefits of possessing such information and externalize all of the harms. As Hardin showed in his allegory, when benefits are internalized and harms externalized, society loses.[72]

A modified example from game theory helps show the ways this phenomenon plays out. The Prisoner's Dilemma (PD) is a classic game-theory approach to understanding how collective-action problems unfold. In the traditional PD setting, we are asked to imagine that two prisoners are being detained by law enforcement authorities in separate interview rooms. If each prisoner remains silent, the authorities are unlikely to gather enough information about an incident for which the prisoners have been arrested to charge them with any significant crime. But that requires each prisoner to trust that the other will remain quiet. If one prisoner comes forward to blame the other, that first prisoner will go free and the other will be charged with the crime. Knowing that the first prisoner might identify the second as the culprit could lead the second to blame the first as well. When that happens, both will face stiff charges. Again, each prisoner must trust the other will not blame them for the crime.[73]

Thinking of digital privacy as a modified PD problem helps us see the imbalance of power in the threat that private entities possessing identity-revealing information pose to collective action. In the modified PD arrangement, it is not that each prisoner can throw the other under the bus. Imagine that the two prisoners as not being held in separate rooms but are detained together. Because of this, they can use this opportunity to communicate, plan for the interrogations to come, and get their story straight. We know from research that certain types of behaviors increase trust and cooperation, like face-to-face communications[74] and overt agreements to cooperate.[75] Thus, putting the prisoners together in the cell is likely to increase trust and facilitate the type of collaboration that will generate the optimal outcomes for the prisoners because it will encourage cooperative behavior designed to advance both parties' mutual interests. All this would seem to suggest that the two prisoners will now be able to coordinate their stories and together walk free. But what the second prisoner does not know is that their cellmate is actually working for the authorities and recording the conversation surreptitiously. That informant will then hand it over to the authorities. When we reimagine the privacy-as-collective-action problem in this way, one party is internalizing the benefits of sharing information about the crime and externalizing all of the harm, letting it rest on the cellmate. There is trust between the two actors, but it is misplaced trust. There is also another problem of asymmetry of information between the two prisoners: one knows they are an informant, the other does not. This misplaced trust and asymmetry of information leads to a form of moral hazard: one prisoner having such damaging information on the other leads the first to engage in action that will benefit him at the expense of the other, that is, the one who divulged damaging information about himself believing it would remain secret.

In the digital world, we have a misplaced level of trust in the companies that possess personal information about us. Dilemmas of collective action often involve intragroup dysfunction, and it might seem strange to consider private companies as being within the group. But when members of a group use digital tools to organize and communicate (and it is hard to think of a contemporary group not using any such tools), they are letting the entities that have access to those tools—the platform operators, the cloud service providers, even the internet and cellular companies that carry the messages—into the group's activities. Such companies can internalize the benefits group members' trust for these providers and externalize the harms by monitoring and divulging the group's private information without its members' knowledge and with no benefit to the group.

The problem of protecting digital privacy can be recast as a collective-action problem to emphasize the need for greater protection for the integrity of identity. Whenever collective action is needed to generate public goods, dilemmas of collective action can plague the endeavor. When private companies have information about our digital selves in their possession, enjoy asymmetry of information about the use of such information, and can internalize the benefits of that information and externalize the harm, it threatens the generation of the goods that can come from cooperative behavior. In addition, there is asymmetry of bargaining power between companies and end users: engagement with the digital world is becoming central to contemporary life, whether it is accessing information to understand current events, to find like-minded individuals, to participate in civic activities, to search for a job, or to find a life partner.[76] These capacities are all central to the formation of social bonds and developing one's identity.[77] As I will discuss in chapter 4, there is also little accountability for privacy abuses, which leads to moral hazard.[78] These phenomena show that the need to protect political privacy and generate the goods that political privacy can engender is a collective-action problem. Collective-action problems arise when it is difficult to monitor and compel cooperation, as is the case today with the behavior of companies that appear to have free rein over our digital information. Guardrails are needed to encourage cooperative behavior and to punish predatory conduct. What makes the need for such guardrails even more imperative is the fact that collective action to reform the privacy rules themselves is under threat when our political privacy is at risk. Without such privacy protections, our ability to affect the laws that protect privacy is itself under threat.

Where and how should we strive to create a legal and institutional framework for protecting the integrity of identity and political privacy in private-law contexts? How might advocates, policymakers, legislators, and regulators choose the right strategies, through the right institutions, to protect political privacy? One approach for identifying the best setting in which to achieve a policy goal is to use the one championed by Komesar (mentioned in chapter 1). Using that method, we might attempt to choose between the best institutional spheres in which to create such a framework: the markets, the political process, or the courts. However, these three institutional settings have failed to protect political privacy in private-law settings; otherwise there would be no need to develop protections for privacy in the era of Surveillance Capitalism. What I hope to show in chapters 4 and 5 is that one of the reasons that we do need to intervene in this context is that each of these institutional spheres generates negative externalities when it comes to political privacy in the private-law context: spillovers into the other spheres that make it more difficult to protect such privacy. Thus, the discipline of Comparative Institutional Analysis fails to offer a clear choice *among* such spheres for the setting in which to protect political privacy when it comes to intrusions upon it by private actors. Instead of choosing among them, we must view the three spheres simultaneously to understand how efforts in one can undermine or strengthen efforts in the others. Only then can we adopt an inter-institutional approach—rather than a comparative approach—to protecting political privacy. In chapters 4 and 5, I examine how the markets, the political process, and the courts have all failed to protect political privacy in private-law contexts. I argue that this failure is not a function of each sphere falling short on its own; rather, this failure is a product of the three institutional settings rendering the others ineffective when it comes to protecting political privacy in private-law contexts. As a result, any approach to protecting political privacy when it comes to private actors will have to not just compare these settings against each other but also consider the ways in which they interact and relate to each other in the broad policymaking context. I will show that effective policymaking in this context (and likely others) is not necessarily a process of choosing *between* different institutional systems but, instead, requires an appreciation for how they are interdependent. As a result, policymaking likely requires a comprehensive view that recognizes this interdependence and attempts to catalyze it rather than face policymaking paralysis because of it.

4

Comparing Institutions

I have tried to make the case that we need to protect political privacy in the United States more robustly than we do at present, particularly in the use and abuse of our private information by private entities and actors. There are many challenges to any effort to protect this form of privacy, whether such protections take the form of changes that businesses adopt voluntarily, regulations or legislation passed through the political process, or legal doctrines that are enforced in courts. Any approach to changing the legal landscape—the institutional landscape, using the term "institution" in the broad sense—will require not only that we, first, map out that privacy-protecting landscape as it currently exists. Second, we will have to develop an understanding of the ways in which privacy is protected or not protected at present. Finally, we will have to develop an appreciation for the different approaches, settings, tools, actors, and organizations that can strengthen the system for protecting political privacy. Before turning to the question of the current state of political privacy, I introduce two analytical tools for assessing the institutional framework that currently structures the protections—or lack of protections—around digital political privacy. The point is to inform the discussion that will follow in subsequent chapters, with the ultimate goal of providing analytical tools to those who might want to advocate for greater protections for political privacy, tools that I use myself throughout the remainder of this book.

Determining the appropriate institution or institutions for regulating political privacy will require not just that we identify appropriate mechanisms for regulating this form of privacy but also that we compare those mechanisms against each other to determine the best approach among a range of different options. Such a methodology requires using the first analytical tool that I will describe in this chapter: the discipline of Comparative Institutional Analysis (hereinafter sometimes abbreviated as CIA). This approach seeks to inform the choice between different institutional settings when one has a desired policy goal. It identifies the market, the political processes, and the courts as the different settings within which one can achieve such a goal. According to this type of analysis, one identifies a desired policy goal and determines the best institutional setting that is most capable of achieving that policy goal based on the nature of that setting. Each such setting—which, again, this methodology identifies as the market, the political process, and the courts—has its own characteristics and logics, and some are better than others at realizing different solutions to complex policy problems. CIA as a methodology provides tools to determine the best choice among institutional settings for resolving a particular problem. But it looks at not just the nature of a single institutional setting; it also looks at the nature of the problem that one is trying to solve to determine the right setting in which to resolve that problem, given the characteristics of the problem and the suitability of the institutional setting for addressing the nature of that problem. I describe this methodology in some detail here and ask whether, given the nature of the problems posed by the challenge of protecting political privacy, there is a specific institutional setting that is appropriate for achieving the desired policy goal of preserving the integrity of identity.

This analysis of the current state of political privacy reveals that choosing between one of the three institutional settings (the market, political process, and courts) to find the most effective one for protecting political privacy may not be so easy, however. Rather, I show that the current practices, laws, and norms in these settings around political privacy have spillover effects on the other institutional settings. Because of that phenomenon, it is difficult to consider one institutional setting in isolation to assess its strengths for protecting political privacy without also understanding the ways that it might influence other settings and, in turn, how other settings may also have an effect on it. It is thus difficult to engage in CIA in this context when, as I show below, the different institutional settings have considerable impacts on the other settings. Because of this fact, there is a lot more noise rather than signal: one cannot really engage in CIA among the market, political process, and courts because one cannot consider them without assessing their relationships to the others and the way actions in one setting can have positive and negative effects on the operations of the others. Again, my goal here is to provide advocates and others with the analytical tools for assessing the possibility of, and generating successful efforts directed toward, social change. This sort of comparative analysis of institutional settings in which change might take place is just one of these methods for building such campaigns.

The second analytical tool I use to assess the state of political privacy is a typology of institutions utilized by political economists Daron Acemoglu and James Robinson, which I introduced in chapter 1. They identify institutions as either inclusive or extractive. Inclusive economic institutions "allow and encourage participation by the great mass of people in economic activities that make best use of their talents and skills and that enable individuals to make the choices they wish."[1] These include an array of property rights, respect for the rule of law, a supportive welfare state, and a government system that enforces the rules in a nonbiased fashion. Extractive institutions do the opposite: they elevate a particular group or groups over the majority of the population, showing bias and favoritism that entrenches and perpetuates hierarchy and inequality. Inclusive economic systems are supported by inclusive political structures and vice versa. An extractive political system favors elites and consolidates power within that elite. I examine the current institutional framework as it relates to political privacy within the context of Surveillance Capitalism with reference to this typology. Viewing the institutional framework around political privacy through this typology strongly suggests that this system is largely governed by extractive institutions and that such institutions have serious and negative downstream effects.

After describing these two analytical approaches, I then turn to the current state of political privacy under Surveillance Capitalism. I examine the evolution of the laws, norms, and practices with respect to our digital information to date. Once we can establish a baseline understanding of the protections that exist—or do not exist—when it comes to protecting political privacy, we can then begin to explore not just what reforms might be necessary to protect this form of privacy but also those that might be possible.

This chapter addresses the first set of questions: What are the current protections for political privacy in private-law settings, and can we identify the appropriate institution or institutions for regulating this form of privacy in such settings? But by engaging in a deep analysis of the institutions that do (or could) protect political privacy, a better method for engaging in this type of institutional analysis emerges. What this review will show is not just that the current institutional framework fails to protect political privacy in private-law setting but also that it is not enough to simply choose among a set of institutions when determining the best approach to protecting political privacy. We must develop an appreciation for the ways in which institutions can sometimes work at cross-purposes when it comes to achieving a desired policy goal, and, if we are to compare the institutions against each other, we must also understand how they also must work together to achieve a goal because of their interdependence. Only after we have such an appreciation for the ways that institutions function in practice can we develop a theory for how they might work to protect political privacy and how we might go about working to ensure that they do. This chapter will explore the current state of political privacy in private-law settings. This sets the stage for the chapters to come, where I examine not just the contours of an institutional framework for protecting privacy in such settings but also a methodology for altering the current framework itself.

Comparing Institutions

Comparative Institutional Analysis as a methodology had its roots in the transaction–cost economics favored by Ronald Coase, but it was championed by legal scholar Neil Komesar. Komesar argued that we should think about the pursuit of policy goals through an institutional lens: it is a process embedded within an institutional framework.[2] Certain types of institutions are better suited to achieve a desired policy goal given the nature of the policy problem one is trying to address and the capacities of the institutional setting in which one might solve it. Komesar identifies three such settings: the market, the political process, and the courts, and each setting has relatively unique characteristics that are better at solving different types of problems. When determining how to address a policy problem, Komesar argues that one needs to compare these institutional settings against each other to determine the optimal setting in which to address the problem. Komesar's significant contribution to the literature around institutions is his assertion that most efforts to address policy problems involve what he calls "single institutional analysis." This type of analysis criticizes how a particular problem is addressed in a particular setting without assessing whether another setting might be better (or worse) than another in achieving a desired policy goal. For Komesar, one can have a critique of an approach to a problem and can critique that approach, but one must also assess the extent to which other institutional settings might be superior or inferior to addressing a problem.[3]

The different institutional settings that Komesar identified have different characteristics, features, and processes, and some are better than others at doing certain things and achieving different goals. In theory, the market might allocate capital efficiently, directing it toward its best and most efficient use. The rewards available to market actors can spur innovation, and market forces can generate what is sometimes referred to as "creative destruction": innovation emerges in light of market signals and results in outcomes that improve economic performance.[4] The political process can help to elevate interests and create an environment in which those who might have less influence within the market can still bring about policy reform, particularly as it relates to the market itself. Courts, too, have their own unique characteristics. For Komesar, it is harder to gain access to the courts (when compared to, say, calling a legislator) because of the rules surrounding who has a right to petition the court (as well as the practical expense of bringing a legal challenge, including the cost of legal representation); the authority of the courts is limited when it comes to resolving disputes; and judges are supposed to have a degree of independence, which in theory insulates them from improper influence from the other institutional settings.[5] The unique institutional role of courts, at least in the American system, is to ensure that political processes are being adhered to and that private parties have a forum in which to resolve disputes.[6] A failure to play their proper institutional role within the broader field, and in relation to the other institutional settings, threatens the very legitimacy of courts as an institution.[7]

As Komesar would do, we can look at the problem of addressing industrial pollution through a comparative-institutional lens to illuminate the value of the methodology in assisting in the choice among the trio of institutional settings for achieving desired policy goals. In the late 1960s, before Congress had passed major environmental legislation like the Clean Air Act, there was a growing appreciation for the need to regulate industrial pollution. The private sector was the source of the problem and showed no signs that it would voluntarily rein in its actions. What is more, industrial polluters had powerful lobbyists who had an ability to stifle any serious effort to regulate industrial emissions. A group of residents in upstate New York sought a different route to address pollution that was emanating from a cement plant in their community. They filed a lawsuit against the plant, claiming it was a nuisance: the toxic fumes discharged by the plant posed an unreasonable risk to the health and safety to the community that surrounded it. The trial court in the case came up with a novel solution, one that New York's highest court would uphold in *Boomer v. Atlantic Cement Co.* (1970).[8] In *Boomer*, Komesar explains that the goal that the court was attempting to achieve was resource allocation efficiency, not equity or environmental protection.[9] Given that policy goal, the judicial view of the dispute was that the economic benefit to be gained by the cement plant's activities was greater than the harm caused to the small number of residents who brought the lawsuit.[10] In order to balance out the benefits and burdens, the court found that it was appropriate to order the plant's owners to compensate the residents for any harms the plant's emissions caused. Since the overall economic benefits of the continued operation of the plant seemed to outweigh the harms it caused, the proper course of action—from an efficiency standpoint—was to come to this result.[11]

When seen through the lens of CIA, with the goal of economic efficiency, the institutional setting that seemed to have the greatest capacity for resolving the dispute in a way that achieved an efficient outcome—one that balanced the benefits against the externalities or harms caused by the plant's activities—was the courts. Where the market would have let the plant operate in an untrammeled fashion, and the political processes were paralyzed by the business interests that stood in the way of any real reform, the judicial setting seemed to serve as the most appropriate institutional setting in which to address this problem. Market actors were unwilling to engage in self-restraint. The political process seemed incapable of achieving appropriate reforms given the intensity of the interests of those who might lobby against pollution controls, as well as the lack of a concerted popular movement to press for them within the political process. The capacity of courts to resolve this type of dispute, then, when compared to the relative lack of an ability of the other institutional settings to achieve a particular policy goal, meant that the courts seemed the appropriate setting to reach that goal.

Of course, economic efficiency is just one of a wide range of goals one might want to achieve. One might have as a goal economic fairness, or one might want industry to act in an unfettered fashion. For Komesar, depending on one's policy goal, one should calibrate and direct one's efforts to achieve that goal based on the features, capacities, and characteristics of a specific institutional setting—the market, the political process, or the courts—to determine the setting that has the greatest likelihood—comparatively—of bringing about that goal.

As a market grows in size, as does the complexity of transactions negotiated within it, monitoring market actors becomes more difficult.[12] Litigation can become more drawn out and sprawling as the number of parties grows, the complexity of the issues increases, and the relief sought is more far-reaching.[13] The field of politics can face challenges in responding to the needs of a diverse population, and rent-seeking elites that are highly motivated and focused on their policy goals can overwhelm a diffuse and poorly organized populace or one that faces greater coordination challenges as the size of a collective entity grows.[14]

An increase in the scope, scale, and/or complexity of problems is likely to make problem-solving and policy advocacy more challenging. In such situations, CIA itself will become more difficult to apply, but that does not mean it should be abandoned altogether.[15] But it might suggest that the simple framework proposed by Komesar—that we must choose between three broad settings when choosing to advance a desired policy goal—fails to capture the fact that there may not be a single setting in which to advance that goal. It also does not take into account a range of other characteristics of these settings, namely that they are not as simple and uniform internally as one might prefer when conducting this sort of comparative work. Nor does it consider the potential for spillover: domination within one setting can have lasting extra-institutional effects. That is, a strong market player, with significant resources, might be able to overwhelm both the political process and the courts and can achieve its own policy goals to the detriment of other actors.

Komesar readily admits that he crafted his methodology to be "as simple, accessible, and intuitively sensible as possible"[16] and did not

offer it as "the last word on the topic."[17] What is more, he also understood that as a policy problem grows in scale and complexity, the task
of Comparative Institutional Analysis becomes more difficult and the
challenges that problem-solving poses within particular settings also
become more difficult.[18] While I will return to the use and application
of CIA to achieve the policy goal of protecting political privacy further
below, there is another institutional issue I want to explore next: one way
of looking at institutions and their impact on society.

A Typology of Institutions

Acemoglu and Robinson classify critical economic institutions as either
being inclusive or extractive. For these authors—who certainly fall on
the side of seeing institutions largely as laws, legal structures, norms,
mores, and habits more than as organizations—inclusive institutions
include: norms, laws, and practices that respect private property; having an "unbiased" legal system that comports with the rule of law; and
having a government that provides public services and thereby ensures
there is a level playing field for economic activity.[19] In contrast, extractive economic institutions tend to do the opposite: they favor a small
group of insiders, privileging their interests over those who are not
among the favored. In such systems, the state fails to provide services
to the community in an unbiased fashion.[20] Inclusive and exclusive economic institutions are often matched with either inclusive or exclusive
political systems: an economic system that is unbiased is usually coupled with a political system that recognizes civil rights and distributes
power within it broadly.[21] Open and inclusive political systems distribute power broadly, with a degree of equality, and subject that power to
effective constraints,[22] whereas extractive political institutions "concen-
trate power in the hands of a narrow elite and place few constraints on
the exercise of this power."[23]

Getting to a point where a society has inclusive institutions is not
easy. There is a constant power struggle among elites, the state, and the
broader population. Acemoglu and Robinson describe the path toward
a well-functioning society, one with inclusive institutions, as a "narrow
corridor," one that both advances economic development and democracy; when operating within this corridor, "state and society do not just

compete, they also cooperate."[24] Such cooperation "engenders greater capacity for the state to deliver the things that society wants and foments greater societal mobilization to monitor this capacity." Achieving this balance requires that the "state and its elites must learn to live with the shackles society puts on them and different segments of society have to learn to work together despite their differences."[25]

Acemoglu and Robinson also argue that a sort of path dependency occurs where the farther one goes down a particular path the harder it is to recover from it.[26] But there is also a virtuous cycle: inclusive institutions beget and extend inclusive economic and political practices.[27] One can certainly stray from the narrow corridor and descend into antidemocratic institutions and practices that favor elites, which, once established, are hard to change because the elites continue to strengthen their position to make it harder and harder to engage in a course correction. At the same time, the more robust the democratic and inclusive institutions, the harder it is to capture them and direct them toward favoring elite interests.

What can we make of the current institutions that protect—or fail to protect—political privacy? In an effort to assess the present state of political privacy in the age of Surveillance Capitalism, the next section provides an overview of the institutions that have emerged that guide practices in the attention economy. As the following discussion shows, it is not difficult to determine that these practices are largely extractive. Moreover, as I also show, there does not appear to be a single institutional setting that is better positioned than another to protect political privacy because they all seem to operate in an interdependent fashion to create an extractive environment where elites are able to draw on and internalize significant benefits from the system while externalizing the harms and imposing them on users.

The Extractive Institutions of Surveillance Capitalism

In chapter 3, I explored the ways in which political privacy is protected by a fairly robust set of laws and norms when it comes to government actors. In many ways, that set of norms has become institutionalized: Americans expect that the government will not spy on them without legal justification or authorization; that they will have remedies against the government in the courts if the state does; and the institutionalization itself has a force of its own, restraining government actors and providing individuals with a sense that they have a degree of space and freedom within which to act in ways that allow them to realize self-determination. Over time, the right to privacy as it relates to private actors has evolved. It emerged first as a private right that an individual can enforce in the courts against another individual when it is violated, and some state and federal laws exist that bolster that right. Second, in the digital space, a set of institutional practices has emerged that has largely immunized private actors from any responsibility for privacy violations that occur in private settings in the digital Upside Down. There are four types of immunities that have emerged in the digital space: *contractual immunity, statutory immunity, adjudicative immunity,* and *enforcement immunity.* I discuss each of these, in turn, next. What is more, an assessment of these immunities leads to the inexorable conclusion that the institutions that affect political privacy, the entire array of them, are extractive in nature under the Acemoglu–Robinson typology.

Contractual Immunity

"Click Accept to proceed." Anyone who has downloaded an app, used a website for services, or logged on to social media has done it. Throughout our digital existence, we are bombarded with terms-of-service contracts; requests that we accept cookies, those bits of code that monitor and track our activities online and feed information back to the companies that place a breadcrumb trail that follows our online movements; and requests that we permit a site or app to know our location, which, it is claimed, is necessary to improve the site's ability to serve us. We are also constantly told that the terms of service required on sites and apps we use frequently have changed, and we can review all we want about those changes, though few ever do. The terms of the permissions we grant to the companies that expect us to accept them are often buried deep in the bowels of the contracts as fine print that few people will ever read, especially if some benefit awaits us just as soon as we click "Accept" to continue. Within these terms of service are, far more often than not, a range of permissions, including that the company providing whatever the service might be can sell the private information shared with the company over the site or app with other companies. Those third-party companies can, in turn, put that information to whatever use those entities, which have no direct relationship to the users themselves, deem beneficial for those companies' own use, with little regard for the needs, interests, or rights of consumers. Legal scholar Nancy Kim has described this form of agreement as being so much more than a shield for companies that secure permission to share our personal data; it is a sword.[28] While the contracts provide an immunity to the company from liability—a freedom *from* liability—it also becomes a freedom *to*—an ability to profit from that user's information however that company sees fit. Yes, we can always reject such terms of service and permissions, but it is far too inconvenient to stop whatever one is doing to read these contracts, which are steeped in legalese. Because of the complexity of the terms, it is not generally clear to the average layperson what it is he or she are accepting, and there is a profound asymmetry of information in these relationships: the companies know and understand exactly what it is their customers are agreeing to, and that is rarely the case when it comes to the customers themselves.[29]

What is more, the so-called attention economy also has a side to it that encourages immediate gratification, channeling online users to accept any terms regardless of the potential impact on privacy. The ubiquity and prominence of digital resources in our lives—whether purchasing tickets to a commuter rail line, ordering from a food delivery service, or streaming a news report or a prestige drama on television—when coupled with our acculturation to a perceived need for convenience and speed in everything we do throughout our day, means that we enter into these sorts of agreements constantly, and we operate under them in virtually everything we do in the digital space. This is what legal scholars Brett Frischmann and Evan Selinger have called "engineered determinism": there is little we can do to escape these contracts when it comes to essential aspects of contemporary life. Indeed, as they describe it (with an appropriate nod to the Borg from *Star Trek: The Next Generation*): "Deliberation is wasteful. There's no room to bargain. Resistance is futile."[30]

These forces all align to create contractual immunity: the entities that provide services in the digital space have largely insulated themselves from any type of liability for breaching customers' privacy. These companies do this by placing immunity in the contracts that serve as the entry point to the perceived (and desired) benefits they offer users. Yes, there are companies, some of them quite large, like Apple, or others that are less popular, like the browser DuckDuckGo, that market themselves as protecting users' privacy. The dominant paradigm in the digital space is that the companies whose products and services we use have largely convinced us, with little effort, to sign away our ability to protect our private actions in digital spaces. Thus, when it comes to the institutional practices of many companies that provide services through digital channels, we have largely granted them immunity, through the contracts we accept, for what most would consider violations of our privacy. There have been efforts to rein in some of the worst abuses of this deterministic system, with the European Union and states like California attempting to curb some of the most prevalent and extractive privacy-breaching practices by improving the disclosures companies must provide. If the terms of the agreements that companies use are not accessible and understandable, however, disclosure that merely directs people to end-user agreements that are still meaningless to the layperson, this will not really rein in contractual immunity.[31] But contractual immunity is not the only kind of immunity that protects companies that have access to our digital information.

Statutory Immunity

Private companies are not the only entities that have gotten into the immunity act. In the early days of the internet, the U.S. Congress passed the monumental Communications Decency Act (CDA).[32] While many aspects of the legislation have been struck down by the U.S. Supreme Court for chilling protected speech,[33] one component has survived challenge after challenge in the courts: Section 230. That provision extends immunity to digital platforms for the content placed on such platforms by third-party users.[34] The purpose behind Section 230 was to ensure that platforms such as Facebook and other social media sites could operate with a high degree of protection from individuals who might claim that someone had posted something on the site that was defamatory or caused some harm to those individuals.[35] As a result, many companies with a digital presence enjoy immunity under Section 230, what I will call "statutory immunity" because of its basis in the law as passed by Congress and upheld by the Supreme Court. In 2023, in two cases before the Court involving horrific acts of violence that, it was argued, were planned over social media, the immunity granted by Section 230 was considered practically airtight: no matter how heinous the offense, a platform could not be held responsible for things that third parties say or coordinate using the application.[36] But the Supreme Court did seem open to the possibility that a site could be held accountable if it mixed user content with its own affirmative acts, like knowingly pushing that content through its algorithms to users in an explicit manner.[37] Still, no company has yet found itself liable to any consumers under this theory.

Adjudicative Immunity

Connected to these first two immunities is what I call "adjudicative immunity": that is, immunity from having to resolve disputes in a setting that is neutral and is not tilted largely in favor of the companies that an end-user might try to sue, for example in the event that the company has breached its own terms of service between the user and that company. Buried in many of these end-user agreements are provisions that require that any dispute under the agreement, where a user might claim a company is in violation of that agreement, must be resolved through the arbitration process. This involves, in effect, resolution in a business-friendly forum that is not governed by the same due process rules that bind the functioning of government courts.[38] Such arbitration clauses often prohibit individual consumers from trying to band together when they have all been the victims of the same practice by a company, displacing the possibility that such consumers might form a class and bring a class action suit in civil court where they might level the playing field.[39] These agreements might even prevent a group of individuals from coming together and trying to bring an arbitration as a class.[40] Channeling such disputes to these forums tends to favor business interests at the outset. As legal scholar Margaret Jean Radin has argued, arbitration is generally favored by businesses for a number of reasons, including that the decisions are generally issued in secret, individual consumers cannot generally form class groups, and the arbitrators themselves are often retired business officials and perceived as favoring business interests.[41] Empirical research of the outcomes of these cases generally tends to show that the results of these disputes are largely favorable to the businesses.[42] What is more, consumers are often hesitant to resort to arbitration because it is costly for an individual to pursue a claim through arbitration. In comparison, other forms of actions, like those involving a class of plaintiffs where the costs of bringing litigation can be spread across the members of the class, are far more cost-effective for the consumer.[43]

Prosecutorial Immunity

The fourth type of immunity that impacts the institutional frame-work for holding private companies accountable for privacy violations is prosecutorial immunity. Perhaps because of the power of the other three immunities, government entities like state attorneys general and local district attorneys have largely refrained from bringing cases against companies for privacy violations related to those govern-ment actors' constituents. But even when they do, their actions will not exactly strike fear in the hearts of companies that might see it as advantageous to capture and sell their customers' private data. The Federal Trade Commission (FTC) has taken some actions related to digital privacy. At the same time, it has largely refrained from taking serious action against some high-profile companies even in the face of significant privacy breaches.[44] The FTC did go after Facebook in the wake of the Cambridge Analytica scandal and secured a $5 billion fine for the actions that led to it. At least one commentator, technol-ogy reporter Kara Swisher, has argued that the fine the FTC imposed was little more than a "parking ticket" when considered in light of Facebook's size and market valuation.[45] As a result, the penalty was unlikely to have any serious deterrent effect that might prevent com-panies as large as Facebook from engaging in similar conduct in the future. While there are examples of state attorneys general tak-ing some actions for breaches of privacy by companies in the digital space,[46] they typically do not have the resources of federal authorities and thus are in a weaker position than the federal government when it comes to policing breaches of digital privacy.

* * *

What I hope is apparent from this description of the immunities that make up the institutional landscape in which Surveillance Capitalism operates is that the framework that might protect digital privacy in private-law settings is weak at best and harmful at worst. This framework not only allows the practices of Surveillance Capitalism to flourish but also likely facilitated those practices in the first place, creating the environment from which Surveillance Capitalism could emerge. And that's one of the features of institutional frameworks: they tend to set a system down a particular path and, once embedded, are hard to change. What is more, as Radin points out, these immunities create a "degradation of democracy," especially when it comes to political privacy: they can strip legislative measures designed to offer some type of protection that are passed through the democratic process of force and effect, further undermining democratic self-determination.[47] We are thus at the mercy of the companies that possess the most intimate details of our lives, are often powerless to try to hold them accountable for breaches of our privacy, and cannot even band together with others to address the current state of affairs.

Another aspect of institutional analysis is to assess them according to the binary typology favored by Acemoglu and Robinson: they are either extractive or inclusive. Looking at these immunities as helping to form the institutional framework of Surveillance Capitalism, it is not difficult to determine on which side of the binary they fall. Returning to the other analytical tool that might help us assess these institutions, given the institutional framework that exists at present, is it possible to engage in a Comparative Institutional Analysis of the settings where we might protect political privacy? Can we choose among institutions to find the best institutional framework in which to center a regime that would protect digital privacy in private-law spaces? Can Comparative Institutional Analysis aid in that process? It is to these questions that I now turn.

Comparing the Institutional Settings Where We Might Protect Political Privacy

If the discussion of the four immunities that currently protect political privacy tells us anything, it is that the current institutional landscape regarding this form of privacy is certainly extractive. But another thing it shows is that the relevant institutions—the norms, practices, and laws—operate in such a way that it is difficult to say whether there is a single institutional setting, even when we take the three into account in the Komesarian approach (the market, political process, and courts), where we might achieve the policy goal of protecting political privacy. The market is clearly not doing enough to protect political privacy, but the logic of the market has something to offer in terms of creating incentives for businesses to provide greater safety and security to users. The political process, at the level of the federal government (the U.S. Congress and the executive branch) appears incapable or powerless to engage in any meaningful efforts to rein in breaches of political privacy. As this book goes to print, privacy legislation at the federal level has been stymied for years, partly a function of legislators not quite knowing how the relevant technology works, but also because of the powerful technology lobby that has long resisted efforts to regulate giant technology companies. What is more, it is important to remember that it was Congress that passed the immunity contained in the Communications Decency Act, which through Section 230 has made it extremely difficult, if not impossible, to hold social media and other platforms responsible for the activity on their sites. When it comes to the executive branch, recent Supreme Court decisions limiting the power of the executive branch to go beyond the express permission granted to it by Congress or the Constitution make it difficult for the president or federal agencies to take anything but enforcement actions for violations of well-established principles, like those involving anticompetitive behavior. Thus, within the political process, the key actors at the federal level—Congress and the executive branch—seem unwilling or unable to take significant action to protect political privacy.

Even if the courts were viewed as a potential venue for the protection of digital privacy, the courts, too, are similarly hamstrung, for a number of reasons. The immunities granted through the terms-of-service agreements are difficult for private litigants to circumvent to hold technology companies accountable for breaches of privacy, unless those breaches are, themselves, violations of the terms of service agreements themselves.[48] Moreover, as stated earlier, Section 230 immunity under the Communications Decency Act also largely insulates technology companies from any responsibility for harmful activity on their platforms, including privacy violations (although an individual user might be able to sue another individual user for such a violation, like sharing revenge porn). But the platforms have no liability themselves, and thus they have no incentive to engage in greater content moderation to prevent such activity from taking place in the first place or to move quickly to remove such content from their sites after the fact. While I have characterized this type of immunity as legislative in nature, a product of the political process, it is also a class of immunity that is enforced through the courts, revealing the inter-institutional nature of these different protections that create the underlying architecture of Surveillance Capitalism.

I hope this discussion makes clear that it is difficult, at present, to engage in Comparative Institutional Analysis in an effort to select an institutional setting from among the Komesarian trio (the market, the political process, and the courts) to find that one that is superior to the others in terms of achieving the goal of protecting political privacy in private-law settings. One of the reasons for this is that, if we analyze the immunities that currently protect technology companies for violating political privacy, they are designed not just to operate within a particular institutional setting. No, they all have cross-institutional effects as well, a sort of game of rock paper scissors, although one in which the providers always win no matter which object they signal. Congress has created Section 230 immunity, which means the executive branch can hardly take action contrary to it and courts are powerless to circumvent it where it applies. Similarly, the market has created end-user agreements that serve as a shield against individuals bringing actions for breaches of privacy in the courts. And courts have certainly done their part as well by upholding these immunities, whether contractual or legislative, and are likely to limit the executive branch in the efforts it might take to rein in violations of political privacy.

So, where does this leave us? Are those who might advocate for greater protections for political privacy in private-law contexts powerless to make change? If it is impossible to choose among institutional settings when seeking to make such change, does that mean change is also impossible? Could we utilize a form of Comparative Institutional Analysis, one that simultaneously draws from and utilizes the best characteristics of the different institutional settings while also accounting for the fact that institutional settings can sometimes work at cross-purposes—as appears to be the case when it comes to political privacy—in order to achieve meaningful reform that protects political privacy in private-law settings? Instead of comparative institutional analysis, perhaps we need a way to find how institutions can *converge*, or come together, to create effective change, because they certainly can converge to prevent change, which seems to be happening when it comes to accountability in the digital space.

What such an effort will require might mean a shift in our analytical tools, one that looks not merely to compare and select between different institutional settings to find the optimal, singular location in which to center actions to further policy change. Instead, such an effort will seek to leverage the most effective elements of the three institutional settings and then ensure that they can be harmonized in such a way that does not have adverse inter-institutional effects.

Strengthening the legal infrastructure that might protect political privacy also requires a deeper appreciation for the characteristics of the institutional settings. As is apparent, they can each have extra-institutional effects. An understanding of the ways in which there can be these institutional spillovers is essential to any analysis that seeks to locate effective policymaking efforts. Such a view might leave one despondent, with a sense that, no matter which successes advocates might have in one setting, those successes might be offset by losses in another. But such a view relies on a perspective on institutional settings that sees them as monolithic. And when one sees them in this way, it is easy to perceive them as likely resistant to change. As I explore in chapter 5, however, institutional systems, in the real world, are *not* monolithic: there is a fair amount of heterogeneity *within* the institutional settings themselves, which makes operating within them more complex and creates more opportunities to leverage institutions for positive change. What I offer in chapter 5 is a deeper analysis of institutions and institutional settings. Through that analysis, I try to foster an appreciation for the varied characteristics of the three institutional settings, including the ways in which they interact with one another, and the ways in which advocates can work to change them from the inside out. Such an appreciation will help set the stage for the creation of a regime for protecting political privacy and also offer a road map for establishing that regime.

The remainder of this book will focus on these two issues. The first is devising an inter-institutional scheme for the protection of political privacy, one that reflects the heterogeneity of institutions, draws from the best features of each institutional setting, and seeks to limit perverse inter-institutional effects. The second is developing a theory of change, steeped in a deep appreciation for how institutions operate, that can help bring that scheme to life. The goal of this effort is to offer advocates not just with a framework for reining in the worst, privacy-abusing practices of Surveillance Capitalism but also a methodology for bringing that framework into existence.

5

Blended Rules, Hybrid Institutions

Our ability to function effectively within a democracy depends upon a degree of liberty to act that includes within it the freedom to think, to inquire, to seek out others, and to communicate with them to advance a collective goal. To describe that cluster of freedoms, and to capture these concepts, I have used the phrase "political privacy." Since this idea of political privacy is so intertwined with our notions of self and identify, protecting the integrity of identity is essential to the democratic project because its preservation is the wellspring of democratic self-actualization and collective self-determination. It is critical to democracy that we have a protected space where the integrity of identity can be realized and the need to create and preserve such a space is more apparent at a time when digital tools and new technologies open up more space for collective action and connection, and such spaces are becoming more and more porous, threatening the very possibility of collective, democratic action. *What* such a protected space should look like, and *how* to bring it about, shall be the focus of the remainder of this book.

Designing a system for protecting political privacy will require not just a goal—that is, a desire to maintain the integrity of identity in the age of Surveillance Capitalism—but also a sense of how to build such a system and where to locate that system within an institutional setting or settings. There is no question that, given the political power of large technology companies—the ones that would have the most to lose by a significant change in the legal landscape of Surveillance Capitalism— the cards are likely stacked against any effort to create a more robust system of privacy legislation. Technology companies already resist efforts to rein in abuses that occur on their platforms, and that can take the form of dismissing concerns that their sites offer breeding grounds for terrorism, domestic and international; or complaining that any effort to address problems related to political privacy will stifle free speech or is simply too difficult to carry out, meaning it will cut into their business model. Adding to the admittedly complicated nature of the problem is the fact that contemporary mobilization efforts require the speed and reach of social media networks. The platforms not only possess the ability to influence legislators due to their economic might, which translates into political might; they also can squelch dissent on their platforms, use algorithms to reduce the prominence of efforts to organize around building a robust political privacy regime, and engage in what one commentator has called "parlor tricks" designed to appear like they are supporting greater regulation around privacy even as they strive to undermine it.[1]

For these reasons, any effort to strengthen the protections around political privacy will need to analyze the current state of affairs with respect to political privacy (which I hope the reader feels I have done already), identify a potential model or models for protecting that privacy, and develop an approach for the widespread adoption of those models. Since I have tried to describe the current state of affairs in institutional terms, and have utilized social movement scholarship that views social change in institutional terms as well, I will attempt to assess, through an institutional lens, what an effort to protect political privacy might look like. The first element, and the main focus of this chapter, is an analysis of the optimal system for protecting political privacy, one that identifies the best institutional setting or settings where policy change can happen and the best array of legal and regulatory protections that will protect privacy in an effective way. I look at two aspects of institutions. First, I assess the broad institutional settings identified by Komesar (the market, the political process, and the courts) to identify the appropriate setting in which to seek policy change in this area. Second, considering institutions also as laws, rules, and norms, I attempt to explore what type of laws or rules are necessary to protect that privacy. Any effort to bring about institutional change requires an analysis of the optimal location or locations where such change can take place and then a sense of what change is desired. This chapter lays out a framework for analyzing the problem of reforming political privacy in institutional terms and I will attempt to identify a potential model for thinking about that reform. In chapter 6, I articulate what that model could be, and in chapter 7 I explore how advocates could think about how to bring that model into existence. This set of concluding chapters can serve as a study of the problem of reforming political privacy, but they also offer a way to think about social change itself through an institutional lens. Any effort to bring about institutional reform (to laws, to institutional settings, and to organizations) in a particular area requires an understanding of how institutions operate within that area, the dynamics that create openings for change or stand in the way of that change, and the methods by which those dynamics can be harnessed to catalyze change or undermined when they might resist it. The remainder of this book is dedicated to developing a richer understanding of those dynamics so that groups committed to reforming the current system of political privacy can strive to achieve such reform. It also serves as a reflection on social change as an institutional enterprise. It is to these endeavors that I now turn.

Choosing Between and Among Institutional Settings

The first step in a process for assessing opportunities for reform is to determine whether there is a setting or settings where advocates might locate their advocacy to drive such institutional reform. Using Komesar's framework, might one look to the markets, the political processes, or the courts as the focal points for such advocacy? Is one of those settings more likely than another to yield to pressure from advocacy efforts? But such an analytical framework, I argue, is incomplete and fails to offer a full picture of not just the inter-institutional effects that one setting can have on another; in addition, it does not take into account the fact that different institutional settings have different internal dynamics as well. In this section, I develop a picture of the different institutional settings to explore the forces that operate between these different institutions (i.e., their extra- or inter-institutional effects), as well as the internal dynamics of these different settings that not only make institutional analysis more complex and rich but also offer more points of leverage where advocacy can occur. In this section, I explain both of these concepts in turn: that institutional settings have inter-institutional effects, and that they have complex internal dynamics. A richer understanding of how institutional settings operate helps to yield a more nuanced understanding of the ways in which such settings function. A more nuanced understanding of institutional dynamics, in turn, makes institutional analysis itself more complex and also generates a more *target-rich* environment for effective policy change and the possibility that one can devise more *targeted* strategies for driving a desired policy change.

Inter-institutional Dynamics

Are there risks that any policy success in one setting might be undermined by gains of an advocacy group's adversaries in another? Any strategy for bringing about institutional change must always attempt to identify not just the opportunities for change within different institutional settings but also the challenges that might arise to reform from other settings. For this reason, advocates must view the whole institutional field and consider the dynamics that operate within institutional settings and those that render cross-institutional effects when seeking policy reform. Given the relationships between and among institutional settings, a focus on making change within one institutional setting might yield few lasting reforms if those gains are easily undermined by forces and actors operating outside of that institutional setting. While all of this may seem highly theoretical, a review of the analysis of the current state of digital privacy helps illuminate this critical point about institutional dynamics.

Indeed, in chapter 4, I utilized the approach of Comparative Institutional Analysis to assess the current state of political privacy in private-law settings to determine whether there was a single institutional setting that seemed appropriate for protecting political privacy. But what that analysis yielded was an understanding that, when one attempts to choose among different institutional settings—again, what the CIA approach identifies as the market, the political process, or the courts—the reality is that no single institutional setting seems immune from harmful spillovers from the other institutional settings. An approach that attempts to identify just a single institutional setting that might serve as the optimal locus of efforts to protect political privacy is insufficient to achieve the desired policy goal because it fails to take into account the fact that those settings do not really offer distinct and discrete fields in which to operate in an effort to achieve that goal. The current state of digital privacy shows that even effective efforts toward the goal of protecting that privacy in one institutional setting [face] the fact that other settings have effectively blocked those reforms. Efforts by the courts to rein in breaches of digital privacy have been undermined by the market; the political processes have only strengthened the hand of business and weakened that of the courts. But the courts, too, have willingly enforced contracts where the parties have wildly disproportionate bargaining power to authorize privacy breaches and even strip the courts themselves of the powers to adjudicate many disputes over digital privacy.

So, even if advocates determined that there is an optimal institutional setting in which they might achieve gains for reform, they would still have to take into account the ways in which other institutional settings could undermine those gains. For that reason, an approach to policy reform that attempts to identify the optimal setting in which to advance such reform must always assess the ways in which the chosen setting might face significant resistance from other settings. A singular focus on making policy gains in one setting might prove unsuccessful if other settings can stymie the reform that might emerge from within that setting.

No matter how effective a setting might appear on paper, when viewed in light of the ways in which other settings can limit that effectiveness, what one might consider a robust setting in which to achieve the goal of protecting political privacy in theory turns out, in practice, to suffer from disabling cross-institutional forces. An approach to institutional analysis that does not take into account these cross-cutting tensions suffers from the same weaknesses that Komesar identified when he criticized so-called single institutional analysis.[2] Comparative Institutional Analysis that does not take into account these cross-institutional effects has similar shortcomings; it views institutional settings as monolithic and not as embedded in a broader institutional field.

When one wants to pursue a policy goal, and wants to choose a field in which to pursue that goal, one has to take into account the ways in which such a goal, and the chosen means to bring it about, might be thwarted by actions taken outside that chosen field. But these institutional dynamics are not just present when it comes to seeking protection of digital privacy. When advocates began to pursue court actions against gun manufacturers for harms caused by the sale, distribution, and use of illegal firearms, legislatures in many states, and even the federal government, passed legislation that largely immunized gun manufacturers from such lawsuits.[3] Similarly, in the mid-1990s, when there was a concern in the U.S. Congress that local and state governments might begin to recognize same-sex marriage, the legislature passed the federal Defense of Marriage Act, which contained provisions that allowed states to avoid having to recognize the marriages and civil unions that individuals secured in those states that permitted them and prohibited the federal government from doing things like granting federal benefits to the surviving spouse of a same-sex union.[4] A victory in one setting (getting states to recognize a same-sex marriage) might be overshadowed or minimized by a loss in another, and thus effective policy change requires a sensitivity to the ways in which institutional efforts can have adverse spillover effects. For these reasons, among others, a nuanced understanding of inter-institutional dynamics is critical to any effort to bring about institutional change. But there are other dynamics at play—the intra-institutional features of different institutional settings—that can also impact such change. Developing an understanding of those forces will also help yield more effective strategies for institutional change, an issue I turn to next.

Intra-institutional Characteristics

Comparative Institutional Analysis attempts to offer an approach to choosing among institutional settings, even though, as we have seen, any effort to do so must also take into account the ways in which one setting may create barriers to effective policy change in other settings. But any attempt to choose *among* these institutional settings also comes up against another challenge. A deeper analysis of how institutions and institutional settings function when it comes to serving as appropriate locations for policy change recognizes that it is *within* institutional settings where there is also a great deal of difference: that institutional settings have many qualities that reveal that they are not siloed as they relate to other settings, but they are also complex within each setting. In order to achieve effective policy change, one needs to develop an appreciation for not just how institutional settings operate in relation to each other; one must also understand the inner workings of the different institutional settings to understand how one can function within them to drive change. Effective social change efforts can also occur within a particular institutional setting, even though it might appear, when the settings are viewed in the aggregate, that there is no hope to effectuate change within it. Moreover, returning to the issue of spillover effects, one can turn that dynamic on its head: an effective campaign for social change within one institutional setting can end up catalyzing change outside of it, creating cross-institutional pressures. I describe some of these intra-institutional differences, and the opportunities they create, further below. Another shortcoming of viewing institutional settings as discrete is that one might ignore the internal dynamics of that setting and thus overlook a potential avenue for effective policy reform. One might write off a specific setting because one believes change within it is hopeless and that efforts directed at change within that setting are bound to fail.

This analysis reveals not only that institutions are not monolithic in relation to each other but also that they exhibit heterogenous, internal qualities. To assemble the most effective components of a policy-achieving approach, one requires a depth of understanding of the different ways in which institutional settings express this heterogeneity. In this section, I attempt to identify the ways that institutional settings exhibit intra-setting differences. An appreciation for such differences will help set the stage for the development of a hybrid approach to achieving the goal of protecting political privacy, one that harnesses institutions in all their complexity to advance protections for political privacy.

To bring about institutional change, a deep appreciation for the way institutions function is essential to driving such change. Using the framework regarding institutional settings—that they are either the market, the political process, or the courts—is a useful starting point for doing so, but it is just that: a starting point. I have already shown how viewing these settings as discrete and operating within their silos has its drawbacks because of the potential that effective policy change in one setting might be undermined by actions taken within another setting. Failing to account for the risk of cross-setting mischief can weaken or neutralize one's efforts at change. At the same time, neglecting to recognize that these settings themselves are not monolithic, that they possess internal qualities that might offer opportunities for progress toward a goal, might mean a campaign for change might overlook meaningful opportunities to advance that goal. One might also miss a chance to work affirmatively within a particular setting to ensure that such adverse spillover effects do not come about. The best defense is, sometimes, a good offense. In order to work institutional change, one must develop an appreciation for the internal workings of institutional settings, both to ensure one can use such settings as offense *and* defense.

An analysis of institutional settings in the American system reveals that they are heterogenous in a number of ways. There is what I will call "horizontal" and "vertical" heterogeneity, as well as differences in roles and interests. There is also "temporal" heterogeneity: a sense that institutions can change over time, so that just as *where* one attempts to bring about change (that is, the institutional setting in which one seeks to drive change) is almost as important as *when* one attempts to do so. I will describe each of these, in turn, below.

The first thing to recognize about institutional settings within the United States is that they exhibit vertical heterogeneity. Government, at least, is explicitly created with federal, state, and local components. This is consistent with our federated, republican, constitutional structure that recognizes that certain centers of government power are better at doing some things than others. The federal government is necessary for collective defense of the nation and can bring more resources to bear during national emergencies. We believe state governments are better suited to deal with property matters, address business functions, and reflect the unique interests and needs of their citizens. Local governments are closest to their constituents and can serve to monitor and address local conditions.

But this type of vertical heterogeneity is also present in the courts and the markets as well. Certain markets—telecommunications and airline transportation, for example—have evolved to be largely national in scope. Tourism that focuses on the unique characteristics of a community—like the gorges of Ithaca, the beaches of Maine, or Jazz in New Orleans—is often considered as state and/or local in focus. The judicial system is not, in fact, one "system." There are federal courts that span the nation and local courts that deal with disputes and traffic infractions in a community. State courts in the United States handle roughly 100 million cases a year, from critical issues related to abortion and voting rights, to small claims cases and consumer debt disputes. In contrast, the federal trial courts handle about 400,000 cases on average each year, also ranging from resolving significant questions of rights to simple business conflicts.[5]

To recognize the vertical heterogeneity of these systems means that one can appreciate that such systems are complex, which, of course, does not make the task of institutional choice easier when it comes to the pursuit of a policy goal. But it is also the case that institutional settings exhibit internal differences that mean that one institutional setting might offer more of an opportunity to serve as a locus of advocacy efforts, when, from the outside, viewing settings as monolithic might suggest such efforts are hopeless. If, for example, one considered that the perceived inclinations of the Justices of the U.S. Supreme Court suggested they would be hostile to a particular claim, that does not mean that there is no room for advocacy within the broader judicial system when one might direct one's efforts to bringing about change in the courts of a state or a group of states where one might stand a better chance of success, assuming one was pressing claims that would not ultimately raise questions that fall within the jurisdiction of the highest court in the federal system. In the area of abortion rights, civil rights, and worker rights, advocates have found ways to press claims under state constitutions and state laws that might not stand a chance of success before a potentially hostile Supreme Court.[6]

Another way in which institutional settings exhibit internal complexity is horizontal heterogeneity. Just as there are different types of courts, there are different types of governments; yes, there are courts, but there are also legislatures and executives, and those executives also include administrative agencies, some of which might operate with some independence from the leader of the executive branch in any given jurisdiction. For example, although it is becoming less common in today's hyper-partisan political environment, the governor of a particular state might be from a different party than its attorney general, or there might be an inspector general, comptroller, secretary of state, head of the board of elections, or a similar entity within the state government who is supposed to act with a degree of independence from the head of the executive branch itself. So, even when we might generally consider that state agencies are an arm of the larger executive branch of the state, even that state government might have different components. With respect to the political process as an institutional setting, then, there are very different components of that setting and it is not monolithic.

The market is also not a single institution. There are businesses, large and small, national and hyperlocal. When we consider the market to include all nongovernmental actors, that includes what is often referred to as all of civil society: businesses, for sure, but also nonprofit groups, religious organizations, civic organizations, and the like. Courts, too, exhibit this type of horizontal heterogeneity, with jurisdictional differences based on the nature of disputes. A federal trial court located in Manhattan will handle disputes that fall within its physical jurisdiction given the nature of the dispute and the parties involved; the same type of dispute, involving different parties, that involved an incident that occurred in Boston would typically be resolved in a federal court in Massachusetts. The judicial system, like the other systems, exhibits both vertical and horizontal heterogeneity.

Actors within different institutional settings will also have very different roles. It is our collective understanding that legislatures make the laws, executive branches enforce the law, and courts say what the law is. Businesses and civic groups play very different roles within the "market." When we speak of courts, they can be trial courts or appellate courts, or they might specialize in handling particular types of cases, like a court for individuals with psychiatric disabilities or veterans. A desire to pursue a change in institutional roles can serve as a form of social change itself, sometimes change that is profound. As political scientists Frances Fox Piven and Richard Cloward argued, institutional life "depends on conformity with established roles and compliance with established rules." When those roles are defied, it may "obstruct the normal operations of institutions." When actors cease to "conform to accustomed institutional roles" and "withhold their accustomed cooperation," they can "cause institutional disruptions."[7]

Just as there are many different types of entities and actors found within each institutional setting, the *interests* of those different elements found within institutional settings are often quite different. Nonprofits and businesses can often work at cross-purposes because they have very different interests and goals. The Obama administration's immigration policy was very different from that of the Trump administration, and that, in turn, was (somewhat) different from that of the Biden administration. (This also shows another feature of institutions: their temporal heterogeneity, as I will show in a moment.) In recent years, it has become quite common that, within the political process, state governments led by elected officials of the party that does not hold the U.S. presidency have lined up to assert those states' interests against the federal government. Indeed, this phenomenon of the American political system is an institutional feature of it, not a bug. It represents how our system operates, even when it might create a great deal of policymaking friction; it can have the effect of limiting more extreme actions that are largely unpopular from occurring because of the checks and balances, the counterweights, that create intra- and extra-institutional tensions.

Those extra-institutional tensions—some of the spillover effects I have described above—also point to the interdependence of institutions, another quality that makes what one might call "one-dimensional" Comparative Institutional Analysis incomplete. A well-functioning market is not one that is completely free of all constraints. Even supporters of a less shackled capitalist class want to be able to use the courts to enforce contracts, and they will lobby government for protections from the anticompetitive behavior of rivals. Institutional systems can certainly work at cross-purposes, as I have shown; but they also must often work in a collaborative fashion, because of their interdependence, to achieve a desired policy goal. An understanding of this capacity for collaboration, which any successful policy effort must achieve, is necessary to leverage institutional settings for positive social change.

Finally, as alluded to above, recognizing that institutions can change over time makes the decision of when to advance a particular policy goal can almost be as important as where to locate it within an institutional setting. Leaders come and go. Businesses pivot. The founder of a nonprofit can retire, ushering in new leadership with a new focus. Elections where a few thousand votes can swing one way or another can alter the course of history. People can change and evolve. The Hoover administration had its own approach to the Great Depression, one that was quite different from that of the Franklin Roosevelt administration. The Supreme Court that the Roosevelt administration inherited first resisted New Deal efforts, then evolved over time to open the door to more comprehensive economic reform. Congress and the Eisenhower administration was not, at first, inclined to take much action in terms of promoting civil rights in the wake of the Supreme Court's decision in

Brown v. Board of Education. A decade later, with Lyndon Johnson in the White House, and as a result of the political agitation of millions of Americans, Congress would pass the landmark Civil Rights Act,[8] Voting Rights Act,[9] and Fair Housing Act.[10] The notion that the Supreme Court would recognize marriage equality in the early 2000s was practically unthinkable; by 2015 it was the law of the land. A lot happened in those intervening fifteen years, which I explore further in chapter 7. But it is important to recognize that institutional settings exhibit a temporal heterogeneity to complement some of the other characteristics of institutions reviewed so far. One day, one [institutional setting] might serve as the location of choice to advance a particular policy goal. The next, another might emerge as superior in achieving that goal. For this reason, time is another critical dimension of institutional analysis and the pursuit of policy goals.

The impact of taking this complex view of institutions yields more places, and times, when effective institutional change can occur. It also yields greater opportunities for crafting institutional change because one can identify multiple entry points for reform efforts, as well as a type of hybridization of these characteristics and functions: we can try to draw the best elements of different institutional settings, ones that are best calibrated to bring about a desired policy change, and potentially apply them within other settings. A description of this approach follows.

Institutional Hybridization

A narrow view of institutions, one that sees institutional settings as discrete, monolithic, and hermetically sealed, might cause one to overlook opportunities for change. One might think that change in, say, the market is impossible: that the only way to rein in certain business practices must come from the political processes or the courts. Alternatively, one might think a government bureaucracy will never change, that legislative or regulatory fixes to a problem could never happen, and thus one looks to the courts or the market for recourse.

Yet policy change can happen when a useful feature of one institutional setting is deployed within a different institutional setting, proving that the different settings are not necessarily monolithic, possessing a discrete set of characteristics and dynamics. One might think the benefits of market-style competition could revitalize government programs and thus seek to adopt a mechanism that draws the benefits of such competition into the functioning of government. Indeed, governments across the United States do this every day when they contract with private entities to deliver public services. These governments recognize that even what might otherwise appear as a purely public function—like providing shelter to the homeless—might benefit from the knowledge and expertise of mission-driven nonprofit groups. Such organizations will deliver those services in a more efficient and effective way because they are more sensitive to and experienced in addressing the needs of that population compared to a government agency.

Thus, another effective method for catalyzing effective institutional change that departs from isolating institutional settings as potential sites for policy change is to draw the best features of different settings to create a cross-institutional approach that maximizes the potential for effective policy change. Instead of considering institutional settings as discrete and monolithic, we might look at the features of the different settings to determine whether there are special characteristics of those institutions that might serve a particular policy goal well, regardless of the setting in which that feature is deployed. We can then reassemble and recombine those features to create a hybrid institutional approach, one that draws the best features of these different settings that are the most useful in achieving one's goal. To do so, though, one needs to analyze and appreciate institutional settings in their full depth and complexity and to understand how the different internal components of institutional settings function.

* * *

Bringing about institutional change is hard. But reliance on an incomplete picture of how institutions function is not likely to yield successful strategies for effectuating such change. A nuanced understanding of institutional settings—the potential locus of institutional reform— builds an appreciation for the complexity of institutions. Grasping that complexity certainly requires a rich understanding not just of the inter-institutional dynamics of such settings but also their intra-institutional characteristics. Once we possess such a nuanced understanding of these dynamics and characteristics, we can begin to identify optimal strategies, deployed in those places most likely to yield to reform, that are calibrated to strengthen the hands of reformers to the greatest extent possible.

Just as Komesar argued that it is challenging to conduct single institutional analysis,[11] I have shown that comparative institutional analysis that utilizes a monolithic or one-dimensional view of institutions also has its shortcomings. To serve as a useful tool for determining how to bring about effective change, Comparative Institutional Analysis must embrace a view of institutions that recognizes them as multidimensional. Such a view, while complex, actually serves to open up more opportunities for achieving one's policy goals in a more effective way. One does not have to write off any institutional setting as one in which change is not possible; nor should one ignore an institutional setting because one believes it is resistant to change if it might be the setting in which one's adversaries are able to create barriers to reform across all institutional settings. A rich understanding of institutional dynamics and characteristics helps to yield a nuanced approach to institutional change that is more likely to generate effective, durable, and sustainable reform, as I will demonstrate throughout the remainder of this work.

In the next section, I explore one more typology, a way to look at regulating conduct, that classifies an array of potential approaches to doing so. If we are to consider reforms to how we protect the integrity of identity, we will have to think not just about the institutional settings in which to bring about such reforms but also the types of reforms that might achieve the desired policy goal. As part of this discussion, I show that, like with Comparative Institutional Analysis, we can also draw from the best features of different approaches to regulation to create hybrid systems. Such systems can both draw from and integrate the best features of the different approaches at the disposal of advocates to ensure that those features are mutually reinforcing as we strive to achieve the desired policy goal of protecting the integrity of identity.

Property, Liability, and Inalienability: Rules for Solving Collective-Action Problems

Thinking about the setting or settings in which one might press for reform is one thing; thinking about what the mechanisms for reform, particularly legal reform, is another critical element of any effort directed at social change. Guido Calabresi, former dean of Yale Law School and now a federal judge, collaborated with legal practitioner and scholar Douglas Melamed to offer a typology for protecting an array of interests where collective-action problems might make it difficult to do so. They argued that different types of rules should be applied to different interests in different contexts. These different rules serve as the mechanisms for advancing the types of changes a group might seek. They characterized these mechanisms as property rules, liability rules, and inalienability rules. Like Komesar, they advocated for an approach that aligns a desired policy goal with an approach in a particular setting. One should choose an approach to protecting different interests—what they called "entitlements"—in accordance with one's goals in any given context. Such goals could include economic efficiency, distributional preferences, or what they call "other justice considerations."[12] In this way, the Calabresi–Melamed typology is similar to Komesar's approach to Comparative Institutional Analysis in that it attempts to align one's policy choices with a set of appropriate institutions. For Calabresi and Melamed, they viewed such institutions as the rules that would achieve one's goals. For the purpose of their argument, they certainly take an institutions-as-rules approach, but within that approach there are implicit and explicit assumptions of the different institutional settings in which such rules are applied. A liability rule—one that compensates a victim of some transgression through the payment of damages by the perpetrator of the harm—is likely applying that rule within a judicial setting. But those assumptions are not always accurate, as I will show further below, because different contexts and policy goals might generate different rules that are enforced in different institutional settings. There is no one setting that is necessarily tied to a particular rule.

Before I go any deeper into the institutional setting in which different rules might be applied, a description of the different types of rules described by Calabresi and Melamed is useful in helping to set the stage for the broader discussion of the rules we might apply to protect political privacy.

Calabresi and Melamed describe a property rule as involving voluntary transactions where "the value of the entitlement is agreed upon by the seller."[13] This arrangement involves "the least amount of state intervention: once the original entitlement is decided upon, the state does not try to decide its value."[14] Liability rules are invoked when the entitlement can be taken away or destroyed by someone "willing to pay an objectively determined value for it."[15] Last, inalienability rules prohibit transfer of an interest even "between a willing buyer and a willing seller."[16] Under each type of rule or approach, the justice system might have a role to play: enforcing bargains when they have been breached, determining the amount of liability one party has to another, punishing those who attempt to sell (or buy) something that is considered inalienable. In the end, like Komesar and his discussion of different institutional settings, Calabresi and Melamed argue that different rules in different contexts help solve collective action-problems and can serve to achieve desired policy goals.[17]

Turning to the institutional settings described by Komesar in which such rules might apply—markets, political processes, and courts—we can see different rules appearing within different settings in different contexts. Legislatures might create a property rule to govern one type of transaction or might state that certain types of transactions are prohibited, meaning they are instituting an inalienability rule. Private parties might enter into a purely market transaction in the exchange of an item for sale, provided such an item is considered governed by a property rule (and its sale is not prohibited by an inalienability rule). But the actions and transactions described here do not operate within institutional silos. The violation of a property rule, say, if a product purchased in an arm's-length transaction has a faulty design that causes harm, we might enforce a liability rule against the party that sold and/or designed that defective product. The market transaction then leads to a dispute within the judicial system. Legislatures might get in on the act to provide stiffer regulations over the design of that product if a pattern emerges regarding the harms caused by the product. We thus see how a picture can emerge in which there are not always clean lines between what type of rule might apply to a given situation or where and how that rule might be created, violated, and/or enforced. Indeed, recognizing that a different type of rule might very well govern the very same product, service, or act—at a different time, in a different context, and in a different setting—helps to frame this typology. Thus, much like institutional analysis more broadly, this typology views the assignment of different rules in different settings as a context-specific task, one where the appropriate rule to apply in a different setting may change, sometimes dramatically, depending on the desired policy goal in that setting. Moreover, adopting such a view of the Calabresi–Melamed typology, much like our view of institutional settings, can lead to an integrated approach to protecting a particular interest. It can also draw from the best features of each, when appropriate, to achieve a desired policy goal. In the next and final section in this chapter, I will show that, in reality, many systems, especially those involving property law, create these sorts of integrated, even hybrid, systems where they deploy all three institutional settings to offer an array of interconnected and complimentary rules—property, liability, and, at times, even inalienability—to create a framework for protecting certain interests and achieving desired policy goals. This discussion will help set the stage for this hybrid approach to protect political privacy, which I explore in chapter 6.

"Supermarket" or Hybrid Institutionalism

A "supermarket" approach is when we, as if we were in a supermarket, can walk down the aisles and pick and choose the things we want to purchase and disregard the things we do not. The Calabresi–Melamed typology suggests that we can use a property rule, a liability rule, or an alienability rule to advance certain interests in different settings depending on our particular goals in relation to that interest.[18] I argue also that such an approach is valuable when choosing the appropriate forum or fora in which to advocate for policy reform, that is, the appropriate setting in which to advance such reform. One is not relegated to choosing between the market, the political process, or the courts when seeking a setting in which to promote institutional change. Not only must one be mindful of the ways that these institutional settings can affect one another; one must also take into account that these different settings are internally heterogeneous. Such an appreciation creates complexity, but it also creates opportunity: one can transpose the different features and characteristics of different components into another setting to create hybrid systems that yield the most effective array of policy interventions that will drive sustainable social change.[19] Taking such an approach also opens up a greater array of locations where advocacy groups can target their advocacy to yield optimal outcomes.

Once again, much of this may seem theoretical, but an analysis of one particular context—the American system of property law—helps to illuminate the concept that we often institute an array of hybrid rules, in hybridized institutional settings, to create a somewhat balanced but certainly integrated and comprehensive regime for solving many types of collective-action problems that always exist when we are talking about property interests. It is these types of hybrid arrangements in the property context that I describe next. This description helps to surface the types of interventions that have evolved over time to balance the array of interests always implicated in a property-law system. But, as this discussion shows, our system of laws and rules that governs real property is not always governed by property *rules* per se. Indeed, different policy goals in different contexts yield different rules, regardless of whether we are talking about the regulation of what we might otherwise consider to be property itself.

Indeed, in the context of that cluster of laws we call "property law" in the United States, we utilize a blend of rules within the Calabresi–Melamed typology to advance desired policy goals in an array of situations. Collective-action problems always arise when we are talking about property. The nature of a collective-action problem in a particular setting will warrant the choice among the different rules; it will suggest the type of intervention—by a specific rule or a collection of rules. The characteristics of those collective-action problems, and the ways in which a community wants to resolve those problems, will often lead to the choice among given rule-based interventions. These characteristics often include asymmetries of information about an interest and asymmetry of bargaining power between or among the prospective parties to a transaction. There are settings that might be subject to moral hazard, like a tragedy of the commons, where the absence of rules governing an interest might lead to rent-seeking and predatory conduct.[20] The nature of the interest at stake might also determine the type of rule to apply.

But in a number of contexts, the rules have evolved in ways that show that we cannot neatly characterize them as either property, liability, or inalienability rules, and this evolutionary phenomenon reveals the fact that solving collective-action problems sometimes requires—as is the case with Comparative Institutional Analysis and institutional settings—not a clean choice between different rules but instead a blended, hybridized, supermarket approach that strives to utilize those features of the rules that serve a particular policy goal. In the contexts I describe next, we see these evolutionary forces in play and the results that flow from the impulses that drive different choices. Once again, viewing these institutions-as-rules approaches as amenable to hybridization shows that policy entrepreneurs have an array of tools at their disposal when thinking about institutional change: they are not restricted in the types of policy interventions, or the locations of such interventions, when they seek a desired policy reform. In this section, I discuss the evolution of the law of property in the United States in several contexts, including landlord–tenant law, the laws governing the mortgage market, zoning restrictions, and restrictive covenants. As this discussion shows, in each of these contexts it is not a single rule that governs each context, and those rules are often applied in different institutional settings. The legal and institutional infrastructure can be seen either as a confusing patchwork or as the result of an evolutionary process by which laws have emerged within this context to create a hybridized system for the resolution of thorny collective-action problems. What this description tends to show is that such hybrid systems can evolve in ways that may serve desired policy goals, even in complex settings where a wide range of interests conflict. I do not believe the evolution of the law in these contexts is optimal by any stretch of the imagination. There are significant social justice concerns that are not always served by the laws as they currently exist. In many contexts, however, and taking the long view, the law has become largely more just and not less, helping to balance out the potential unfettered interests of property owners in the use and disposition of their land and other critical interests, like the protection of civil rights. The system is by no means perfect; nor would I defend every aspect of it. What an analysis of this system does show, however, is that hybrid institutions-as-norms and blended institutional systems can evolve in the service of desired policy goals. We are not relegated to choosing merely among a distinct collective of institutional settings or a narrow set of rules to achieve a desired policy goal. Once again, this complexity, with the potential for novel combinations and interoperability, creates greater opportunities for creative efforts designed to advance positive social change. A description of these different property-law contexts that help to reveal some of this hybridization follows.

Landlord–Tenant Law

For centuries, tenants had little bargaining power in the landlord–tenant relationship.[21] As urban populations grew in the United States and placed greater pressure on tenants because less housing stock was available to them, it increased the asymmetry of power in that relationship.[22] The typical approach to rental housing had been caveat emptor: "buyer beware" or, in the rental market, "tenant takes the property as-is."[23] The far greater bargaining power residing in landlords, and the asymmetry of information when it came to the quality of the property to be leased, combined to put tenants in an even weaker position.[24] Courts began to enforce what has come to be known as the "warranty of habitability," requiring that, in residential settings, the landlord had to warrant— promise—that the leased premises was fit for human habitation.[25] Even if the landlord did not agree in a lease or other contract that the property was habitable, a tenant could enforce that requirement in a court of law.

This approach exhibits a range of features from within the Calabresi– Melamed typology but does not necessarily yield a singular rule. A leasehold is clearly a property transaction. The warranty of habitability holds the landlord liable for violations of the promise that the dwelling is suitable as a place to live. It even makes certain lease transactions illegal (that is, inalienable): one could not rent a tenant an apartment that was entirely uninhabitable, for example. Such protections originally have evolved largely through judicial decision-making, but many of these types of protections have been incorporated into local and state housing laws and regulations. In addition, federal regulations concerning housing conditions apply to housing either provided by or funded by the federal government.

But the landlord–tenant relationship is not simply regulated based on whether the premises that the tenant wishes to lease is suitable as a place to live. The relationship itself is one to which antidiscrimination laws also apply, like the federal Fair Housing Act[26] and the Americans with Disabilities Act.[27] These federal laws, which often have state and even local corollaries, prohibit certain discriminatory behavior and impose liability rules in the event these prohibitions are violated. Federal and state agencies are supposed to police such behavior and can often pursue administrative enforcement actions or bring cases in state and federal courts to curb such behavior through injunctions and punish it through damages awards.

This description of just some of the laws that govern the landlord–tenant relationship—a relationship that so clearly implicates a "property" interest in a leasehold—shows that the relationship is often regulated by liability rules as well as property rules (and even some inalienability rules thrown in for good measure). Upon deeper inspection, what appears at first blush to be a property interest is—in reality—an interest that has implications for other interests and policy goals as well: the desire to balance out asymmetries of information and bargaining power, the desire to protect civil rights, and so on. Out of a desire to solve the collective action-problem of ensuring tenants can overcome the asymmetries of information and bargaining power, a series of blended or hybrid rules have emerged to cover virtually all residential real estate leaseholds when it comes to the services landlords must supply to tenants.[28] Similarly, in order to prevent housing discrimination, restrictions on the unfettered rights of landlords to rent out their properties to whomever they choose yielded to the need to root out such discrimination. That, too, is a collective-action problem because landlords, left to their own devices and without any restrictions on their decisions with respect to whom they will accept as tenants, will feel free to exclude members of groups disfavored by those landlords, and such individuals and families will find it extremely difficult to find housing. Without some restrictions on such behavior, the situation that would ensue would create significant negative externalities (to put it in coldly economic terms), and such effects are at the center of most collective-action problems.

In this description of the institutional order affecting landlord–tenant relations in the United States, we see a range of rules deployed to regulate the landlord–tenant relationship as well as an array of institutional settings in which these relationships are regulated. Those rules and settings exhibit the type of heterogeneity described above in this chapter. The lease of property involves a market transaction that is private in nature yet has been the subject of judicial and legislative interventions. The relationship is certainly governed by property rules, but liability rules have also been imposed, the violation of which will result in the payment of money damages after the fact. These rules and laws that govern the relationship between landlord and tenant are set at the local, state, and even national levels. We thus see in this context the evolution of blended rules and hybrid institutional settings emerging to create an integrated system for regulating the landlord–tenant relationship. Again, it is not a perfect approach, and does not yield perfect results, as the current state of homelessness in America shows. But it is one in which different types of interventions, carried out in different institutional settings, have addressed just some of the potential collective-action problems that can arise in this context. It is also not the only area within property law where we see this type of approach.

The Laws Governing the U.S. Mortgage Market

Similarly, in the mortgage market, which grew dramatically in the United States after World War II, prospective homeowners also had to deal with significant asymmetries of information.[29] In addition, individual borrowers, acting alone, might not become aware of the potentially discriminatory behavior of a lender if the borrower did not know of the practices of that lender with respect to other borrowers.[30] As a direct product of agitation by the Civil Rights Movement and consumer advocates, Congress passed an array of laws designed to address not just these asymmetries of information but also discrimination itself, including the Fair Housing Act,[31] the Equal Credit Opportunity Act,[32] the Truth in Lending Act (TILA),[33] the Real Estate Settlement Procedures Act (RESPA),[34] and the Home Mortgage Disclosure Act (HMDA).[35] These were intended to provide prospective homeowners and mortgage borrowers with information about the practices in the mortgage market and help uncover patterns of potentially discriminatory conduct.[36] Because of these laws, prospective borrowers receive information about the terms of mortgage transactions; as Congress noted when it passed RESPA, "significant reforms in the real estate settlement process" were "needed to ensure that consumers throughout the Nation are provided with greater and more timely information on the nature and costs of the settlement process."[37]

Through HMDA, mortgage lenders must report aggregate demographic data on the borrowers to whom they extend or deny mortgages.[38] While an injured borrower cannot sue for relief under HMDA,[39] when information revealed through HMDA shows a potential pattern or practice of discrimination, that can give rise to an action under the Fair Housing Act. Similarly, violation of the requirements of TILA and RESPA can lead to fines and damages claims, among other remedies.[40] Congress thus utilized an array of tools to address asymmetries of information and bargaining power in the mortgage market, from information-forcing tactics to liability rules for violations of at least some of these laws.

As in the landlord–tenant context, there are many additional protections that govern mortgage transactions that are established at the state level. States have traditionally been the locus of laws governing property in general and the sale of real property in particular. State law also governs real estate transactions, and many states have their own laws that prohibit discrimination in mortgage transactions. Like with their federal corollaries, these laws, which clearly govern a property transaction, operate like liability rules in the Calabresi–Melamed typology. As with the landlord–tenant context as well, they are also enforced through actions by administrative agencies or private parties. They thus reflect a hybrid set of rules as well as a hybrid system where those rules are promulgated and enforced. We do not simply regulate mortgage transactions by a property rule alone and through the courts. No, regulation of the mortgage market is a hybridized affair along the two dimensions we have talked about here. It enlists different types of rules and different institutional settings to carry out the policy goals that the system is designed to advance. We see this type of hybrid system in two more property-law contexts that I describe together in the next subsection: zoning and restrictive covenants.

Zoning and Restrictive Covenants

A similar blended set of rule types is applied through the technique known as "zoning." When American cities and their surrounding suburban areas began to grow around the turn of the nineteenth century to the twentieth century, it became clear that liability rules—in the form of what are known as "nuisance remedies"—were not enough to prevent untrammeled development that thwarted the emergence of thoughtful, planned communities that balanced a range of interests effectively. As legal scholar Rachel Godsil explains: "By the early twentieth century, it became clear that nuisance law alone was insufficient to resolve the tensions between a rapidly industrializing economy and the individual's property rights and enjoyment of property."[41] A collective-action problem arises when landowners might want to engage in practices on their property that harm the interests of neighbors and the larger community.[42] The law of zoning emerged and combined all aspects of the Calabresi–Melamed typology: it blends property rules, liability rules, and even alienability rules to create a patchwork quilt of tools to guide and control the uses of land.[43] While such a system is typically enforced at the local level, within an institutional framework set by the states, different jurisdictions will deal with the issue of zoning differently and locate authority over zoning differently, with local planning commissions having a great deal of sway over zoning decisions; but state courts are often invoked to enforce zoning restrictions. Some zoning rules can even implicate federal and state constitutional provisions, leading to litigation in those different contexts based on the nature of the alleged violation. Zoning decisions are typically made at the local level, but the authority of those local authorities is often set at the state level. In other words, there is not one institutional setting in which the hybrid rules baked in to zoning laws and regulations are promulgated and where and how they are enforced. Once again, we see a mix of rules, embedded in an array of institutional settings: another example of institutional hybridization.

And even when a local government does not apply restrictions on the use of land through zoning, owners of private property can voluntarily choose to regulate the ways in which they will all use their respective properties and can bind future purchasers of tracts affected by such restrictions through what are known as "restrictive covenants." They do so through the full array of rules found within the Calabresi–Melamed typology and help to solve collective-action problems in the process.[44] The legal commitments made by those who enter into such covenants include property rules, as well as liability rules and even inalienability rules when certain uses are prohibited or sales of property are restricted without the consent of other members of the group that are parties to the covenant. There is also a sort of "reverse-inalienability" rule that has also emerged in the law governing covenants and even zoning: certain restrictions are prohibited in zoning rules and covenants if they would result in the exclusion of certain classes of individuals from purchasing or renting property.[45]

Once again, though, while these restrictive covenants generally emerge as private agreements, they are enforceable in the courts (typically state courts) as contracts, but they can also implicate federal constitutional provisions. A perfect example of an instance of a seemingly simple market transaction—a private restrictive covenant—having broader institutional implications is the U.S. Supreme Court's ruling in *Shelley v. Kraemer*.[46] There, in a decision issued six years before *Brown v. Board of Education*, one that civil rights advocates saw as a potential harbinger of broader opportunities to fight discrimination in the courts, the Supreme Court intervened to find a private restrictive covenant that prohibited homeowners affected by the covenant from selling to African American buyers violated the Equal Protection Clauses of the Fifth and Fourteenth Amendments. It reached that conclusion even with no government actor directly implicated in the transaction. This otherwise private transaction would generally not be subject to any type of equal-protection requirements because there was no government entity that was party to the transaction. The Court found, nevertheless, that there was so-called state action—an essential ingredient in any equal-protection challenge—because courts were being asked to enforce these otherwise private covenants. Because of that, the contracts themselves were unenforceable in the courts. This arrangement, seemingly governed strictly by the market, having different and larger implications— constitutional implications—due to the nature of the remedy (which had to be carried out within the judicial system), triggered federal constitutional questions that were adjudicated by the highest court in the federal system. Thus, in this context, we see the phenomenon of multidimensional, institutional hybridization in high relief.

* * *

The evolution of the law that governs landlord–tenant relations, the mortgage market, and certain other land-use contexts reveals that effective collective-action problem-solving measures can include an array of property, liability, and alienability rules. These rules are then enforced in, through, and by a wide range of institutional settings and actors, recognizing that those settings exhibit a range of different characteristics.

We see the warranty of habitability (a creature of judge-made common law), enforced in state courts. It is also established in federal law in housing contexts involving federal funding, and such provisions are enforced in federal *and* state courts. In addition, fair housing protections that exist in federal, state, and even local laws cover property transactions that are typically governed by property rules per se, but they are also subject to liability rules, which are enforced in state and federal courts and by state and federal agencies as well as private actors.

This description of the ways in which "property" is governed by an array of different rules, and that is generally considered to be a uniquely private and local interest, reveals that even such an interest is subject to different types of rules and that those rules are promulgated—and enforced—in many different institutional settings. This system of hybrid rules, with the shared institutional settings in which they play out, has evolved over time to address a range of collective-action problems, and that evolution has been the product of countless hours of efforts across the country to create a better—albeit imperfect—system for protecting rights critical to well-being, like the right to enjoy decent, safe, and sanitary shelter and to be free from discrimination in the housing context. Partly because of the centrality of stable and discrimination-free housing to human flourishing, this system has emerged as, by all possible accounts, a hybrid system of different types of rules and institutional settings in which those rules are enforced. At the end of the day, the "boxes" that typically exist around housing—that it is a form of property, is a uniquely local institution, and its lease or sale is generally considered no more than a mere private transaction—yield to the reality that such an interest or subject of regulation is so much more than this narrow, and simple, array of features. Thus, an interest we might commonly refer to as "property," one that is local and private, is subject to different types of rules and different types of institutions. Despite this seemingly narrow set of superficial characteristics of the interest at stake, through effective advocacy, where larger interests are at stake and such interests implicate essential elements of human flourishing, institutional reform is possible, and such reform is not relegated to single institutional interventions.

What this recounting of these phenomena can also offer is a model for not just a hybrid approach generally—as to both rules and settings—to issues of digital privacy but also one that is based on the concept of zoning in particular. That is, can the lessons from property-law contexts, especially those in which blended rules and hybrid institutional settings are put to work to advance a desired policy goal, serve as effective vehicles for effective policy interventions when it comes to strengthening digital privacy and protecting the integrity of identity? In chapter 6, I introduce an approach for protecting political privacy that I call "digital zoning." This approach draws from the full range of approaches outlined in the Calabresi–Melamed typology and also utilizes a cross-institutional, hybrid methodology for doing so. It is this model for protecting political privacy to which I turn next.

6

Zoning Cyberspace

Whether democracies can continue to function in the age of Surveillance Capitalism, artificial intelligence, misinformation, and manipulation remains to be seen. The threats to democracy across the world are significant. In the United States, the world's oldest democracy, authoritarianism and threats to the rule of law are real and increasing in force. Today's technology-fueled media environment, because of disintermediation, social media, and artificial intelligence, poses significant threats to the preservation of the American form of democracy, one in which a delicate balance of institutions—public, private, civic, communicative—operates to help citizens achieve individual and collective self-determination. In turn, these institutions are reflections of the popular will. I have shown in previous chapters and in past work the symbiotic relationship between institutional change, the ability to communicate, and social movements. What is more, that relationship is constantly changing, as the technology that enables and shapes communication, as well as society and the citizen, is also changing. When that technology is placed within democratic societies, the connections run even deeper, but so does the possibility that such technologies can be used not just to advance democracy but also to undermine it. For these reasons, the need has never been greater to ensure that the communications tools of today and tomorrow are not weapons that can strike at the heart of democracy but rather tools to help realize it.

In a 2022 work,[1] authors Zac Gershberg and Sean Illing trace the relationship between democracy, political speech, and communications technologies over several millennia, from the Greek city-state to the present. They argue democracy as a form of government, as it emerged as a system more than two thousand years ago, operated through two interrelated concepts: the equal opportunity to participate in public discourse,[2] and "the right of individuals to say anything they wanted, whenever they wanted, and to whomever they wanted."[3] For these authors, such a system "does not automatically translate into wise counsel or fair treatment,"[4] however. Indeed, they claim that democracies, because of their openness, are always potential "breeding grounds for tyranny."[5] The authors call this the "paradox of democracy": the openness of free and open communications environments "invites exploitation and subversion from within"[6] and can also "lead to the consolidation of autocratic and oligarchic power just as easily as it can lead to more representative political systems."[7]

What is more, according to Gershberg and Illing, democracies are "shaped in real time by the communicative choices of individual citizens and politicians,"[8] and today's media environment makes the threats even greater because new forms of media are "evolv[ing] faster than politics" and "resulting in recurring patterns of democratic instability."[9] In prior eras, even during the early age of mass media, "media gatekeepers and politicians hashed out a norms-driven discourse of information and debate in the public sphere."[10] In turn, citizens then "absorbed what they read, listened to, and watched, registering their approval or disapproval at the polls."[11] Today's media environment and the technologies that enable it "let citizens in on the act of forging discourses and choosing what news they prefer."[12] This has resulted in "a more democratic and less liberal world."[13] Because of these phenomena, democracy "presents not just a collective-action problem but a genuine existential dilemma: it demands that we take responsibility for the situation in which we find ourselves."[14]

So how would advocates concerned about this state of affairs take action that might protect political privacy in the age of Surveillance Capitalism, when democracy itself seems to be at risk? In this chapter, I lay out a model for how we might protect the integrity of identity within the current technological environment. It draws from some of the concepts that I have discussed so far, concepts that help us not just build a model from an institutional perspective but also leverage institutional dynamics to create an effective system for preserving the integrity of identity.

Creating an Institutional Framework for Protecting Political Privacy

In previous chapters, I examined several approaches to achieving desired policy goals. The first of these assesses the settings in which policy change can happen. The second looks at different tools for achieving such goals. In this chapter, I describe an approach to achieve the desired policy goal of protecting the integrity of identity in the digital world and, by so doing, preserve a private space where one can realize one's political self and collaborate with others to achieve individual and collective self-determination. The two approaches described previously—Comparative Institutional Analysis and the Calabresi–Melamed typology—offer a sort of framework within which to operate, but neither should be seen as offering a range of options, options that are themselves siloed. That is, we should not look at either approach as dictating that we must choose one institutional setting (from CIA) or one rule (from Calabresi–Melamed) and call it a day. Such an approach is unlikely to work for several reasons. As I have shown previously, institutional settings can have extra-institutional effects, meaning one setting might take measures that offset the gains advanced in another. What is more, a range of characteristics of different settings—the policy tools they offer, the incentives they create, the ways in which they exhibit heterogeneity within them, the fact that one setting might be more appropriate to achieve a policy goal at one time as opposed to another, and so on—might serve a desired policy goal well, while other aspects of that setting might also serve to offset the advantages one setting might have over another. In such a case, selecting the effective tools that one setting offers and combining them with those of others that might also achieve a particular policy goal is an approach that can prove effective in advancing policy change.

Similarly, different rules—liability, property, and inalienability—might work in different ways in different settings, but together they can still be utilized to advance a chosen policy goal if we can tailor them and use them surgically at the right time, in the right place, to channel desired actions toward a policy goal. In both instances, a hybrid approach to policymaking—one that draws from the most useful aspects of a specific setting and sets different rules around a range of behavior in certain contexts—can offer a comprehensive framework for achieving a desired policy goal like the protection of political privacy.

Finally, against the backdrop of any approach to regulating in private-law contexts is the First Amendment's free speech protections. That is, when government seeks to impose rules on speech, even in private-law settings, the First Amendment is implicated. So, any government effort through regulation or laws, even to rein in action and speech in private-law contexts, must not run afoul of free speech protections. At the same time, we must continue to recognize that the First Amendment does not constrain private actors who operate digital platforms from regulating the speech of others who use those platforms. The system I propose here is useless if it cannot avoid imposing unconstitutional protections. Accordingly, the proposed approach, which borrows from other contexts, strives not just to offer a method for protecting political privacy but also to operate well within the bounds of the First Amendment.

Considering how we regulate political privacy in private-law contexts and assessing that approach according to both the CIA framework and the rules-based typology offered by Calabresi and Melamed, we see that we largely regulate this form of privacy in private-law contexts through liability rules—torts for invasion of privacy—with a smattering of federal statutory law. So, mapping these approaches onto our two frameworks, we protect digital privacy in private-law contexts already through a hybrid approach that utilizes some state law–based principles developed by the courts using liability rules and some federal statutory protections that blend liability and inalienability rules. A party that violates this blend of protections is answerable in the courts, both state and federal, and is held liable for such infractions. But we must also recognize that even these protections are limited in their ability to restrain privacy infractions by the immunities described in chapter 4. Whether it has been the development of contracts that permit the holders of private information to share that information, or statutory protections found in the Communications Decency Act[15] that insulate internet platforms from liability for abuses on their platform, any liability rules, regardless of their source, are largely counterbalanced at present by offsetting immunities, which are the product either of the market finding a way of protecting commercial activity within it or of the political process providing cover to privacy-breaching conduct. In addition, even the courts have not been the greatest champions of digital privacy, even when it has implications for political privacy, by reading the immunities baked into the system in broad ways, as opposed to limiting their applications. To the extent that this system—which is simply Surveillance Capitalism operating at full speed and with practically no guardrails or even brakes— undermines political processes through which rights and interests are advanced, diminishes the individual's capacity for self-determination, and limits the ability for civic activity by groups, it is bad for democracy, and it inhibits that form of human flourishing that is found in collective endeavors directed toward political self-realization. If the existing system fails to protect the privacy of individuals when they access the vast digital world, this state of affairs has profound implications for personal dignity and even democracy itself. The central feature of liberal democracies is that they strive to protect the autonomy of the individual to engage in acts of self-determination and to act collectively with others to realize such self-determination together. A system that undermines that enterprise by infringing on the integrity of identity is not just bad for individual well-being; it is bad for democratic society as a whole.

The existing hybrid, extractive system—one that activates features from different institutional settings and uses an array of rules and principles derived from those rules—largely protects those actors and entities that might infringe upon the integrity of identity. To respond to and rein in this system, we will need a similarly hybridized, integrated, complimentary, and comprehensive system for *protecting* political privacy. It will also have to minimize immunities currently afforded those who would infringe upon this form of privacy. What follows is an approach that draws from the best features of the different institutional settings and appreciates and embraces their complexity and heterogeneity while doing so. It also strives to activate property, liability, and inalienability rules at the right time, and in the right place, to create a system for preserving the integrity of identity. The goal is to catalyze individual and collective self-determination while preserving and advancing critical democratic, inclusive values. It is to that system that I now turn.

Hybrid Rules for the Protection of Political Privacy

Since Warren and Brandeis first identified the so-called right to privacy toward the end of the nineteenth century, we have mostly protected privacy interests through liability rules: measures that provide for protection of interests for violations after the fact, through the payment of damages. Might we look to property rules, or hybrid systems that blend property, liability, and alienability rules like those described in chapter 5, to create a similarly blended approach to protecting political privacy in private-law contexts? We have already seen that institutional settings have a range of characteristics that might lend themselves to just this sort of hybridization. Like with institutional settings, is it possible to draw from the essential characteristics of different rules and institutional systems to apply them in strategic ways to different contexts and by doing so achieve desired policy goal in this context? Can such an approach inspire and empower advocates to take meaningful and effective action to achieve that goal?

Calabresi and Melamed argued that it was the policy goals of a system that should dictate the rule one might deploy to protect an interest, based on the values society ascribed to that interest, rather than how we might think about that interest;[16] in other words, what we might commonly think of as property, like a piece of land, does not dictate that we must protect it through a property rule. If someone trespasses on your *property*, the trespasser is liable to you for damages: that is, we protect property through a liability rule in that context. Should that trespasser want to purchase that property from you, you might negotiate a price for doing so. The person might even negotiate with you to purchase a right-of-way that would enable that person to cut across your property to get to something on the other side of it. That trespass is no longer a trespass; instead, it is an invitation. Without that right-of-way, however, that property is guarded again through liability rules; yet the sale of the property or the permission slip are negotiated through property rules. The same piece of land is thus protected by both property and liability rules depending on the context. Similarly, with another interest we might typically consider "property," like a home, Calabresi and Melamed demonstrate that we protect that interest by both liability and property rules as well. If the government wants to seize that home through eminent domain, or a neighboring property owner is engaged in acts that might constitute a nuisance under the law, we impose what are, in effect, liability rules.[17] Much like Komesar's assessment that the cement plant in the *Boomer* case had to pay neighboring property owners the cost of its pollution, and such an outcome advanced the value of efficiency, in these settings the efficient thing to do is to resolve the conflict through recourse through liability rules rather than property rules. Forcing the government or the cement plant to negotiate with each homeowner leads to holdouts, and bargaining in such contexts would likely outweigh the ultimate benefits of the particular activity.[18] Economic efficiency certainly does not have to be the touchstone or policy goal of a given institutional framework for protecting and advancing different interests, however. When it is, in these contexts at least, a liability rule might better serve that goal than a property rule.

Another way to think about the best approach to regulate the use of our private information is whether we think about either an *ex ante* prohibition on or *ex post* punishment for that use. That is, do we create restrictions on the use and abuse of that information prior to an individual or entity engaging in some prohibited act? Or do we punish it after the fact, once we know of exactly what that use was? Both approaches can have a deterrent effect; both require sufficient monitoring for violations. The benefit of an ex ante rule is that it tends to send a clear signal as to what is prohibited and what the consequences will be for violating the rule. It might also chill otherwise legitimate activity for fear that one is violating the prohibition when one is not. The upside of an ex post rule is that one will know the full scope of the harm caused because it has occurred; the obvious downside is that someone suffers a violation of the interest, and compensation after the fact may not be sufficient to compensate the victim for the harm caused.[19] In the context of developing protections that might impact free speech protections (and any matter involving the government regulating privacy will always implicate such rights), prior restraints on speech (that is, ex ante protections) are generally disfavored, while ex post remedies are sometimes inadequate to deter violative conduct or make the victim whole for the violation. Thus, finding the proper balance among these approaches is essential to any measure that might seek to protect political privacy.

Protecting digital privacy and, with it, political privacy, as we have seen, has largely been attempted through liability rules: there is some punishment after a violation occurs, making them thus ex post measures. What is more, in order to limit a different sort of prior restraint—that which might chill innovation out of fear of litigation and liability—the rules that have largely existed to date consist mostly of disclosure requirements, which are really consent requirements. Based upon these requirements, entities that possess our private information or track our behavior online get us to agree to their near unfettered use of end-user data. (This poses a question: If end-user data has a life beyond an individual user's use of a site or application, are they really an end user? It would seem the company is the true end user, but I digress.)

The current regime, as directed by requirements imposed by the European Union and some states, relies heavily on disclosures. But even disclosures that comply with these mandates often bury the terms regarding consent to the use of information and the tracking that might occur of one's behavior online in complex and opaque user agreements. At present, in order to comply with the obligations under existing systems, most sites indicate that the end user has to consent to the company's cookies policy (the tools that are used to track consumer activities online). The end user can then review the entity's policy related to cookies, but, as research consistently shows, even in this new disclosure regime, which was designed to protect consumers, most consumers simply click "Accept" without reviewing those disclosures and end-user agreements that relate to cookies and other items that the European Union and other governments require of companies. Even for the consumer who does read a site's cookie policy, the disclosures tend to be as opaque as most other end-user agreements. The end result is that the consumer is unable to discern the terms of these agreements, is unwilling to take the time to scour the end-user agreement, or finds such agreements difficult to understand. As a result, they typically simply throw up their hands and click "Accept," rendering the somewhat more robust disclosure regimes that demand this type of disclosure somewhat toothless.

Could clearer disclosures convince users to be more mindful of the extent to which companies might use their personal information? Legal scholars Ian Ayres and Alan Schwartz have argued that clearer, simpler disclosures, particularly when it comes to the unfavorable terms buried within many contracts, would serve as more effective mechanisms for protecting consumer interests.[20] They also suggest creating consumer feedback loops that would inform the decisions about what information to disclose and how.[21] Other research suggests that structuring the format of disclosures to make sure they convey information to the user in an effective way can ultimately result in greater consumer understanding of the terms to which they are agreeing.[22] Other legal scholars have also argued that, in many consumer settings, disclosure regimes generally fail, although they admit that simple disclosure mechanisms, when coupled with expert advice, can sometimes aid consumers in understanding complex information.[23] At present, the disclosure regime relating to consumers' online and other digital activities is one that companies entrusted with end users' information can easily comply with, but that compliance often serves as little more than window dressing as they continue to mask the ways in which they use their customers' data behind disclosures that are difficult to comprehend. Is something more than disclosure needed then?

There are those who have argued that we should impose property rules to protect such interests. The idea here is that such an approach will require those who wish to exploit our data to make payment for such use before they do so.[24] Early in the digital age, legal scholar Lawrence Lessig,[25] later joined by Paul Resnick,[26] suggested that we might try to utilize a system, like zoning, to protect our private information, but they would recognize that the technology likely did not exist then that could facilitate such an approach.[27]

Others have also proposed requirements that go beyond mere disclosure, that we should consider those in possession of digital data to have a fiduciary obligations to protect it, which typically brings with it liability protections for failure to uphold those duties.[28] Still others argue that consumers should be paid for their data, another type of property rule.[29] Any such approach has led to the objection that, if this digital information is subject to a price, it will only further commodify the self.[30] Indeed, this sort of phenomenon is common in settings where one might consider a "fine" through a liability rule (that is, an award for violation of that rule) merely becomes a "price" through a property rule (what is, in effect, a cost for purchasing an item, whether or not it is actually bargained for). In a famous study of an Israeli day-care center, when the owners of the center wanted to curtail late pickups by parents and guardians at the end of the day, the center imposed a relatively modest fine for doing so. This actually *increased* the number of late pickups because those parents and guardians felt the cost imposed by the center was worth paying: it was transmogrified from a fine to a mere price, moving from a liability rule to what was, in effect, a property rule.[31]

Looking back on some of the contexts described in chapter 5, a blend of liability and property rules (with a smattering of inalienability rules) protects what many would consider property in a number of contexts. This is done to balance out asymmetries of information and unequal stores of bargaining power. What is more, liability rules sometimes back up or complement information-forcing rules, like disclosures in the mortgage and lending contexts. These disclosure regimes help to balance the asymmetries in a system protected by property rules. They then can also lead to liability in a number of ways: such information can expose certain illegal patterns and practices that result in damages awards for violations of civil rights, or they can bring about other remedies for a failure to follow the specific disclosure requirement that bolstered the property-rule regime.

So far in this discussion I have focused largely on considering the institutions that might protect privacy from the institutions-as-rules perspective. But, as explained in chapter 4, rules alone are not sufficient to protect privacy. We can have a system of perfect rules that then are weakened or undermined by different institutional actors. Returning to the different settings in which those actors operate (the market, political processes, and courts), to create an effective system for protecting political privacy will require not just effective rules for protecting political privacy; it will also have to ensure that institutional actors within these systems cannot undermine the protections afforded under those rules. Any system that protects political privacy and the integrity of identity will not just have to have an effective set of laws, rules, and norms that protect that privacy but also restrain efforts to undermine those protections within the institutional settings where those rules must be carried out and enforced. As with the current regime as it relates to online activity, we have seen that private actors and lawmaking bodies have engaged in practices (e.g., contracts through which users consent to certain uses, or legislators creating immunities for certain online behavior) that have made it increasingly difficult for the third institutional system—the courts—to enforce privacy rights that might otherwise exist. Thus, any approach to protecting political privacy must account for, and strive to counteract, the extra-institutional effects that can undercut any effort to protect political privacy, where market actors, legislators, or even the courts might weaken the ability of different institutional actors to enforce the protections afforded consumers through a privacy-protecting regime.

What I propose is a system that utilizes simple and mandatory disclosures that make it clear to consumers how entities that possess their data use it.[32] Such disclosures would not involve complex, difficult-to-understand end-user agreements that are so prevalent today; instead they will involve a form of digital zoning. Entities covered by this regime would have to self-identity and self-classify their practices based on how they use our data: whether they protect privacy and the integrity of the identity by making clear the array of practices they use when handling our data and the types of accountability measures they accept when they fail to do so.

Such a regime would contain the following components and require disclosure by entities that possess our personal data as to what particular features and practices they utilize when handling our data. The array of protections those companies provide (or do not provide), and the manner in which they use our personal data, would have to be disclosed in an accessible, understandable format, one where the companies will have to be clear about their practices. They will not be able to hide those practices behind opaque, difficult-to-understand end-user agreements. They will have to declare quite clearly exactly what it is they do with respect to a number of highly specific practices. The proposed system then clusters the practices based on those that are more consumer-friendly and those that are not; those different clusters become an easy-to-understand array of "zones." By indicating what package of protections an entity offers consumers, the system then associates that entity with a particular zone. The zone with which the entity is aligned is then communicated to the world every time a user uses the site or the application. Users can then decide whether they want to access that site or service once they learn of the zone within which the site operates: that is, the array of protections the company accepts is communicated quickly and easily to consumers in a simple and easy-to-understand fashion.

Such a system will be imposed by legislators and enforced by courts when a company fails to comply with either the disclosure regime itself or does not honor the types of protections it says it offers its customers. At the same time, it will also give companies a high degree of flexibility: it will offer them a choice of the types of protections they will afford consumers. To the extent that a company does not want to protect consumers in a particular way, it does not have to, but what that company will have to do is make clear to consumers that the company has no plans to protect consumer data in any way.

An approach built on digital zoning would require that any entity that has access to an individual's data, including activities on the entity's website, would have to identity the uses that entity makes of that individual's data. It would also have to make clear how that data is stored and used and identify the types of accountability mechanisms end users have with respect to the handling of their data. Instead of asking such entities to simply disclose this information, which they can do by burying it in confusing end-user agreements, those entities would have to identify exactly what their practices are with respect to several key items, like the following: search history, use of consumer data, and the accountability measures available to consumers for breach of their privacy. An array of protections and uses will be clearly spelled out with respect to these areas, and the entities will have to make evident exactly what their practices are as they relate to these important privacy-related issues. Those protections and uses will be clustered according to numerous practices that are more consumer-friendly and those that are less so. Based on the cluster of practices to which the entity adheres, it will identify itself as operating within a specific zone. For the end user, the zones serve as a heuristic, a quick rule of thumb that allows him or her to know, immediately upon entering a site, whether that site's practices are more consumer-friendly or less so. Armed with that knowledge, an end user can determine whether that site or service engages in practices with respect to user data that the consumer would prefer or those that might be harmful to the consumer. Instead of a relatively thin system that simply requires disclosure of the policies of a particular entity, even if those policies are buried deep within difficult-to-understand end-user agreements or statements of a company's use of cookies, the end user will be able—at a glance—to determine whether the entity operates in a fashion that is more consumer-friendly or less so. One could also anticipate controls that consumers choose where they—or their children—will not enter sites that do not agree to the more robust protections of the "higher" zones.

Thinking about the types of protections that consumers should want in such a regime (though, I understand, setting the express contours of such a system should go through a robust policymaking process in which consumers play a central role), a number come immediately to mind, and still others are ones that consumers *should* want, whether or not they know it. First, consumers' activities as they search on the internet should be afforded significant protection. Consumers probably would want to know exactly what information is collected, beyond just their search activity. But other protections are also important and are likely top of mind for many consumers, like wanting to know how an entity might use the information it possesses about consumers. Does it use that information merely to recommend products to consumers? Or does it sell such information to third parties, regardless of those third parties' intended use of that information? Other information might also be important to know, even though it might not be something most consumers think about all that often. For example, to what type of dispute-resolution mechanisms will a company submit? Will consumers, should they seek recourse against the company, have to go into arbitration with the company or sue them in a faraway location? Another is whether the company will compensate consumers if there is an unauthorized breach of the company's data such that users' information maintained by that company is exposed. Similarly, consumers might want to know whether the company uses algorithmic mechanisms for promoting information to the individual and, if so, what types of information is pushed to them using such algorithms. Again, if it is an algorithmic system that promotes products to the consumer, that would be one thing. If it is sending radicalizing or manipulative content with the goal of keeping the person engaged and online, that is another. Last—and this is also not something a consumer might think about all that much—an effective system would require companies to disclose whether they serve as a fiduciary over customers' data. That is, do they put customers' interests in preserving that data ahead of their own in terms of the use of that data such that only those uses that are in the best interests of the consumer will be those in which the company is engaged? In turn, a breach by the company of its fiduciary obligations toward the individual will subject the company to liability for that breach. The exact contours of such a system, and the types of information that should be disclosed, and how it should be disclosed, are obviously subject to negotiations, lobbying, advocacy, and fine-tuning. Still, some of the broad elements of such a system are described more fully in the next section.

The Elements of Digital Zoning

In this section, I lay out the basic components of a digital zoning regime. While the precise features and elements of a such a system should be worked out through dialogue with all stakeholders, especially consumers, the following can serve as the building blocks and core organizing principles for this system.

Protect Information-Related to Search

First, consumers would need to know how such covered entities utilize those consumers' browsing data generally and movements within their sites. The first piece covers companies that offer "search," like Google and similar sites, but search is also a phenomenon on social media and online retail stores like Amazon. Certainly some of the things we have talked about must be protected, like an individual who is looking for people like them, but real harm can come to individuals even when they are shopping for specific items and that information can be used against them, like when a family learned a teenager was pregnant because of her search history and the company's marketing of products for infants that followed.[33] Similarly, it was revealed that the messaging app ToTok (not a typo) was used by security officials in the United Arab Emirates so they could "track every conversation, movement, relationship, appointment, sound[,] and image of those who install it on their phones."[34]

This protection is probably of the greatest importance when it comes to protecting privacy in general and digital privacy in particular. We need to have an ability to explore concepts and ideas that would help us shape our own identities. This freedom is essential to the process of forming that identity. People should have the ability to consider different ideas, different ways of viewing the world, and different ways of being in the world. People should have that freedom without fear that, should they even examine different viewpoints and different identities, the mere fact that they searched for such concepts might be exposed to the public. Such fear of exposure would chill the very identity-constitutive acts that are essential to individual self-determination: the ability to become who we want to become and ensure an alignment with who we believe we are or should be.

Such threshold activities online also have significant downstream effects. This inquiry into identity-related information becomes a gateway to finding others who are like us, examining the way in which they operate in the world, and joining with them in collective endeavors, including group action directed at advancing social change. For that reason, protecting search is also essential to collective self-determination, even if it extends only to the actions of individuals in their otherwise private online activities. Thus the cluster of activities we consider "search" entails all of this—the search for information that can help one form one's identity as well as the process by which one identifies with others, connects with them, and joins together to bring about a change to the broader institutional order.

Once again, political privacy is a critical democratic institution itself, one that makes institutional change possible. The actions one takes online are essential to both individual and collective self-determination. One's identity is very much tied up with this activity. We then activate this identity in our engagement with others, especially that engagement that is directed toward collective acts designed to advance and realize change in the world that is consistent with that identity. Because of this, it is difficult to ignore the role that search plays in the formation of individual and collective identity. In turn, preserving the protection of our search activities is thus essential to individual and collective self-determination. And if it is essential to those forms of self-determination, it is also essential to the functioning of democracy itself. As a result, it is entitled to extremely strong protection. For this reason, it sits at the highest point in the "pyramid" of activities that digital zoning is designed to protect.

In addition, companies can track a consumer's activities online in a number of ways, including search engines that monitor the consumer's queries through those engines and follows the consumer around the internet as the consumer explores the answers from those queries. A site can also record the consumer's activity on that site or follows the consumer through so-called cross-site tracking. There are thus many ways in which our online activities are monitored and recorded. While consumers' general lack of awareness about such monitoring might mean that the potential chilling effects of that surveillance might be of little consequence, there is a growing fear that individuals will be subject to harassment if they engage in certain types of online activity, like searching for reproductive health care. Should consumers learn more about the extent to which their online activities are being surveilled and might subject the most intimate information about them to distribution and exposure, it is likely that it will discourage them from engaging in such activity in the first place. Ifconsumers curtail their online activities as they develop a greater awareness of the extent to which their online activity might put them at risk, this will necessarily lead to those consumers choosing not to engage in behavior that might help them participate in the exploratory efforts designed to discover their identity and then find others with whom they share that identity. And if that activity becomes chilled, it warps the democratic process itself. While the ability to seek out one's identity and find others who share it has never been stronger in all of human history, it is not without risks. And protecting that process by protecting search is a core threshold element of any robust system that would protect the integrity of identity and, in turn, democracy.

Reveal What Is Gathered and What Is Stored

Companies that gather and store personal information about their customers and those who access their digital products and services should have to disclose just what type of information those entities gather about their users and whether they maintain that information on their own servers or those offered by cloud-service providers. This is particularly important for entities that provide web-browsing services. They will have to disclose whether they gather that information, store it, pass it along to a cloud-service provider, or sell any or all of it to others. For services provided through the internet or the internet of things writ large (like vehicles, biometric monitoring devices, GPS systems, or anything that tracks location), entities that possess this information will have to reveal what information is tracked, like activities on the site, health information, users' location, and so on. Some of this information is important for a provider to gather and store. In fact, it might be the point of the site that the entity provides in the first place. One might use a system like Dropbox for the precise reason that one wants to store information on it. One might use an activity tracker and the purpose of the tracker is to monitor and record one's steps or other actions over time to allow the consumer to see or monitor behavior to help spot trends, identify weaknesses, and encourage improvement.

In any event, consumers should be made aware of the extent to which a site or digital service gathers and stores data on its customers. Coupled with company reporting on cross-site tracking (described above), it should also report the extent to which it gathers data on its customers that use other sites as well. Just as a location tracker baked in to something like a navigational app might also monitor users' activities even when they are not using that app, websites track activities of customers even when they are not on that website itself. Companies that engage with users online should have to reveal what information they gather about their customers and whether they do so just while the user is on that company's site or app or if that company engages in any cross-site tracking of customer behavior.

An issue related to the question of what information is gathered about a consumer is the extent to which information is automatically deleted after a period of time or whenever the customer asks the entity to do so. The search engine DuckDuckGo makes it incredibly easy to clear one's search history by having an icon positioned prominently on the browser interface that permits the user to do so simply by clicking on that icon. One could imagine a system that automatically deletes one's browser history whenever the browser is closed. One could also imagine a system by which no data is maintained, let alone stored. Companies would argue—correctly—that they might want such information for their own use to determine what types of messages or advertisements on their websites receive the most attention, how consumers are using their websites, and what is the last thing the consumer looked at before they left the site. Companies will say they need this information to improve the user experience, and they clearly have a point. But that gets into the ways that these companies use this data, a matter I turn to next.

Disclose the Use of Private Data, Including Whether Data Is Sold

Any entity with access to a consumer's digital information must disclose how it uses that information. Will it use that information only for its own use? If so, for what purpose? More important, will it disclose that information or sell it to third parties? While most companies use some sort of cloud-service provider, the company's arrangements with those cloud-service providers must indicate whether that provider itself maintains the information securely and does not, in turn, disclose it to others.

It is clear that some of these uses are innocuous, even if annoying. When one engages with an e-commerce company, most consumers probably do not mind if, based on their activities on the company's site, they receive information about products that might meet their needs or even ones that the company wants to promote. If a company is using a consumer's search history on the site to recommend a new product, or to remind the consumer that it might be time to renew an old order for pet food that might be running low, few consumers object. Nevertheless, companies should disclose to consumers the use to which they put any information they gather about their customers. Again, in the e-commerce area, when a company is using the data about its users for its own internal purposes, to recommend products to those customers, or to help the company gauge market trends, there is little cause for alarm.

But if that data leaves the company's control in any form, the company should make that clear to the consumer. While it might not bother many consumers to know that an e-commerce company might sell some of its user data to other companies who wish to understand consumer trends, data brokers gather a lot of information about consumers, and that information can be used to advance political causes as well, not just products. In the Cambridge Analytica scandal introduced in chapter 2, the data about the social media activities of millions of consumers was sifted through to create political profiles of individuals to determine what kinds of information—and misinformation—to pass along to them in an effort to persuade them to support a particular political candidate. This type of profiling is often based on online activities, and this type of information is often sold to interested third parties. In turn, knowledge about users' activities can lead to information and misinformation being shared with them with the hope that it will drive them to ever more intriguing, enraging, and even radicalizing content, all with the express goal of chasing continued online engagement. For these reasons, companies should have to disclose how they use the data they do collect on consumers, especially whether it is for their own purposes or whether they sell it to third parties. Admittedly, it might be difficult to differentiate among some of the internal uses that a company makes of the data it collects. Does it do so to market additional products to its customers? Is it trying to track market trends on its own site? Is it trying to determine whether a customer might be amenable to entering into subscription services the company offers? One could consider these uses, if all are internal to the company, as "private" uses of the company. If, however, the company sells it to third parties, that use is no longer private. So, there is a fairly bright line here that companies would have to disclose: Are they using the data they collect for their own internal purposes to improve their products and services and marketing? Or are they selling it to or otherwise sharing it with third parties?

Disclose Uses of Algorithms in Treatment of Customers

Even if companies are using data for their own purposes, to what extent are they using algorithms in determining how that information is used and what information is then pushed back to the consumer? This could be another area ripe for disclosure. Again, certainly few might object if a company uses algorithms to decide what product to market to a consumer using the company's site, or for a streaming service to recommend a new television show to a consumer based on that consumer's viewing habits. But what about when a company pushes content to a consumer in order to keep them engaged on the site and then, in order to maintain that engagement, sends content to that consumer that might be manipulative or even radicalizing? It also might send outright misinformation precisely because that is just the kind of information that might preserve that engagement. One area where there are some who suggest platform companies should not receive broad immunity under the Communications Decency Act is when they do not merely host content posted by others but actually promote it. This was the subject of recent litigation before the Supreme Court, but the Court was not ready to hold companies liable in light of the Communications Decency Act, even when they might do more than merely host information.[35] While companies say that these algorithms are proprietary and the companies should not have to expose their algorithms to review, at a minimum they should have to disclose whether they use algorithms at all to promote information to users and what the purpose of those algorithms is.

Identify Accountability Mechanisms

Entities that provide digital services and maintain digital information should have to disclose how disputes with that entity are resolved, that is, whether it is over the maintenance of digital information itself or some other disagreement a consumer has with the company, like a canceled flight that was secured over an airline ticket broker or a piece of pottery purchased online arrives to the consumer broken. Entities will have to disclose whether they require that all consumers go through arbitration and whether that arbitration bars collective action. Of course, if a company does not require disputes to go through arbitration and instead agrees that it will resolve any contract claim or other type of issue in a court of law where due process rights are guaranteed, such an approach on the part of the entity is sometimes referred to as a "first, trusting move," one that signals that the entity is trustworthy, likely encouraging consumers to do business with that company.[36]

Disclose Status as Information Fiduciaries

One easy way to protect consumer information would be to require all companies to serve as fiduciaries for their customers' data, which would mean those companies would have to place the interests of the consumer ahead of their own. Should companies breach this obligation, consumers could hold them liable for harm caused by that breach. This would require quite a stroke of legislative intervention, one that is not likely to occur any time soon. Nevertheless, companies could be expected to disclose the extent to which they are acting as fiduciaries for the data they collect and maintain. They could also avoid this type of disclosure if they simply do not maintain any such personal data about their customers and others who use their digital services. This is an awfully high obligation for companies to take on, for sure. But they could satisfy a high level of consumer protection simply by agreeing not to collect any data on their customers.

Disclose Breaches of Customer Information and Offer Clear Remedies for Such Breaches

At present, companies are required to disclose data breaches, particularly publicly traded companies where such breaches could have an impact on the value of their stock price. But not all companies must disclose such information, and remedies are not consistent across industries for such breaches. The disclosure regime considered here would require companies to say whether they will inform consumers when those companies' data systems have been compromised and describe what remedies they offer to customers when such breaches occur. Such remedies could include actual damages—compensation for the harms the consumer experiences because of that breach—or a form of liquidated damages: the company agrees to pay a set amount to each consumer for any such violation, even where the consumer cannot establish any actual damages. In contexts where actual damages are hard to prove, or the consumer may never even become aware of the uses to which their otherwise private information has been put, liquidated damages—the idea that the company will have to pay a set amount to consumers regardless of whether they can prove harm—not only can make it easier on consumers to obtain some relief but also has a powerful deterrent effect on the company, ensuring they take serious measures to prevent the type of activity that could lead to liquidated damages. Under the robust disclosure regime imagined here, companies offering the consumer-focused suite of protections would agree to notify consumers of any unintended disclosures of private information, make clear whether the company agrees to be held liable for any actual damages that occur should the company be found responsible for the breach (because it was negligent or otherwise failed to take appropriate care to safeguard its customers' data), and disclose whether it will agree to pay liquidated damages in the event of a breach. While no system can prevent cybersecurity breaches, consumers should know which companies are agreeing to be held accountable—and in what form—should such a breach occur.

A Clear Regime

This is a lot to digest, especially if all of these disclosures are buried deep in the complex and opaque end-user agreements that have bedeviled the institutional framework around digital privacy for decades. That being said, after instituting such a robust disclosure regime, two important moves are required after that. The first is to cluster those actions that are considered to be more pro-consumer along a continuum, from most favorable toward consumers to least favorable. We would then require the entities to choose among those clusters, or what I have called "zones," as we might in a land-use zoning context. These items would form a hybrid disclosure-with-zoning system, one that is largely consistent with the principles contained in the U.S. government's so-called Fair Information Practice Principles regime.[37] Entities would agree to accept a bundle of protections found in one of the zones. They would then identify their practices based on the zone within which they operate and then label their site or digital functions according to the bundle they have accepted. Agreeing to provide an array of rights consistent with a particular zone would permit an entity to identify itself as operating within that zone in a clear and easily understandable way; what is more, if the entity failed to honor that suite of protections, consumers could hold it accountable for that breach. Even with today's byzantine end-user agreements, when providers actually violate those agreements, as favorable as they are to providers, courts can hold them accountable for doing so.[38]

While these are the broad categories that would serve as the basis for a robust disclosure-based regime for the protection of digital privacy, the next section explores just how such a system might work. Again, companies would identify the types of consumer protections they afford their customers along the lines described above. They would then disclose those protections in an easy-to-understand way, one that most consumers will be able to grasp intuitively. The following section describes the core elements of such a system, and then I describe how it would be enforced, enlisting a cross-institution system for adoption and monitoring. In chapter 7, I explore ways in which activists might work to bring such a system into existence.

How Would Such a Digital Zoning Regime Work?

A disclosure-plus-zoning approach, one where companies made it clear what collection of protections they offer their customers, could look something like the following. A company would clearly communicate to consumers the "zone" within which it associated itself upon the consumer visiting a site or opening an app. This information could even be communicated to consumers as they use search to find a site before they even go to the site itself, much like Google communicates whether a search result is a promoted site or an advertisement. Consumers could also be afforded the opportunity to rank their search results such that those sites that afford the consumer the greater range of protections will be ranked higher in the search results, much like a travel site might rank the flights or hotels for which one is searching based on the least expensive options available based on a consumer's search parameters.

The exact details of these different zones will have to be negotiated, of course, but here is one approach that clusters the most consumer-friendly and protective measures in the higher zones and those that are less beneficial to consumers in the lower zones. To reiterate, this zoning regime would require companies to report on the extent to which they monitor consumers' search activities; what information they gather and maintain on their customers; to what use they put that information; how they might use algorithms in their actions toward the end users of their digital activities; what sort of accountability measures they have in place or do not have in place; whether the company has agreed to serve as a fiduciary for its customers' information; and what sort of remedies the company affords its customers for breaches of consumer data the company experiences. Each of these categories of protections would be clustered according to the extent to which a practice within a category is more or less consumer-friendly. Companies would then disclose which cluster of protections they will afford their customers and then that information will have to be disclosed whenever a consumer enters that site or even when the site comes up in a search. The different zones might look something like the following:

Zone 1—*Full Protection.* Any entity agreeing to operate in this zone does not store, track, identify, or sell any personal information about users. Since there is no use of that data, companies in this zone do not have to disclose how the information is used and when and how it is deleted. Similarly, since no data is maintained on customers, companies that operate in this zone will not be expected to act as fiduciaries toward customers' information and thus will not have to disclose their status as fiduciaries. The companies in this zone do not use algorithms to promote products or information to their end users. These entities also do not require disputes to be resolved through arbitration in any form and agree to be held liable for damages in the event of any privacy breaches that occur. They would also agree to afford consumers liquidated damages or actual damages, depending on the consumer choice.

Zone 2—*Strong Protection.* An entity might store and track usage by consumers on its own site and for its own purposes (like to monitor activity on its site or to keep track of market trends that its users' activities might reveal), but it does not share that information with third parties. It also agrees to serve as a fiduciary over any customer information it does store. In addition, the entity does not require arbitration to resolve such disputes and recognizes that damages are appropriate for breaches in limited circumstances, including liquidated damages. It might use algorithms to market its own products to its customers, although not to push any other form of content on those customers. It could also automatically delete information after a short period of time, like thirty days.

Zone 3—*Moderate Protection.* An entity operating in this zone both stores and tracks consumer usage on its site for its own ends but also shares that information with third parties—but only such third parties as may be necessary for the entity to function, like a cloud-service provider. At the same time, the company warrants that any third party used has agreed that it, in turn, does not use or share such information with additional parties. The site may mandate arbitration for some disputes but does not prohibit consumers from seeking class arbitrations to resolve disputes. It does not agree to pay damages in the event of a breach of private information but maintains insurance to indemnify users if one should occur. It does not agree to serve as a fiduciary for customer information. The entity might use algorithms to market its own products to its customers but not to push any other form of content on its customers. It will delete consumer information upon request.

Zone 4—*Weak Protection*. In this zone, *almost* all bets are off. The site stores, maintains, and tracks consumer usage and shares information with third parties but agrees that any such information will be anonymized before sale. When it comes to accountability, entities operating in this zone require arbitration, prohibit class or collective arbitration, and do not disclose whether they maintain insurance. They use algorithms to push products and content to their customers and subscribers. They do not agree to serve as feduciaries over customer information. They will have no policy on deleting consumer information.

Zone 5—*No Protection*. All bets are off. Any user activity is tracked, sold, and not anonymized in any way. The entity does not disclose whether it offers any accountability measures. It does not serve as a fiduciary. It uses algorithms however it pleases.

Importantly, the disclosure methodology regarding the zones must be simple and in a format that is accessible and understandable;[39] it could operate in a way similar to the rating system used by the National Highway Traffic Safety Administration to communicate its assessment of the safety of automobiles and trucks[40] or what some U.S. cities use to grade restaurants on whether they satisfy health and safety requirements.[41] As Woodrow Hartzog argues, warnings such as these are "useful in making people generally skeptical," and if "the goal isn't to transmit information but rather to discourage behavior or simply facilitate a mind-set, the full panoply of notice techniques is available to regulators." They can include "notice through design in the form of symbols, interface aesthetics, feedback mechanisms, sound, haptics, and any other notice that might not convey substance but will affect you on a deep, intuitive level."[42] At present, Google search results typically reveal when an entry is an advertisement or the fruit of the search itself.[43] A similar type of grading and disclosure regime could accompany our digital activities, where entities have to select what level of protection they will afford their consumers and then communicate that information to their customers in an easy-to-understand way.

A disclosure-plus-zoning regime could accomplish several things effectively.

- It would provide clear notice to consumers regarding when digital activities are private and when they are not. Simple disclosures help to overcome the problem that many consumers generally do not read end-user agreements.[44]
- By requiring entities to pick a zone, it will give consumers an easy way to compare different company practices and create a "race to the top": sites will compete to provide more privacy-enhancing practices, not fewer.[45]
- A disclosure-plus-zoning regime will preserve individual autonomy, one informed by real disclosures that help to overcome asymmetries of information.
- Such a regime would not mandate any particular activity by companies. They get to choose what types of protections they wish to afford their customers, and that choice drives market behavior. Let innovation work to encourage healthy competition that drives behavior toward greater protection, not less.
- The system would be adopted by legislators, harness market forces, and enlist the courts to enforce it. The integration of these three institutional settings working toward the same goal will limit the extent to which one setting might undermine the operation of any other in the enforcement of this regime.
- The system will also likely spark a dialogue—both before adoption and after—about the proper array of protections that will both protect political privacy effectively while also winnowing out the practices that are not essential to the proper functioning of digital services.

Institutional Accountability in the Digital Upside Down

When it comes to the institutional settings through which these protections would be extended and protected, each different setting—the market, the political processes, and the courts—has a role to play in bringing this system into effect, enforcing it, and ensuring that it is not undermined. While it is possible that some private companies might willingly utilize such a system, or that some private entity could develop this system and encourage companies to submit to a review of their practices consistent with this system, to make the program mandatory it would have to be passed into legislation through the political process. Courts would have to enforce violations, primarily around misrepresentations a company might make about its practices. While I explore how to accomplish passage of legislation that would incorporate some of the ideas shared here in chapter 7, any system that is ultimately adopted will require effective enforcement mechanisms and some degree of assurance against entities evading responsibility for infractions by seeking the types of immunities described in chapter 4.

When it comes to the immunities that might emerge in such a system, admittedly a disclosure-based regime like the one proposed here is at least partly built around a degree of immunity: it allows companies a wide degree of freedom to choose what kinds of protections it will or will not afford its customers. It simply requires that those companies disclose—in a clear, comprehensive, and easy-to-understand way—just what protections it will afford consumers and those it will not. Companies can take a minimalist view and choose to offer no protections to consumers; presumably, such companies will receive less traffic to their websites, consumers will be less inclined to shop for their products, and users will be less likely to utilize their platforms. As we are currently seeing with the service formerly known as Twitter, when the pool is polluted, fewer swimmers (advertisers in this metaphor) wish to swim in it, and advertising revenue plummets. That sort of market dynamic is one that a disclosure regime seeks to activate and harness, but it would be worthless if companies could simply misrepresent the suite of protections they afford their customers. Accordingly, any generous disclosure regime, one that affords companies a great deal of leeway as to what type of protections they offer their customers, must also bring with it strict punishment for companies that seem to comply with the disclosure regime but misrepresent the level of protection they actually offer their customers. Where, as here, at least some measure of this compliance will come from self-reporting, there will have to be a system for regulating that self-reporting, one that includes incentives for internal whistleblowers from within these companies to come forward but also punishes companies for tampering with or otherwise manipulating data that would make it appear a company is following the disclosure regime when, in reality, it is not.

Legislation typically often carries with it remedies when it is violated. But we also support efforts to monitor violations of the law and punish actors who might engage in activity designed to evade the law itself.

In the employment discrimination context, employees should not face punishment for complaining about discrimination in employment and could have a separate retaliation complaint if they face any sort of adverse employment action by virtue of their having complained about such discrimination.[46] Similarly, many travelers are aware that federal law now makes it illegal to smoke anywhere on an airplane; it is also illegal to tamper with the smoke detectors that airplanes must have in the bathrooms on the plane.[47] And how is it that we know of this relatively obscure federal law? Its existence is announced at the beginning of every flight, that is, we have it disclosed to us by a voice (literally) of authority. Finally, the automobile manufacturer Volkswagen was fined billions of dollars for creating a diabolical system on its so-called clean diesel engines where those engines could detect when they were being inspected for compliance with emissions standards. When the engine was being monitored by regulators, it would operate in a way that was consistent with the requirements of the law, even when those engines did not do so when operating under normal conditions (i.e., when they were not being inspected by regulators).[48]

What these examples reveal is that any system for regulating digital privacy will have to ensure that it is not easily evaded and that one institutional setting is not working to undermine the functions of the others when it comes to the operation of that system. In the current regime governing digital privacy and activity, different institutional settings have proven that they are capable of working at cross-purposes when it comes to other institutions; in a disclosure-plus-zoning regime, the markets, the political processes, and the courts must work collaboratively, drawing from the best elements of each to ensure the functioning of a comprehensive, integrated, and holistic system that protects political privacy and does not make it easy to evade the system because those institutional settings are not functioning with the same goal in mind. At present, end users, federal regulators, and state law enforcement officials have had some limited success in taking technology companies to court when they engage in actions that violate even the very low bar of their own end-user agreements; with digital zoning, the bar will be raised and should have real consequences for failing to live up to its requirements.

* * *

While there may be some consensus that something needs to be done to protect digital privacy in a more robust fashion, given the state of American politics it might seem difficult, if not impossible, to institute such a system such as this for protecting such privacy. In chapter 7, I again utilize an institutional lens not just for assessing the prospects of change in this area but also for exploring how to activate an institutional perspective on how to make social change, even when change is hard.

7

Institutional Convergence

It is one thing to provide a vision for a system that might regulate political privacy. It is another to institute, or to institutionalize, that system. In this concluding chapter I weave together some of the concepts regarding institutions and institutional change discussed previously in this work to present what I hope is a coherent theory that not just takes an institutional lens to the concept of political privacy in the age of Surveillance Capitalism but also harnesses such an institutional perspective to catalyze the change necessary to protect the integrity of identity, the wellspring of individual and collective self-determination. The approach I introduce is *institutional convergence.* The prism offered by institutional theory as used throughout this work exposes the different ways that citizens, lawmakers, judges, and technologists can see the importance of protecting the integrity of identity, the impacts it has on the institutions of democracy, and the ways in which those institutions can be leveraged to bring about real change. But if one is to advocate for change, one needs a theory for how change happens. Legal scholar Paul Brest has described a theory of change as any "empirical basis underlying any social intervention."[1] As I show here, when advocates are able to bring institutions into convergence, such change is possible. Before I introduce a theory of change around institutions, I describe another theory of change that centered around a different type of convergence, what the theorist called "interest convergence." The discussion of this theory will serve as a foil for subsequent discussions centered around institutions.

One theory of social change was that advanced in legal scholarship by the late Harvard Law School professor Derrick Bell. His thesis of "interest convergence" emerged in the wake of the U.S. Supreme Court's decision in *Brown v. Board of Education*[2] as a way not just to explain but also to justify the approach taken by the Court in that decision. Bell's thesis, which I will describe in greater detail below, posited that the Court had reached a defensible decision because the interests of advocates for civil rights *converged* with those of white elites: the desire for civil rights was consistent with the foreign policy needs of the elites in government. The United States was waging the Cold War with the Soviet Union, and the treatment of African Americans in the Jim Crow South was providing ammunition to America's foes abroad as they attempted to garner support within the developing world. Bell's thesis—that social change happens when the interests of those who seek such change align with the interests of those in power, particularly those enjoying some kind of racial hegemony—has spurred many to attempt to utilize an interests-based approach to catalyzing change. It has also drawn critics, like those who balk at the notion that a campaign can advocate for change only by convincing elites that it is in their own interest to accept the change desired by a movement. Taken at face value, it is also a potentially disempowering vision, one that removes agency from those who might seek such change but not hold positions within elite circles. As I argue here, it is also incomplete. It does not explain well *how* change happens or offer a clear road map to those who might attempt *to bring about* change without catering to elite interests and needs. It not only fails to recognize the heterogeneity of interests found *within* elites; it also neglects the ways in which real change occurs despite opposition *from* elites. One of the reasons the Interest-Convergence Thesis is incomplete as an effective vision and playbook for change is because it does not take institutions, and the process of institutionalization, seriously enough.

This chapter shows that a model built on institutions and institutional change—that is, institutional convergence (with an obvious nod to and out of my deep respect for the late Professor Bell)—operates in a way that appreciates and leverages the complexity and heterogeneity of institutions described throughout this work; offers a better description of the process of social change; empowers those who might serve as agents of change even if they are not themselves elites; and does not require that change takes place only when consistent with the interests of those elites. Nor does it always require change at the apex of any institutional system, like securing a victory at the Supreme Court or winning an election for the U.S. presidency. Rather, a bottom-up strategy that focuses on creating change within institutions, with all of their heterogeneity as described in greater detail in chapter 5, is a more empowering one and helps to chart a path forward that does not rely on waiting for the interests of elites to come around on a particular issue. It is also a more accessible strategy for social change, one that average citizens can deploy effectively to advance real change. After I describe an approach based on institutional convergence, I will also describe how one might use it to advance protections for political privacy and the integrity of identity.

The Interest-Convergence Thesis

Derrick Bell's legal career included serving as a lawyer in the U.S. Department of Justice and then for the NAACP's Legal Defense and Educational Fund before joining the faculty at Harvard Law School, becoming its first African American professor to earn tenure there. Bell introduced this notion of interest convergence as a response to another legal scholar, Herbert Wechsler, who had argued that the decision in *Brown v. Board of Education* could not be justified on what Wechsler called "neutral principles"—that is to say, when a court "reach[es] judgment on analysis and reasons quite transcending the immediate result that is achieved."[3] Wechsler believed the freedom of association for the African American community that the *Brown* decision would vindicate ran counter to the interests of some in the white community who did not want to associate with African Americans.[4] With a clear nod to the importance of associational rights, even if it represented a warped view of them, Wechsler would criticize *Brown* as positing that, where the state "must practically choose between denying the association to those individuals who wish it or imposing it on those who would avoid it, is there a basis in neutral principles for holding that the Constitution demands that the claims for association should prevail?"[5]

Ceding ground to Weschler and accepting the neutral-principles frame, for Bell the neutral principle that could justify the decision in *Brown* was the convergence of interests between the white majority and the black minority.[6] That interest was the need to counter the narrative on the international stage that the United States had discriminatory policies toward the African American community at a time when the Soviet Union and the United States were vying for influence throughout the world, primarily in the developing world. There, many rightly saw

Jim Crow policies in certain states as discriminatory, which was not aiding in the promotion of U.S. interests abroad.[7]

Bell used the Interest-Convergence Thesis to explain and justify the Court's decision in *Brown* along a so-called neutral principle.[8] Others have tried to use the thesis to do more: to explain how social change happens.[9] For some, the thesis reveals not only how social change has happened retrospectively but also how it can be harnessed to spur that change prospectively.[10] In order to advance social change, one needs to look for opportunities where interests across communities, sectors, and government agencies align. In the context of the Civil Rights Movement's desire for change, the narrative that Bell claimed was a reflection of the shared interests across different social groups was the idea that U.S. foreign relations suffered from the persistence of institutionalized racism, especially in areas of the world where populations of countries where the United States was trying to gain influence might associate themselves with the African American community in the United States. By finding common ground between those who wanted to end segregation because of its devastating impact on the African American community and those who wanted to promote U.S. foreign policy goals that were undermined by that segregation, Bell argued that the Court in *Brown* found a way to advance landmark social change at the constitutional level.[11]

To bring about social change, then, if Bell's Interest-Convergence Thesis holds water theoretically and one also wants to use it in an instrumental fashion, to bring about change, one needs to identify when interests align, particularly when a change agent can identify those interests within elites, most commonly racial elites, that comport with a desired change. But the thesis, even if it does have both explanatory power as well as predictive, instrumental power, raises significant questions around identifying interests and catalyzing change. The most significant questions are: Whose interests matter? And is there a single group of "elites" that all have the same interests? A small group or collection of groups gain little legal or political traction on their own or even working in concert. Even if they could work together, they might find it difficult to create the type of pressure that the alliance of civil rights advocates and white elites applied to combat and overcome *de jure* desegregation. But just because a position might enjoy majority support does not always mean advocates of that position will secure victory in the courts. In the area of firearm regulation, for example, most Americans endorse stricter laws than the Supreme Court's Second Amendment jurisprudence seems to permit.[12]

Bell asserted that the persistence of institutionalized racism obviously negatively impacted the African American community, but it also damaged the standing of the United States in international relations.[13] The desire to end Jim Crow segregation established common ground between two sectors of society: civil rights advocates and white elites. The latter had concerns regarding the reputation of the United States abroad; the former wanted to end segregation because of its devastating impact on the African American community. The *Brown* Court would ultimately favor dramatic constitutional change,[14] and for Bell it was this convergence of interests that gave the Court the impetus, and the constitutional justification, for doing so. But for some, the ability of the Court, through its decision in *Brown*, to actually accomplish the goals of the Civil Rights Movement is subject to significant debate. And if the Court's decision in *Brown* alone did not secure an effective end to segregation, can Bell's thesis serve as a useful guide and road map for inducing change? What is more, if the vision of change is especially disempowering because it means that advocates must wait for elites to come around and share those advocates' goals, it is not much of a theory of change and more a recipe for frustration. Thus, the Interest-Convergence Thesis, as a methodology for inducing change, suffers from at least two potential shortcomings: one that fails to recognize the heterogeneity in interests, primarily among the elite, and a second that removes agency from social change advocates who might not enjoy shared interests with elites, even when such interests are more complex than Bell might have envisioned. I address each of these concerns next.

Heterogeneity of Elite Interests

The first issue that arises in any analysis of elite interests is the fact that powerful elites and the interests they might have are not monolithic. Wealthy investment bankers, captains of industry, and financiers support conservative and liberal causes alike. Some provide financial support to candidates for elected office to undermine any effort to rein in industry, particularly regarding environmental regulation. They also fund advocacy groups that to fight climate change and lobby for stiffer laws to protect the environment. Bottom line: there is not one elite, and it does not have a single set of interests. Looking back on the effort to fight school segregation, there were certainly some elites in power that believed the United States needed to end segregation in the United States to advance national interests abroad. Historian Mary Dudziak has found strong support for the notion that at least some elites believed segregation had to end in order to advance those interests.[15] Certainly not all American elites believed this to be the case; otherwise, Southern elected officials, judges, and community leaders would have supported the end of Jim Crow. Instead, at least in the South, these leaders largely resisted desegregation efforts, even though there were some whites, even in the South, who supported the Civil Rights Movement's efforts. Federal judges in Southern states were some of the strongest allies of efforts to desegregate schools and other institutions, but even that group was not uniformly supportive of civil rights litigation, and some were more aggressive than others in enforcing decisions like *Brown*.[16]

Accepting the Interest-Convergence Thesis's descriptive utility, what advocates were able to do was convince the Justices of the Supreme Court to act in accordance with the perceived interests of at least some elites (i.e., that American foreign policy required a dramatic change to domestic policy). Chief Justice Earl Warren bent over backward to come up with a decision, and an enforcement scheme, for ending segregation in education, one that would garner unanimous support from the other Justices on the Court.[17] In some ways, this "least common denominator" approach is a reflection of an interest-convergence strategy: one seeking to find some common ground among potentially divergent interests might water down one's demands in order to make them more palatable to a larger audience. In *Brown*, the Court's decision would find that segregation violated the U.S. Constitution's Equal Protection Clause, but it also delayed a decision on enforcement for a year. Even that subsequent ruling, also unanimous, was weak at best (and might have been unanimous precisely because it was weak). It permitted Southern states to essentially drag their feet and take a range of actions designed to undermine the holding.[18] And this is another risk with the interest-convergence approach alone: people might find themselves catering to such a wide audience in playing to a broad array of interests, finding where they converge, that the prospect of real change diminishes.[19]

What the decision in *Brown* does point to is that with respect to at least one institution, the Supreme Court, some interests did, in fact, converge. All of the Justices agreed that segregation was unconstitutional. Those who might have wanted to slow-walk efforts to end segregation had their interests respected as well.[20] The Chief Justice may have felt that the Court needed to send a clear message about segregation, and he was willing to play to the desires of the more conservative Justices by preparing an opinion that did not develop clear guidelines or a rapid timeline for compliance with the ruling.[21] What is more, that institution reached a tipping point. Whereas a mere four years earlier, in the *Sweatt v. Painter* decision, the Court had enforced the separate-but-equal framework first adopted by the Court in *Plessy v. Ferguson* to require the state of Texas to integrate the flagship law school of the state university system when the alternative school for African Americans was woefully unequal to its whites-only counterpart,[22] a change in personnel at the Court (a new Chief Justice) led the Court to reject that framework when it ruled in *Brown*.[23] Looking at the Supreme Court as an institution, and evaluating the characteristics of institutions described in chapter 5, we see a range of interests among its members and the fact that, with the passage of time, the makeup of the Court changed. In 1954, the Court had reached a tipping point in terms of addressing Jim Crow segregation, so much so that all Justices on the Court ruled to end it, even if their decision left much to be desired in terms of its approach to enforcement of its own ruling.[24]

Reviewing the road to *Brown* as a Supreme Court decision, and looking at it through an institutional lens, just as there were differences among the Justices when it came to the approach to enforcement, the institutional setting of the courts as a whole exhibited differences as well: the *Brown* case involved a number of cases that had worked their way through lower courts where litigants had challenged segregation in educational settings.[25] Most of those lower courts, except one, had ruled against the plaintiffs and in favor of preserving segregation.[26] Those that upheld segregation likely did so because they did not perceive themselves as having the authority to overturn the Court's prior precedent in *Plessy v. Ferguson* that enshrined the separate-but-equal doctrine in law.[27] Returning to the range of characteristics that institutional systems exhibit, trial courts, intermediate-level appellate courts, and state and federal courts all operated under the shadow of the Supreme Court's prior ruling, and thus the "judicial system" writ large was not, itself, monolithic. Different courts had different interests, different powers, and different personnel. What made *Brown* possible was that a particular set of judges, sitting on a particular court, made a particular decision at a particular time. The lessons for advocates in this situation is to understand the complexity, and heterogeneity, of institutions and to determine when and where to try to create an institutional tipping point (a concept I explore just below). What advocates have to decide is: Where is it appropriate to push—in the right way, at the right time, with the right institution, with the right personnel—to create the desired change? But what was that change that was achieved by the Civil Rights Movement? And when and how did its most important accomplishments come about? I will revisit the goals of the Civil Rights Movement and what was ultimately accomplished in the long wake of the Court's decision in *Brown* below. A focus on elite interests in the interest-convergence approach fails to recognize the potential differences within elites when it comes to those interests, which means it has less descriptive value. When one considered its prescriptive value—its ability to serve as a playbook for social change—it also has a potentially harmful consequence. Instead of empowering change agents to think about ways to advance social change, it can have the opposite effect: it can lead such agents to discount their own agency, their power to effectuate change.

A Disempowering Vision

If perceived as a social change strategy, the Interest-Convergence Thesis also instructs those who might seek to bring about such change to either cater to the perceived interests of elites, which can limit the type of change one might seek, or to give up on such change when one cannot find elites whose interests align with those who seek to bring about that change.[28] This is a largely disempowering vision, one that undermines those change agents' potential belief in their own efficacy, which is an essential ingredient of any social change effort.[29] Recognizing that elite interests might change over time, it also suggests to activists that they must wait until elite interests come around, if they come around at all. So, if one were to try to construct a movement around an interest-convergence approach, one would likely have to water down one's goals to appeal to elite interests, wait for elite interests to align with one's own, or forego any efforts if one could not find a way to appeal to such interests. Again, this might turn out to be more of a recipe for paralysis and the perpetuation of the status quo.

If the Interest-Convergence Thesis does, in fact, have descriptive, if not instrumental, value, but if a group were to look at it as a formula for social change, it has the potential to undermine social change efforts. But what if it fails in a descriptive sense as well? While there is historical support for the position that at least some elites believed an end to segregation was in the national interests of the United States,[30] what were the true goals of the Civil Rights Movement in advancing the litigation in *Brown*? And did that decision accomplish those goals? If it did not accomplish the movement's goals at the time, or if those goals were advanced at a different time and under a different set of circumstances, might we look to that time for a better strategy for accomplishing change than the Interest-Convergence Thesis offers? For an assessment of the effectiveness of the courts, standing alone, as a means of advancing civil rights, I turn to the work of legal scholar Gerald Rosenberg in at attempt to begin to address this question.

By Litigation Alone: The "Hollow Hope" of Single Institutional Analysis

When we think about the Civil Rights Movement and the gains it made in the 1960s, the decade *after Brown*, the notion that social change requires more than just a convergence of interests emerges.[31] In Rosenberg's work *The Hollow Hope: How Courts Can Bring About Social Change*, he highlights the gains that the Civil Rights Movement made by stressing what occurred in the 1960s when compared to the 1950s.[32] He looks at the change that came about as a result of the Court's decision in *Brown v. Board of Education*, and assesses gains in such areas as education and voting rights, after the court's decisions in 1954 and 1955 in that case. He argues that, in terms of significant advances in civil rights, the more significant gains occurred in the 1960s, roughly a decade after the court's decision in *Brown*. He assesses the impact that decision had on the culture, the media, and educational and private institutions, among other sectors.

For Rosenberg, one can have two views of the Court when one thinks about its potential impact on social change. First, there is the constricted view, which holds that courts have very little power in bringing about social change. The second is the dynamic view, which suggests courts can play a significant role in bringing about such change. He contrasted the 1950s and the 1960s and the effects that judicial actions had in civil rights in those two decades respectively. He argues that the dynamic view of the court was much more consistent with reality only in the 1960s, when the courts, aligned with the efforts of other institutions, like the U.S. Congress and the executive branch, among others. It was then that these other institutions were much more engaged with and had much more effect on advancing civil rights than the judiciary. The constricted view, where courts are seen as having much less of an effect on social change, was much more consistent with the role of the courts in the 1950s, when those *other* institutions played a smaller role in advancing civil rights. The Rosenberg thesis, then, is that courts can play a more dynamic role in advancing social change when they are working in conjunction with other institutions. In the case of the civil rights achievements of the 1960s, the work of the courts aligned with that of the federal executive branch and Congress. Thus, social change, in Rosenberg's view, can develop with court support when there are other institutions that are also functioning to pursue the goals that advocates might seek.

According to Rosenberg, then, the more important victories of the Civil Rights Movement did not emerge after the Supreme Court's decision in *Brown*. Rather, it was only after other institutions began to take action in support of civil rights that the movement secured more significant change. In other words, it was the convergence of *institutions*, and not merely interests, that led to the broader social change accomplished by the Civil Rights Movement in the 1960s, which largely overshadowed gains made in the 1950s. A range of factors, of course, led to those changes. The televised attacks on civil rights advocates in Birmingham and Selma; the murder of Freedom Riders; the innumerable acts of millions of rank-and-file activists; the assassination of President John F.

Kennedy; the role that President Lyndon B. Johnson played in being a strong and vocal supporter of civil rights—these all contributed to the more dramatic changes that took place in terms of the advancement of civil rights in the 1960s when compared to those that the movement accomplished in the 1950s. Certainly an argument can be made that the decision in *Brown* offered a useful frame for advancing civil rights more broadly. It became a yardstick against which the practices of educational institutions could be measured. It strengthened the position that segregation and disparate treatment were inconsistent with the Constitution, and perhaps that framing helped to galvanize support for the desegregation of areas other than public education.[33] All of this is consistent with the Interest-Convergence Thesis. But the more significant gains in terms of advancing civil rights certainly occurred in the 1960s when it was not just interests that converged, but institutions: like the Congress, with the Office of the President of the United States also joining forces in a full-throated way. If this is the case, does an approach based on institutions, rather than interests alone, help to provide a more effective, durable, and empowering vision for social change?

Bringing Institutions Back In

In the decades after *Brown*, scholars from different disciplines who study social and institutional change advanced different theories of how interest groups and social movement organizations operate to advance such change. Many included in their analysis ideas that paralleled Bell's focus on interests. In the 1950s, an approach to understanding policymaking and governance known as "Public Choice Theory" emerged that led theorists to argue that, in democracies, individual preferences became multiplied within groups; the larger the group, the more powerful was its sway over politics. As explored in chapter 3, Mancur Olson would challenge this view and introduce the concept of the free rider: the notion that individuals pursue their own self-interest, pitting those interests against the possible well-being of the group. The free rider allows others to do the work while reaping the benefits of their labor. This led to the development of Resource Mobilization Theory, an approach to social movement advocacy that says that the leaders of such organizations have to appeal to their members' self-interest and convince them that their labor is well spent: that the overall benefits of cooperation outweigh the costs.[34] This type of cost-benefit analysis would also inform the New Institutional Economics school. One of its main proponents, Douglass North, would argue that change occurs when institutions (which he saw only as norms) interact with organizations that form on the basis of those norms and also "shape[] the direction of institutional change."[35] Change occurs when entrepreneurs understand that it is in their self-interest to attempt to bring about norm change: that is, they perceive "they could do better [economically] by altering the existing institutional framework."[36] In other words, it is in their interest to engage in what Sunstein calls "norm entrepreneurship" and to change the existing norms to their advantage.[37]

But a more nuanced understanding of what leaders must do, how members see themselves within social movements, and how social movement organizations operate has developed that goes beyond this narrow rational view of institutions and interests. Such a view recognizes that individuals do not always engage in calculative, self-interested decision-making when choosing what actions they will take toward a goal. This more nuanced view, as set forth in greater detail in chapter 2, recognizes that social change has distinct institutional features that are both symbolic and material. Such features involve individuals and the associations of which they are a part creating social movement organizations (a type of institution in the material sense). Such organizations often form around more symbolic concepts like identity, which is so much more than just interest. What is more, such organizations, particularly the more successful ones, follow institutional norms and practices that engage their members in meaningful ways. Such practices might lead the organization to success, while an approach that does not do so can risk failure.[38] Ultimately, those institutional practices are often directed at and can lead to a change to the institutional order—the informal norms and formal laws, rules, and systems that construct society.

How social movements can catalyze, operate within, and strive to reshape the institutional order is the focus of the remainder of this book. The Civil Rights Movement would not merely achieve significant gains in the 1960s, a time when different formal institutions came together to realize real change; it would also have significant extra-institutional effects on other social movements. Indeed, it would either reinvigorate or inspire the emergence of other advocacy movements, like the movement for women's rights, the environmental movement, and the movement for gay liberation, all of which continue to make real change in society, sometimes in fits and starts, and sometimes in dramatic fashion. I will return to the successes of one of those movements, which involved efforts to advance marriage equality, further below and use it as a case study for advancing social change through an institutional lens. But another movement, largely made up of elites themselves, would also seek to gain insights from the gains of the Civil Rights Movement. At least one important voice within that movement viewed the change that was afoot in the nation through a very institutional lens. This perspective, admittedly from the perspective of economic elites, helps us draw additional lessons from the Civil Rights Movement, lessons that show the role that institutions can and do play in advancing social change and how at least one commentator believed they should be harnessed to bring about such change.

Making the Theoretical Real

The successes of civil rights groups did not just attract the attention of advocacy organizations and scholars interested in understanding the dynamics of social change. In the early 1970s, a well-connected conservative lawyer at the time, Louis Powell, who represented tobacco companies and would one day serve on the U.S. Supreme Court, prepared a strategy memo that he would share with a neighbor who worked at the U.S. Chamber of Commerce. For some, this memorandum changed history. Others believe it had little to do with the conservative revival of the 1970s that would help usher in Ronald Reagan's presidency in the next decade. At a minimum, it might stand as a reflection of some of the thinking of conservative-leaning interests, particularly those representing business interests, because it coincides with the birth of some of the conservative think tanks, those that would borrow some of their tactics from the liberal and progressive groups that had formed around the same time.

Powell would title his memo "Attack on American Free Enterprise System."[39] The so-called attack on the economic system in the United States was "broad"[40] and its sources "varied and diffused."[41] He certainly believed that who he would describe as revolutionaries on the far left were a part of this attack, but he also argued that "perfectly respectable elements of society," which included institutions of higher education, church leaders, the "intellectual and literary journals, the arts and sciences, and . . . politicians," were also behind these changes.[42] In addition, Powell blamed the media, which "voluntarily accords unique publicity to these 'attackers,' or at least allows them to exploit the media for their purposes."[43] He placed a great deal of blame on television, which, Powell argued, "plays such a predominant role in shaping the thinking, attitudes and emotions of our people."[44] He also identified consumer advocate Ralph Nader by name, claiming that he had effectively used the media, was the "single most effective antagonist of American business," and had become a "legend in his own time and an idol of millions of Americans."[45]

Powell argued that the "painfully sad truth" was that business interests took these attacks lying down: "[B]usiness, including the boards of directors and the top executives of corporations great and small and business organizations at all levels, often have responded—if at all—by appeasement, ineptitude and ignoring the problem."[46] Powell claimed business leaders were not trained to "conduct guerilla warfare with those who propagandize against the system, seeking insidiously and constantly to sabotage it."[47] Instead, they have focused on creating jobs, being community leaders, serving charitable organizations, and being "good citizens." Powell believed they had performed these tasks "very well indeed," but they have "shown little stomach for hard-nose contest with their critics, and little skill in effective intellectual and philosophical debate."[48] Powell thought this had to change: "The time has come—indeed, it is long overdue—for the wisdom, ingenuity and resources of American business to be marshaled against those who would destroy it."[49]

The Powell memo then recommended a strategy for commercial interests to defend themselves and the American economic system. Powell believed that such a strategy should center around the Chamber of Commerce and its broad network of local affiliates. He wrote: "Strength lies in organization, in careful long-range planning and implementation, in consistency of action over an indefinite period of years, in the scale and financing available only through joint effort, and in the political power available only through united action and national organizations."[50]

Powell's approach identified areas where the Chamber and businesses would fight back against the hostility toward business interests. They should start with college campuses and develop sympathetic scholars and speakers' bureaus that could advocate a probusiness message.[51] Powell promoted efforts to monitor texts used on campuses with an eye toward "restoring the balance essential to genuine academic freedom."[52] For Powell, this would "include assurance of fair and factual treatment of our system, its accomplishments, its basic relationship to individual rights and freedoms, and comparisons with the systems of socialism, fascism and communism."[53] Powell believed this review of the textbooks was necessary because analysis of the different economic systems were typically "superficial, biased, and unfair."[54]

He believed similar tactics were being used effectively by the Civil Rights Movement and by labor unions. For Powell, civil rights groups "insist on rewriting many of the textbooks in our universities and schools."[55] And labor unions "likewise insist that textbooks be fair to the viewpoints of organized labor."[56] While he thought such activities were "constructive" in a democratic society, "[i]f the authors, publishers and users of textbooks know that they will be subjected—honestly, fairly and thoroughly—to review and critique by eminent scholars who believe in the American system, a return to a more rational balance can be expected."[57] Similarly, Powell thought that "national television networks should be monitored in the same way that textbooks should be kept under constant surveillance."[58] On television, "'news analysis' . . . so often includes the most insidious type of criticism of the enterprise system."[59] This criticism, whether it "results from hostility or economic ignorance," brings about "the gradual erosion of confidence in 'business' and free enterprise."[60]

Powell also charged the business community with engaging more in the political arena, where the American business executive, in his words, was "the 'forgotten man.'" Business interests, he argued, needed to engage in the political process. Once again, Powell would turn to the history of successful social movements for guidance. The business community must "learn the lesson, long ago learned by labor and other self-interest groups": that is, "political power is necessary; that such power must be assiduously cultivated; and that when necessary, it must be used aggressively and with determination—without embarrassment and without reluctance which has been so characteristic of American business."[61] Powell insisted that, although political activism may be "unwelcome" to the Chamber of Commerce, that body needed to "consider assuming a broader and more vigorous role in the political arena."[62]

While Powell's assessment likely suffers from some of the same infirmities as Bell's theories when it comes to serving as an accurate description of the state of the American political landscape in the early 1970s, what we can see is that he certainly took a decidedly *institutional* perspective on social change, one gleaned from the success of other social movements. He believed that college campuses, various forms of media, and religious organizations were all lining up to undermine the American free enterprise system. Only a concerted effort to infiltrate these institutions and serve as a counterweight to progressive forces, and even to create and strengthen their own institutions to do so as well, was essential to business interests.

Powell's analysis drew from the successes of the Civil Rights Movement and unions and tried to reverse-engineer a strategy and tactics that would undermine the perceived gains those groups had achieved, which Powell believed came at the expense of American businesses. His prognosis and prescription took on a decidedly institutional cast; he recommended that business interests should work through institutions like colleges and universities, the media, and even the textbook publishing industry to strengthen the hand of economic elites. Whether such elites took such guidance to heart is subject to some debate.[63] Today, the existence of groups like the Federalist Society and the Washington Legal Foundation, among others, and the recent controversies around speech on college campuses, seem to indicate that Powell's prescription is playing out in real time.

But Powell is not the only individual to have deployed an institutional lens to assess social change and to attempt to formulate an approach to catalyzing such change using an institutional perspective. Indeed, theorists who have studied antiauthoritarian movements have taken a similarly institution-centric approach to an analysis of the success of such movements. What I argue for here is that it is possible to reverse-engineer their prescriptions for how to *confront and undermine* authoritarian regimes and use an institutional approach to *advance and construct* positive social change, an approach I turn to next.

Reverse Engineering the Antiauthoritarian Playbook (Just like Powell Did)

In work surveying protest movements from across the world, Erica Chenoweth has attempted to document quantitatively how social movements have successfully undermined authoritarian regimes.[64] Chenoweth analyzes dozens of examples to point to the importance of "civil resistance," or peaceful efforts designed to draw support away from the leaders and institutions of such regimes. What has drawn some attention in this work is that Chenoweth quantified the percentage of a population that purportedly is required to mount a successful campaign of civil resistance. According to Chenoweth, there is a "3.5 percent rule": "[N]o revolutions have failed once 3.5% of the population has actively participated in an observable peak event like a battle, a mass demonstration, or some other form of mass noncooperation."[65] Thus, when more than 3 percent of the population is actively involved in a protest movement, that has often proven the difference between success and failure of such movements. But a deeper look into Chenoweth's analysis shows that, while quantity does seem to matter for the success of a movement, the *quality* of such efforts—how they go about eroding support for such regimes, and to whom they direct their efforts—does matter. And such tactics also have a decidedly institutional cast to them.

Chenoweth explains that, in carrying out effective civil resistance, "many activists and organizers have found it useful to conduct a 'pillar analysis' . . . as they develop a campaign strategy."[66] In such an approach, "movements map out which groups or sectors prop up the status quo and are therefore blocking the movement's progress."[67] Chenoweth identifies the key pillars that support a regime as the military, business elites, civil servants, state media, and the police.[68] Chenoweth goes further to point out, echoing the institutional analysis described in chapter 4 stressing the heterogeneity of institutions, that "a wide variety of people from the broader population are involved in each of these groups or institutions."[69] They all "have their own personal interests, which may or may not align with [those of] their superiors."[70] Activists then "try to examine different influential subgroups within each 'pillar'" and determine "the movement's potential for affecting or disrupting people in each of these smaller groups."[71]

Chenoweth's prior work with Maria Stephan attempted to compare the effectiveness of violent and nonviolent resistance, showing that the latter was generally more successful, in the long run, than the former. They explain why: "[R]ather than effectiveness resulting from a supposed threat of violence, nonviolent campaigns achieve success through sustained pressure derived from mass mobilization that withdraws the regime's economic, political, social, and even military support from domestic populations and third parties." Such nonviolent resistance gains leverage against antidemocratic regimes "when the adversary's most important supporting organizations and institutions are systematically pulled away through mass noncooperation."[72] Chenoweth and Stephan point to the literature that identifies the different institutional pillars that might support a regime and show that what public demonstrations can do—if they are large enough—is undermine the support of those pillars by revealing to the individuals who make up those institutions that public backing of that regime is flagging. As they would conclude: "[O]ur central point is that campaigns that divide the adversary from its key pillars of support are in a better position to succeed."[73] Another scholar of antiauthoritarian movements, Gene Sharp, one of the researchers to whom Chenoweth and Stephan turned in their own analysis, concluded that that the three most important factors in determining the degree to which government power will or will not be controlled include the desire of the populace to rein in that power, the strength of independent institutions, and the population's ability to "withhold their consent and assistance" from the government.[74] Most of the movements that Chenoweth and Stephan studied involve prodemocracy movements that sought to topple dictators and autocrats, but their analysis can serve other types of efforts as well. As I explore next, their institutional analysis cannot just serve to topple autocratic regimes; it can also serve in a constructive way—to build support for a movement for social change. By reading the antiauthoritarian playbook from back to front, so to speak, one can start to build support for social change by *creating* institutional support painstakingly, in much the same way one might seek to take it away from a dictator or authoritarian regime, as the following discussion shows.

From Outlaws to In-Laws

The campaign for legal recognition of same-sex marriage, or the fight for marriage equality, came to its conclusion in some ways differently from the fight to outlaw segregation and to undermine the Jim Crow system. In that earlier context, although the lawyers advocating for an end to segregation in schools had slowly chipped away at a system seeking to enforce the separate-but-equal doctrine, they would ultimately prevail at the Supreme Court in the decision in *Brown* in 1954, which found that doctrine unconstitutional. But, as Rosenberg's analysis shows, that victory required another decade at least of advocacy to build institutional support to pass laws that would prohibit segregation in public accommodations; to protect the right to vote; and to ban discrimination in employment, housing, and credit decisions. It was the culmination of an array of phenomena, actions that were deeply situated within an institutional framework, that led to these achievements: continued pressure of civil rights activists from within civil rights groups and civil society organizations, like churches; the work of advocates in such campaigns as were found in Montgomery and Selma; and the championing of civil rights efforts by President Johnson. Efforts directed toward gaining institutional support, which occurred within an institutional framework, tipped different institutions, and helped to build a firm base from which to secure the legislative changes that remade the economy in a way that at least ended de jure segregation. The decision in *Brown* was a significant victory, and it helped to set the stage and galvanized support for these other victories, but securing the outcome in *Brown*—that is, winning at the Supreme Court—might be seen as the starting point. Or, to put it another way, and to borrow the words of Winston Churchill from the early days of World War II, after Great Britain had largely held off the threat of invasion of the British Isles by Nazi Germany: "This is not the end. It is not even the beginning of the end. But it is, perhaps, the end of the beginning."[75] With *Brown*, the landmark it established was, perhaps, the starting line, not the finish.

For some advocates for LGBTQIA+ rights over recent years, starting in the 1980s, the main goal of any effort to secure such rights had to center around securing a victory at the U.S. Supreme Court that would recognize same-sex marriage and prohibit state restrictions on such unions. Like many advocates before them, they saw a decision like *Brown* as serving as a sort of blueprint for how change happens: through activist lawyers, working through the courts, to convince activist judges in ways that—to borrow from the words of Dr. King—bend the moral arc of the universe toward justice. But there was not uniformity of opinion within the advocacy community regarding tactics, let alone goals. Some believed the fight for marriage equality was a worthwhile one in itself; others thought that securing the freedom to marry would have broader impact and would help legitimize same-sex relationships and signal acceptance of such relationships in the broader community. Others thought it was not a fight worth having, nor one worth winning: that same-sex relationships did not require greater acceptance from the broader community and state-sanctioned legitimacy was not something the community should seek. Still others thought it might be a worthwhile goal, but the threat of backlash should the community secure victories in the courts might set the advocacy community back and create real harm for members of that community. Some might look to the Supreme Court's 2015 decision that prohibited states from not recognizing same-sex marriage, *Obergefell v. Hodges*, as, to borrow from Churchill once again, the end of the beginning. And one could certainly see it as a critical inflection point that helped launch new campaigns for trans rights and workplace rights for the LGBTQIA+ community. In many ways, though, it was the culmination of more than two decades of painstaking advocacy built on institutional convergence.

The first legal effort to secure recognition of marriage equality (i.e., same-sex marriage) in the United States took place in the state of Hawaii in the early 1990s.[76] Toward the end of the decade, other campaigns took place in states like Vermont and Massachusetts to secure recognition of civil unions, which often occurred through cases won in state supreme courts. Some of these victories were undermined by legislation and ballot initiatives in these states, as well as by campaigns in other states to prevent such efforts from taking root within them.[77] Any victory at the state level had a Pyrrhic quality to it, especially when the U.S. Congress passed the Defense of Marriage Act,[78] which provided that states that did not have to recognize same-sex marriages entered into from other states and prohibited the federal government from doing so as well, in programs like employment benefits that heterosexual married couples enjoyed and the right to file joint tax returns.

What is more, the topic of marriage equality became a central focus of the culture war in the early 2000s. Not only did then-Mayor Gavin Newsom of San Francisco begin to recognize marriage equality; the specter and spectacle of same-sex couples getting married became a flashpoint in electoral politics. Conservative activists, in an effort to boost voter turnout in the election of 2004, placed referenda on the ballot in many states that would prohibit legislation that would recognize marriage equality and prevent local governments from doing the same,[79] and most of these ballot initiatives would succeed, even in states where the electorate is generally seen as roughly divided equally between the two major political parties.[80] Four years later, when conservative activists sought to place a referendum for voters' consideration in California in 2008, another presidential election year, the LGBTQIA+ community believed the opponents of marriage equality had gone too far: the voters of the generally liberal state would certainly reject it.[81] On a night that saw the nation elect its first African American president, who would win California in a landslide, Proposition 8, which banned same-sex marriage in the state, would narrowly pass,[82] much to the shock of the LGBTQIA+ advocacy community.[83]

The loss would spark a review of the campaign that failed to defeat Proposition 8,[84] including an exploration of the strategies and tactics they used in that effort.[85] What the review showed was that the campaign's flaw was that it was using legalistic arguments about visitation rights in hospitals for same-sex couples and the ability to inherit property after a loved one's death. This campaign led at least some voters to think that the marriage equality advocates wanted special treatment, a collection of rights that was different than what heterosexual couples enjoyed. As author Arlie Hochschild shows, this sort of campaign can appear as what she refers to as "line cutting": when interest groups are seen as seeking special treatment and do so "out of turn," it can lead to a backlash and resistance to such efforts.[86] In rethinking their strategy moving forward, advocates begin to stress that what they were pursuing was marriage *equality* for the LGBTQIA+ community and not something different from what heterosexual couples enjoyed.[87]

What is more, some thought a broadside legal challenge in the courts to the adoption of Proposition 8 in California could potentially lead to the U.S. Supreme Court taking up the question of state-level prohibitions against marriage equality and ruling to uphold the right to marriage equality. And some legal heavy-hitters teamed up to lead such a campaign.[88] For others within the advocacy community, however, there was a concern that the Supreme Court itself was not quite ready to outlaw such prohibitions; more important, if it failed to do so, it could set advocacy efforts back for a generation. Instead, what leaders within groups like Freedom to Marry thought was that the right approach was to focus on states where it was believed that the marriage equality message would resonate. Even in a state like Maine, which had defeated a marriage equality measure in 2009, advocates believed they could turn the tide and engaged in a yearslong door-to-door effort at hundreds of thousands of homes throughout the state to rally support for the initiative.[89] In May 2012, President Obama, in the midst of his campaign for reelection, publicly pronounced his support for marriage equality, marking an evolution of his own position on the topic.[90] Momentum began to grow. On election night 2012, just eight years after a wave of initiatives passed in states across the country that prohibited recognition of same-sex relationships, advocates won state ballot initiatives in Maine, Maryland, and Washington that recognized marriage equality and defeated one in Minnesota that was a throwback to the 2004 initiatives that sought to prohibit it.[91]

These victories in the states revealed two important developments. Certainly, support for marriage equality was gaining steam. But what they also showed, to those who might oppose marriage equality or who might have been neutral on the topic, that marriage equality can happen without any real negative ramifications. In spring 2015, one religious leader stated in the midst of significant progress on the question of marriage equality that "citizens in 36 states and Washington, D.C., already have marriage equality, and the sky did not fall."[92] In addition, in community after community throughout the United States, individuals were feeling emboldened to come out and reveal their sexual orientation and identity. As the number of openly gay characters in popular culture increased, people became even more comfortable making their identity public, which helped to put a human face on the experience of members of the LGBTQIA+ community.[93] It was becoming harder and harder for those who were opposed to rights for that community to rally support to their side.

In 2013, the Supreme Court addressed a technical legal question: Was a provision of the Defense of Marriage Act, which prevented the surviving spouse in a same-sex marriage, where that marriage was recognized in the state in which they were married, from earning federal benefits unconstitutional? In *United States v. Windsor*,[94] the Supreme Court would answer that relatively narrow question in the affirmative, ruling for the marriage equality advocates. While this applied only to one component of the Defense of Marriage Act, it did not prevent Justice Antonin Scalia from fulminating in his dissent in the case that such a ruling would likely open the door for advocates to challenge state bans on same-sex marriages.[95] But the *Windsor* ruling was both a watershed moment *and* an incremental step, not unlike the Legal Defense and Educational Fund's efforts in cases like *Sweatt v. Painter*, which preceded *Brown* and helped lead the way to broader victory. But the campaign kept on track and continued to press for gains at the state level to create what it considered to be a tipping point, where the Supreme Court would feel compelled to rule in favor of marriage equality writ large because the general national sentiment seemed to be in favor of it. While the Justices of the U.S. Supreme Court probably do not want to appear as if they are influenced by public opinion, legal scholars sometimes argue that the Court is "nationalist" in the sense that it tends to move with broad shifts in sentiment, even if more recent rulings seem to belie this position.[96]

Indeed, in 2015, the Supreme Court would, in fact, rule in a way that was consistent with this apparent shift in national sentiment, as evidenced by the growing support for marriage equality, when it issued its landmark decision in *Obergefell v. Hodges*.[97] Recognizing that the marriage equality effort was not one involving line-cutting but rather merely sought equal treatment, Justice Kennedy, writing for the majority, would state that exclusion from the "institution" of marriage "consign[s]" same-sex couples "to an instability many opposite-sex couples would deem intolerable in their own lives."[98] That exclusion means "that gays and lesbians are unequal in important respects."[99] He would provide further that it is "demean[ing to] gays and lesbians for the State to lock them out of a central institution of the Nation's society. Same-sex couples, too, may aspire to the transcendent purposes of marriage and seek fulfillment in its highest meaning."[100] We thus see how the Court encoded such important concepts as individual and collective identity and dignity onto marriage. It thus embedded them for same-sex couples within the broader cultural and legal institution of marriage itself by recognizing their unions as no different from marriage unions between heterosexual couples. What is more, the marriage equality advocates, by building support across various institutions simultaneously, used an institutional-convergence approach that would, in turn, restructure the larger institutional order.

What the campaign for marriage equality accomplished was to open the institution of marriage to equal access for the LGBTQIA+ community. The advocates who secured that victory, which culminated in the *Obergefell* decision but did not begin there, did so with an institutional lens in mind. It built up support for the campaign by constructing a framework made up of various pillars: state laws and state courts, the media, popular support, and elected officials. These institutional pillars and the way in which they all converged created the momentum that was necessary to foster an environment where the Supreme Court was more likely to follow popular sentiment rather than to try to drive it. In the late 2000s, even after the Supreme Court had ruled in favor of lesbian and gay rights in cases such as *Romer v. Evans*[101] and *Lawrence v. Texas*[102] (which, respectively, found that state legislatures could not override local ordinances protecting the rights of the LGBTQIA+ community or that outlawed anti-sodomy laws), the Court was not viewed as being ready for a full-out challenge to laws against marriage equality. Instead of seeking such a ruling, advocates built up a groundswell of support, institutional support, that would create the environment that made a pro–marriage equality decision more likely.

The edifice that the advocates created serves as a reflection of institutional convergence in action, gathering support from across a wide range of institutions. It also leveraged the heterogeneity of institutions: using the courts, but largely those found in the states, at least at first; using the political process, but not just legislatures, and not at the federal level; and harnessing civil society and the media. This type of institutional-convergence strategy, one that catalyzes the heterogeneity of institutions and their complexity rather than seeing those qualities as an impediment to change, is a more empowering vision than one that relies on interest convergence alone. It is this type of approach—institutional convergence—that is a reflection of how change happens that can also help reveal a path forward for protecting the integrity of identity and political privacy. Next, I explore the institutional-convergence approach in greater depth and what it can mean for advocates. I then address how to activate such an approach to protect political privacy in the age of Surveillance Capitalism.

The Institutional-Convergence Rubik's Cube

Returning to Derrick Bell's Interest-Convergence Thesis: we saw how that approach may not have much descriptive force in terms of explaining how social change works, but it also is somewhat limiting for another reason. As should be apparent, a group that is unable to harness elite opinion in its favor, even if "elites" can clearly be identified and "elite interests" are something worth aspiring to secure, will believe social change is elusive, and if it is seen in that way, it can undermine the perceived efficacy of the group. And efficacy—the belief in the group's prospects for success—is an essential element of any social change effort.[103]

So, according to the Interest-Convergence Thesis, if a group is unable (or unwilling) to wait for elites to come around, is change not possible? What an institutional approach to social change tells us, particularly one that recognizes the heterogeneity of institutions and of institutional systems, is that groups can engage in what Chenoweth calls a "pillars analysis" but run it in reverse. In other words, according to a pillars analysis, one seeks to find the pillars of support that prop up a regime and try to erode them. The institutional-convergence approach tries to build up pillars of support from within an institutional framework. One can start with those settings, and those institutions, that hold out the most promise, like the efforts by marriage equality advocates who sought to identify states where pro–marriage equality referenda might pass and start in such locations, using such measures to begin to build wider support for the cause. But one is not limited to choosing between state and federal strategies.

An institutional-convergence approach starts with an analysis of the institutional settings where one can bring about the desired change. It looks at the different settings but appreciates them for the wide heterogeneity they exhibit. One can try to secure a victory at a local town council where one might find the elected members of that body sympathetic to one's cause. One can try to secure a victory in a judicial forum. One can try to convince a local, state, or federal agency to look at a specific problem in a new way, or to conduct an investigation, to try to pass regulations that will rein in unwanted behavior. A tactic one deploys using an institutional-convergence approach always includes finding the pressure points within the institutional systems and across their different levels and components. Instead of a one-dimensional array of monolithic systems, one sees these systems more like one might view a Rubik's Cube: each institutional system has different components, dimensions, and depths. One should identify the location within the system that might yield a positive result, then build from there.

What is more, instead of waiting around for broad interests to converge and hope for support from elite interests, one can change the forum to one in which the notions of elites and majority might change. We see this type of campaign emerging around the country in a number of different areas. When it comes to raising the minimum wage, a campaign solely directed at convincing the U.S. Congress to raise the federal minimum wage, which it has not done since 2009, may seem unlikely to succeed. But advocates have proven quite adept at fighting at the state and local levels to raise the minimum wage throughout the country, so much so that, in certain jurisdictions today, it is over twice the national minimum wage, which serves as a floor below which states cannot go. Advocates for increasing the minimum wage have largely advocated at state and local levels to push for increases in the minimum wage in areas where public sentiment is supportive.[104] Similarly, there is a movement underway across the nation that is seeking to ensure that tenants facing eviction in housing court receive legal representation to defend against such cases. This campaign has proven successful in cities where renters tend to outweigh homeowners and where the notion of a right to counsel in the relatively complex landlord–tenant context is popular.[105] Advocates are pressing in such jurisdictions and trying to make the case that not only is the right to counsel in such proceedings a critical element of fundamental due process rights; it also makes good fiscal sense. If the local government will have to house families that get evicted through housing court should they become homeless, it is far less expensive to provide a lawyer to defend them in court to stave off that eviction in the first place. While advocates may want a right to counsel to apply to all tenants in all housing courts at all times across the country, and to set national policy, they likely realize that such a goal is not possible at this time. Instead, they are starting in those places where such change *is* possible.

It is this possibility for change, and the receptivity of different institutions, in different settings, and at different times, that makes an approach centered around institutional convergence more attractive and effective than one based on interests alone. When we look merely at interest, we fail to recognize the depth to which institutions exist. Interests are just one facet of the immaterial aspects of institutions. They are just ideas. It is possible that they can be institutional ideas that animate people to action, but they are still just ideas. An institutional-convergence approach to social change would recognize both the extent to which interests may help to animate action and the extent to which institutions, in their material sense, count to foster social change and bring such change about in concrete ways. Revising interest-convergence theory as institutional-convergence theory opens up new ways of looking at social change. When we recast interest convergence as institutional convergence it helps us to appreciate the multidimensional ways in which social change occurs, on both the material and the immaterial levels. Interest convergence does not take into account how change occurs with respect to institutions in their material form. It also fails to consider the role that immaterial concepts like identity play in serving as a mobilizing force within social movement organizations.

Through an approach based on institutions, one can identify those places where the balance of opportunity tilts toward change. Instead of waiting for public sentiment (meaning elite interests) to come around to one's way of seeing things, one can take positive action and bring about change where it is possible. Such successful efforts can breed further successes and lead eventually, perhaps, to a broader tipping point. When this type of support builds across institutions, what can occur is what sociologists Clemens and Cook refer to as "institutional thickening," when new institutional norms emerge and gain strength.[106] As advocates secure support through different institutional elements—a court here, a town council there, maybe even a state legislature—it can begin to create the sort of norm cascades that Sunstein describes, building momentum that tips the scales in the favor of that group's desired change.

While Chenoweth might argue that successful social movements engage at least 3 percent of the population, where advocates direct their efforts, and how they go about tilting institutions, are also essential elements of social movement success.

When exactly this tipping point, or institutional thickening, occurs is difficult to say. Is it simply a question of securing a majority of the institutions in an institutional setting, or across institutional settings? If one "shrinks the change" and identifies a location within a particular setting, that can begin to have ripple effects within that system, as when a state legislature that advances worker protections in its state thereby encourages advocates in other states to say, "We'll have what they're having." Sunstein's view of norm cascades captures this concept, but he does not necessarily articulate a sense of when and how the tipping occurs. For him, in order to advance social change, "some kind of movement" that is "initiated by people who say that they disapprove" of a norm will succeed when "some kind of tipping point is reached."[107] Similarly, although journalist Malcolm Gladwell has an entire book titled *The Tipping Point*, he fails to go beyond defining that point other than to say it is when change happens "all at once."[108] Or, as Ernest Hemingway had one of his characters describe the process of falling into bankruptcy: "'Gradually, then suddenly.'"[109] But there is a sort of physics to it, just as one might imagine the toppling of a pillar or a dictator or solving a Rubik's Cube. The right move in the right place at the right time eventually brings the sides into alignment, and solving the puzzle on one side necessarily has effects on the other sides as well. But instead of saying that advocates have to build momentum on a national scale—across all institutions all at once—they can work to secure victories where such victories are possible, then strive to build momentum toward larger successes across institutions and institutional settings, until finally the new norm is institutionalized in a comprehensive way.

Leveraging Institutions to Protect Political Privacy

So, what would an institutional-convergence strategy look like in any effort to protect political privacy and the integrity of identity? We have already seen that the digital zoning framework described in chapter 6 strives to leverage some of the most effective elements of different institutional settings, while recognizing their respective shortcomings, in the path toward an effective system for protecting political privacy. But how does one get there?

Using the institutional-convergence framework, there are several core institutional groups that one might catalyze for meaningful change in this area. Some state governments and even individual institutions, like private and public colleges, are taking steps to address the perceived threat posed by certain social media apps.[110] Such efforts should continue and can certainly begin to start a conversation about the threats social media pose to digital privacy. It is at the state level where we can and should continue efforts designed to protect digital privacy. We see this already in a range of states, and this group does not reflect the typical red state/blue state divide.[111] States have passed legislation around digital privacy, with somewhat different approaches, though most enlist a disclosure-style regime favored by California and the European Union.[112]

Advocates should continue to push at the state level, where such legislation might stand the best chance of success. One could also imagine campaigns around digital privacy that emerge as ballot referenda, not unlike the type that were used in the marriage equality context and that abortion access advocates are starting to deploy with some success, even in traditional red states.[113] This is likely to create a groundswell of support for a national privacy law—but not for the reason that marriage equality ultimately came to a head at the Supreme Court.

By pushing state legislation to protect political privacy, it is likely to create support for national legislation, albeit from an unlikely source: industry itself. The main reason that this would occur is that companies affected by a patchwork of state laws governing privacy are likely to push for national legislation that would do two things at once: it would provide a uniform, national standard, and it would also likely be weaker than those state laws and could completely preempt them. In the minimum-wage context, federal legislation creates a floor and not a ceiling. As a result, states are free to create a minimum wage that is higher than the federal minimum wage, and many states do. With federal privacy legislation, it is likely that industry would seek to do the opposite: create a ceiling and not a floor. That is, it will seek to prohibit states from passing legislation that goes above and beyond that which federal law provides.

Indeed, the privacy legislation industry might support would likely not just prevent states in the future from passing legislation that went beyond what federal law says but also would likely preempt state laws already on the books. In other words, even if states pass strong privacy legislation now, Congress could, in the future, displace it, saying that any laws that offered greater protections than what the federal law provides are void. Thus, like with the approach to minimum-wage laws, advocates should work to make sure that federal privacy legislation, should Congress ever generate any, should create a floor, not a ceiling. It would permit states to go beyond those protections afforded through federal law.

Advocates will thus have to work in the states to push privacy legislation where state legislatures are receptive to such efforts, but they will also have to be mindful that, even if they have great success in convincing such legislatures to protect political privacy, there is a strong chance that industry will step in and advocate at the federal level for "strong" (that is, weak) protections that will displace those state laws that offer more protection than any federal law might afford consumers. If enough states pass robust privacy legislation, the notion that a federal law might actually undermine the benefits of those state efforts might meet public resistance. Those protected by such state laws might lobby their elected representatives not to support federal measures that would take away existing state-based rights. Economists talk about "prospect theory," or the idea that we care more about losing things we already have than not obtaining things we do not already possess, even when those things have the exact same monetary value.[114] Activists could seek to leverage this phenomenon and press federal legislators to preserve those rights citizens enjoy through state laws.

This sort of pressure from states passing privacy legislation of their own already seems to be working when it comes to the development of national legislation, but the risks that it will not strengthen—but actually weaken—the overall privacy landscape are very real. As this book goes to print, Senator Maria Cantwell of Washington State and Representative Cathy McMorris Rodgers, a Democrat and Republican respectively, have begun to circulate what they are currently calling a "discussion draft" of a proposed national privacy bill: the American Privacy Rights Act of 2024.[115] This bill has a long way to go before ultimate passage, and it contains some references to legal liability for those who would breach consumers' privacy as well as provisions that protect robust state privacy laws, but a lot can happen to this bill before it becomes law, if it does at all. Advocates will have to maintain pressure to ensure that any such federal legislation that might come about through this effort actually expands privacy protections and does not undermine it.

In addition, while state legislatures could get in the act to expand state laws regarding digital privacy, private nonprofit actors and academic institutions could analyze what information is currently available through company end-user agreements and begin to develop a system that graded company privacy policies in a way that was similar to the type of zoning system described in chapter 6. There are a number of private certification models in existence in the United States, including some, like the kosher food system, that have existed for centuries.[116] Recently, groups have created the LEED system for recognizing the environmental impacts of building construction, and B Lab has developed a method by which companies can seek B Corp certification, an assessment of company practices along a number of progressive metrics, including, among others, employee compensation and environmental impact.[117] One could envision an entity, like the Electronic Frontier Foundation, which already makes digital tools available to consumers to protect their privacy, spearheading an effort that might grade companies' digital practices for consistency with the type of guidelines set forth in the zoning regime outlined in chapter 6.

What is more, when it comes to protection of political privacy, there is the possibility that advocates on the left and the right, and those within industry, might actually join forces to bring about the type of zoning framework introduced above because it offers a "mere" disclosure regime and does not mandate any type of protection. It strives to harness market forces to create a race to the top. "Good" industries will seek to achieve a higher rating within the zones. In this way, it might lead to a division within the technology industry and the business community more generally, splitting that pillar of institutional support that might resist this type of legal framework for digital privacy. Some businesses might see a strategic advantage to this sort of rating: a business that already protects consumer privacy on a number of dimensions will gain a market edge over competitors that do not, and the signals digital zoning will send will help consumers recognize the advantages such privacy-protecting businesses offer, which will likely drive up their market share.

A strong digital zoning framework, even at the national level, could create the sort of institutional convergence that I have shown offers advocates the opportunity for real change—but only if they recognize how the framework functions, how institutions and institutional settings are not monolithic, and how to leverage and catalyze that framework to bring about real and lasting change.

* * *

Institutions come in many shapes and sizes, and it is the richness and complexity of our institutions, and the ways we come to find ourselves being shaped by such institutions, that help to give meaning to our lives and makes it worth living. It is also the heterogeneity of institutions that helps us shape those institutions and allows us to bring about social change. That heterogeneity also offers both challenges and opportunities when it comes to such efforts. Those who are able to identify the right institution to move at the right time and in the right way can create institutional convergences that lead to wider institutional—that is, social—change. It is my hope that this work has established not just the importance of the institution of political privacy for the functioning of democratic society but also how individuals can utilize an institutional lens and framework to catalyze institutions in ways that will protect political privacy. Democracies require privacy, and the integrity of identity is essential to individual and collective self-determination. An approach to protecting that identity that harnesses institutions in ways that can construct support for that essential element of democracy is one that might stand the chance of preserving the broader democratic endeavor. In the end, institutional convergence is democracy in action and a means to secure that individual and collective self-determination, especially when it comes to protecting political privacy. Protecting that political privacy is a starting point for all other truly democratic action and the lifeblood of democratic societies. Without it, no other democratic action is possible. Securing it, then, must become a central focus of those who would see democracy flourish, even as Surveillance Capitalism runs amok. But we have a choice to rein in its worst excesses while ensuring we have the digital tools that make life more interesting and engaging and social change more possible than ever. Our democratic future may just depend on it, and it is not too late to secure that future. I hope this book, in a small way, can help to provide some insights as to how advocates might do just that.

ACKNOWLEDGMENTS

This work is the product of many hands, especially my research assistants on this project: Alice Broussard, Andrew Fay, Miller Fina, and E. Conor Graham. Barbara Jordan-Smith and Sherri Meyer, my legal assistants at Albany Law School, also offered unwavering and cheerful support. The team at Albany Law School's law library, including David Walker and Pegeen Lorusso, also provided invaluable assistance and support. Without the team at New York University Press, especially the visionary and intrepid Clara Platter, this project would have never come to fruition. In addition, my colleagues at Albany Law School are a constant source of support and strength, in this project and in others, especially Pam Armstrong, Ava Ayers, Ted De Barbieri, Keith Hirokawa, Rosemary Queenan, Patricia Reyhan, and Sarah Rogerson. Support from the administration at Albany Law, especially current President and Dean Cinnamon Carlarne, and former President and Dean Alicia Ouellette, has allowed this initiative to come to life. This work also benefits from comments I received on previous drafts from Ian Ayres, Sandra Braman, Jon Mandle, David Turetsky, and Ariel Zylberman. All errors and omissions are, of course, mine. Finally, another colleague, Robert Heverly, has been a consistent supporter of this project over the years, though he probably does not agree with much, if anything, written here, but the project is better for that skepticism. Friends also offered constant encouragement throughout this process, especially Tom Bongiorno, Graham Boyd, Adam Bramwell, Dana Carstarphen, Charles Chestnut, Chris Coons, Beth Garrity-Rokous, Gates Garrity-Rokous, Mitch Glenn, Mark Napier, Richard Newman, Kurt Petersen, Richard Pinner, Nicole Theodosiou, and Mike Wishnie.

More than anyone, though, the unwavering support of my family, especially my spouse, Amy Barasch, and son, Leo Brescia, makes everything I do even remotely possible, especially this work.

NOTES

1. POLITICAL PRIVACY AND THE INTEGRITY OF IDENTITY

1 Ray Kurzweil, How to Create a Mind: The Secret of Human Thought Revealed 261 (2012); Ray Kurzweil, The Singularity Is Near: When Humans Transcend Biology 7 (2005).

2 Marissa Gunther, *Invading the Darkness of Child Sex Trafficking*, Stan. Soc. Innov. Rev. (2020), https://doi.org/10.48558/71H4-NG74.

3 Cecilia Yap, *Policy Brutality Trends as Philippines Murder Video Goes Viral*, Bloomberg (Dec. 21, 2020), www.bloomberg.com/news/articles/2020-12-21/police-brutality-trends-as-philippines-murder-videogoes-viral.

4 Hamza Shaban, *Facebook to Reexamine How Livestream Videos Are Flagged after Christchurch Shooting*, Wash. Post (Mar. 21, 2019), www.washingtonpost.com/technology/2019/03/21/facebook-reexaminehow-recently-live-videos-are-flagged-after-christchurch-shooting.

5 Ronen Bergman and Farnaz Fassihi, *The Scientist and the A.I.-Assisted, Remote-Control Killing Machine*, NYT (Sept. 18, 2021),www.nytimes.com/2021/09/18/world/middleeast/iran-nuclear-fakhrizadeh-assassination-israel.html.

6 Craig Silverman et al., *Facebook Hosted Surge of Misinformation and Insurrection Threats in Months Leading Up to Jan. 6 Attack, Records Show*, ProPublica (Jan. 4, 2022), www.propublica.org/article/facebook-hosted-surge-of-misinformation-and-insurrection-threats-in-months-leading-up-to-jan-6-attack-records-show#:~:text=Facebook%20groups%20swelled%20with%20at,The%20Washington%20Post%20has%20found.

7 Woodrow Hartzog & Neil M. Richards, *Privacy's Constitutional Moment and the Limits of Data Protection*, 61 Bos. Coll. L. Rev. 1687 (2020).

8 Jessica Bursztynsky, *Roger McNamee: Facebook and Google, Like China, Use Data to Manipulate Behavior and It Needs to Stop*, CNBC (June 10, 2019), www.cnbc.com/2019/06/10/roger-mcnamee-facebook-and-google-like-china-manipulate-behavior.html.

9 Ari Waldman calls this the "virtual self" that emerges online. Ari Ezra Waldman, *Durkheim's Internet: Social and Political Theory in Online Society*, 7 N.Y.L. Sch. J. of L. & Lib. 345, 392–415 (2013) (describing the virtual self).

10 George Orwell, 1984, 19 (1949).

11 Daniel J. Solove, The Digital Person: Technology and Privacy in the Information Age (2004) (hereinafter Solove, The Digital Person).

12 MARSHALL GANZ, WHY DAVID SOMETIMES WINS: LEADERSHIP, ORGANIZATION, AND STRATEGY IN THE CALIFORNIA FARM WORKER MOVEMENT 32 (2009).

13 Ari Ezra Waldman, *Privacy as Trust: Sharing Personal Information in a Networked World*, 69 U. MIAMI L. REV. 559 (2015).

14 Pamela E. Oliver & Gerald Marwell, *Mobilizing Technologies for Collective Action*, *in* FRONTIERS IN SOCIAL MOVEMENT THEORY (Aldon D. Morris & Carol McClurg Mueller eds. 1992).

15 ALAN F. WESTIN, PRIVACY AND FREEDOM 12–15 (1967).

16 W. J. M. MACKENZIE, POLITICAL IDENTITY (Penguin Books, 1978).

17 Steven M. Buechler, *Beyond Resource Mobilization? Emerging Trends in Social Movement Theory*, 34 SOCIO. Q. 217, 228 (1993).

18 SHANNON WATTS, FIGHT LIKE A MOTHER: HOW A GRASSROOTS MOVEMENT TOOK ON THE GUN LOBBY AND WHY WOMEN WILL CHANGE THE WORLD 6–8 (2019).

19 *Id.*, at 19.

20 YOCHAI BENKLER, HAL ROBERTS & ROBERT FARIS, NETWORK PROPAGANDA: MANIPULATION, DISINFORMATION, AND RADICALIZATION IN AMERICAN POLITICS (2018).

21 EZRA KLEIN, WHY WE'RE POLARIZED (2020).

22 SHOSHANA ZUBOFF, THE AGE OF SURVEILLANCE CAPITALISM: THE FIGHT FOR A HUMAN FUTURE AT THE NEW FRONTIER OF POWER (2019).

23 The Rolling Stones *(I Can't Get No) Satisfaction*, on The Rolling Stones: The London Years (ABKCO 1989). And there, the Stones seem to understand this connection between advertising, communications, and identity. The "man" pushing different products on the radio couldn't, in fact, be a man in the metaphorical sense, because he didn't "smoke the same cigarettes" as Mick Jagger.

24 Dante D'Orazio, *Uber Is Tracking Its Drivers in China, Will Fire Anyone Attending Taxi Protests*, VERGE (June 14, 2015), www.theverge.com/2015/6/14/8778111/uber-threatens-to-fire-drivers-attending-protests-inchina.

25 Zoe Schiffer, *Apple Just Banned a Pay Equity Slack Channel but Lets Fun Dogs Channel Lie*, VERGE (Aug. 31, 2021), www.theverge.com/2021/8/31/22650751/apple-bans-pay-equity-slack-channel.

26 *See The Facebook Files*, WALL ST. J. (Oct. 1, 2022), www.wsj.com/articles/the-facebook-files-11631713039.

27 Erving Goffman, *The Territories of the Self, in* RELATIONS IN PUBLIC: MICROSTUDIES OF THE PUBLIC ORDER 38–40 (1971).

28 SIDNEY G. TARROW, THE POWER IN MOVEMENT: SOCIAL MOVEMENTS, COLLECTIVE ACTION, AND POLITICS (3rd ed. 2011).

29 William Gamson, *The Social Psychology of Collective Action, in* FRONTIERS IN SOCIAL MOVEMENT THEORY 71–72 (Aldon D. Morris & Carol McClurg Mueller eds. 1992).

30 Philip E. Agre, *Introduction, in* TECHNOLOGY AND PRIVACY: THE NEW LANDSCAPE (Philip E. Agre & Marc Rotenberg eds. 1997).

31 *See, e.g.,* Paul M. Schwartz, *Internet Privacy and the State,* 32 CONN. L. REV. 834 (2000).

32 Danielle Keats Citron, *Sexual Privacy,* 128 YALE L. J. 1870 (2019).

33 Citron, *supra* note 32, at 1880.

34 *Id.,* at 1888–91.

35 *Id.,* at 1882.

36 DANIELLE KEATS CITRON, THE FIGHT FOR PRIVACY: PROTECTING DIGNITY, IDENTITY, AND LOVE IN THE DIGITAL AGE 44–45 (2022).

37 *Id.,* at 44.

38 Isaiah Berlin, *Two Concepts of Liberty, in* FOUR ESSAYS ON LIBERTY 118, 118–22 (1969). *See also* ROBIN L. WEST, CIVIL RIGHTS: RETHINKING THEIR NATURAL FOUNDATION 156–57 (2019).

39 Elettra Bietti, *A Genealogy of Digital Platform Regulation,* 7 GEO. L. TECH. REV. 1, 55 (2023).

40 Salomé Viljoen, *A Relational Theory of Data Governance,* 131 Yale L. J. 573, 580 (2021).

41 ROBIN DUNBAR GROOMING, GOSSIP AND THE EVOLUTION OF LANGUAGE (1997).

42 RAY BRESCIA, THE FUTURE OF CHANGE: HOW TECHNOLOGY SHAPES SOCIAL REVOLUTIONS (2020).

43 PAUL STARR, THE CREATION OF THE MEDIA: POLITICAL ORIGINS OF MODERN COMMUNICATIONS 66 (2005).

44 BRESCIA, *supra* note 42, at 13–14.

45 DANIEL WALKER HOWE, WHAT GOD HATH WROUGHT: THE TRANSFORMATION OF AMERICA, 1815–1848, 847 (2007).

46 THEDA SKOCPOL, DIMINISHED DEMOCRACY: FROM MEMBERSHIP TO MANAGEMENT IN AMERICAN CIVIC LIFE 205 (2004).

47 ANIKO BODROGHKOZY, EQUAL TIME: TELEVISION AND THE CIVIL RIGHTS MOVEMENT (2012).

48 MARSHALL MCLUHAN, UNDERSTANDING MEDIA: THE EXTENSIONS OF MAN 1 (Terrence Gordon ed. 1994).

49 SKOCPOL, *supra* note 46, at 37–41.

50 *Id.* at 40–41.

51 BRESCIA, *supra* note 42, at 37.

52 SKOCPOL, *supra* note 46, at 40–41.

53 Margaret Weir & Marshall Ganz, *Reconnecting People and Politics, in* THE NEW MAJORITY: TOWARD A POPULAR PROGRESSIVE POLITICS 149–71 (Stanley B. Greenburg & Theda Skocpol eds. 1997).

54 MCLUHAN, *supra* note 48, at 19.

55 BODROGHKOZY, *supra* note 47.

56 PAUL KIX, YOU HAVE TO BE PREPARED TO DIE BEFORE YOU CAN BEGIN TO LIVE: TEN WEEKS IN BIRMINGHAM THAT CHANGED AMERICA (2023).

57 *NAACP v. Alabama* ex rel. *Patterson*, 357 U.S. 449, 460 (1958), and *NAACP v. Button*, 371 U.S. 415 (1963), discussed in Chapter 3.

58 David J. Garrow, The FBI and Martin Luther King, Jr.: From "Solo" to Memphis (2015).

59 Joseph M. Adelman, *A Constitutional Conveyance of Intelligence, Public and Private: The Post Office, the Business of Printing, and the American Revolution*, 11 Enterprise & Soc'y 709, 733 (2010).

60 Lyman Beecher, The Memory of Our Fathers Sermon, Plymouth, MA, 27 (Dec. 22, 1828).

61 David P. Currie, The Constitution in Congress: Descent into the Maelstrom 1829–1861 24–25 (2005).

62 Richard R. John, Spreading the News: The American Postal System from Franklin to Morse 256 (1998).

63 I discuss the evolution of privacy law, and its relationship to changes in technology, in some depth in Chapter 3.

64 Sara Morrison, *A Surprising Number of Government Agencies Buy Cellphone Location Data: Lawmakers Want to Know Why*, Vox (Dec. 2, 2020), www.vox.com/recode/22038383/dhs-cbp-investigationcellphone-data-brokers-venntel. *See also* Citron, The Fight for Privacy, *supra* note 36, at 58–60 (describing data brokers and their collaboration with government entities). *See also* Christopher Slobogin, *"Volunteer" Searches*, Vanderbilt Law Research Paper No. 23–18 (Aug. 22, 2023), https://papers.ssrn.com/sol3/papers.cfm?abstract_id=4548412. (using the phrase "volunteer searches" to describe the practice of private companies sharing personal information of their users with government agencies without those agencies first seeking a warrant for such information).

65 Rosa Ehrenreich, *Privacy and Power*, 89 Georgetown L. J. 2047, 2052 (2001).

66 Daniel J. Solove, *A Taxonomy of Privacy*, 154 U. Pa. L. Rev. 477, 487–88 (2006).

67 Sarah J. Jackson, Moya Bailey & Brooke Foucault Welles, #Hashtag Activism: Networks of Race and Gender Justice (2020).

68 Zeynep Tufekci, Twitter and Tear Gas: The Power and Fragility of Networked Protests (2016).

69 Paul M. Romer, *Economic Growth, in* The Concise Encyclopedia of Economics 131 (David R. Henderson ed. 2007).

70 Charlotte Garden, *Meta Rights*, 83 Fordham L. Rev. 855 (2014).

71 Emily Stewart, *Lawmakers Seem Confused About What Facebook Does—and How to Fix It*, Vox (Apr. 10, 2018), www.vox.com/policy-and-politics/2018/4/10/17222062/mark-zuckerberg-testimony-graham-facebookregulations.

72 Woodrow Hartzog, *Body Cameras and the Path to Redeem Privacy Law*, 96 N.C. L. Rev. 1257, 1269 (2018).

73 Ari Ezra Waldman, *Privacy Law's False Promise*, 97 Wash. U. L. Rev. 773, 776 (2020).

74 47 U.S.C. § 230(c)(1).

75 Anupam Chander, *How Law Made Silicon Valley*, 63 Emory L. J. 639 (2014).

76 Tim Wu, The Attention Merchants: The Epic Scramble to Get Inside Our Heads (2017).

77 Lee Fang, *Silicon Valley-Funded Privacy Think Tanks Fight in D.C. to Unravel State-Level Consumer Privacy Protections*, Intercept (Apr.16, 2019), https://bit.ly/3j7pWYJ.

78 Lawrence Lessig, Code: And Other Laws of Cyberspace (1999).

79 Solove, The Digital Person, *supra* note 11, at 103–04.

80 Chloe Aiello, *Tech Pioneer Jaron Lanier Says Companies Should Pay for Data: 'Let's Get Out of the Manipulation Business'*, CNBC (June 21, 2018), https://perma.cc/NR6A-PR4H.

81 *See, e.g.*, Tomiko Brown-Nagin, Courage to Dissent: Atlanta and the Long History of the Civil Rights Movement 136–64 (2011) (describing tensions between local advocates and national leaders within the Civil Rights Movement); Kix, *supra* note 56, at 79–80 (describing local leaders in Birmingham, Alabama, who pushed national leaders in the SCLC for more aggressive efforts in the campaign in that city in the spring of 1963); Constance Baker Motley, Equal Justice Under the Law: An Autobiography 62–69 (1998) (describing demands by local advocates to desegregate public golf courses in Atlanta over the objection of NAACP leadership, who wanted to focus on other priorities).

82 Daron Acemoglu & James A. Robinson, Why Nations Fail: The Origins of Power, Prosperity, and Poverty 73–83 (2012).

83 *Id.*

84 Neil K. Komesar, Imperfect Alternatives: Choosing Institutions in Law, Economics, and Public Policy 1–28 (1997).

2. POLITICAL PRIVACY AND INSTITUTIONS

1 Sheera Frenkel & Cecilia Kang, An Ugly Truth: Inside Facebook's Battle for Domination 149–59 (2021).

2 Paul Lewis & Paul Hilder, *Leaked: Cambridge Analytica's Blueprint for Trump Victory*, Guardian (Mar. 23, 2018), www.theguardian.com/uk-news/2018/mar/23/leaked-cambridge-analyticas-blueprint-for-trump-victory; Alvin Chang, *The Facebook and Cambridge Analytica Scandal, Explained with a Simple Diagram*, Vox (May 2, 2018), www.vox.com/policy-and-politics/2018/3/23/17151916/facebook-cambridge-analytica-trumpdiagram.

3 Brad Smith & Carol Ann Browne, Tools and Weapons: The Promise and the Peril of the Digital Age 144 (2019).

4 Shaun Walker et al., *Pegasus Project: Spyware Leak Suggests Lawyers and Activists at Risk Across Globe*, Guardian (July 19, 2021), www.theguardian.com/news/2021/jul/19/spyware-leak-suggests-lawyers-and-activists-at-risk-across-globe.

5 Margaret Renkl, *Tell Me There Isn't a Witch Hunt in Tennessee*, N.Y. TIMES (July 3, 2023), www.nytimes.com/2023/07/03/opinion/tennessee-trans-lgbtq-health-records-vanderbilt.html?smid=nytcore-ios-share&referringSource=articleShare.

6 Byron Tau, *Antiabortion Group Used Cellphone Data to Target Ads to Planned Parenthood Visitors*, WALL ST. J. (May 18, 2023), www.wsj.com/articles/antiabortion-group-used-cellphone-data-to-target-ads-to-planned-parenthood-visitors-446c1212.

7 Michele Gilman, *Will My Period Tracking App Betray Me? Menstrual Surveillance in a Post-Roe World*, MS. MAGAZINE (May 9, 2022), https://msmagazine.com/2022/05/09/period-tracking-app-menstrual-surveillance-roe-v-wade-abortion. It is also likely that other states will follow Texas in incorporating similar provisions in their own laws.

8 Zak Doffman, *Black Lives Matter: U.S. Protesters Tracked By Secretive Phone Location Technology*, FORBES (June 26, 2020 11:22 AM) www.forbes.com/sites/zakdoffman/2020/06/26/secretive-phone-tracking-company-publishes-location-data-on-black-lives-matter-protesters/?sh=7632d9bb4a1e.

9 Marisa Iati and Michelle Boorstein, *Case of High-Ranking Cleric Allegedly Tracked on Grindr App Poses Rorschach Test for Catholics*, WASH. POST (July 21, 2021), www.washingtonpost.com/religion/2021/07/21/catholic-official-grindr-reaction.

10 Drew Harwell, *Pharmacies Share Medical Data with Police without a Warrant, Inquiry Finds*, WASH. POST (Dec. 12, 2023), www.washingtonpost.com/technology/2023/12/12/pharmacy-records-police-privacy-abortion/.

11 *See The Facebook Files*, WALL ST. J. (Oct. 1, 2022), www.wsj.com/articles/the-facebook-files-11631713039.

12 Igor Derysh, *Despite Parler Backlash, Facebook Played Huge Role in Fueling Capitol Riot, Watchdogs Say*, SALON (Jan. 16, 2021), www.salon.com/2021/01/16/despite-parler-backlash-facebook-played-huge-role-in-fueling-capitol-riot-watchdogs-say.

13 TIM WU, THE ATTENTION MERCHANTS: THE EPIC SCRAMBLE TO GET INSIDE OUR HEADS 259–60 (2016).

14 Hannah Ellis-Petersen, *Facebook Admits Failings Over Incitement to Violence in Myanmar*, GUARDIAN (Nov. 6, 2018), www.theguardian.com/technology/2018/nov/06/facebook-admits-it-has-not-done-enough-to-quell-hate-in-my-anmar#:~:text=Facebook%20has%20admitted%20it%20did,harmful%20and%20racially%2Dinflammatory%20content (describing Facebook's role in stoking violence directed toward racial and religious minorities in Myanmar).

15 Keach Hagey and Jeff Horwitz, *The Facebook Files: Facebook Tried to Make Platform Healthier. It Got Angrier Instead*, WALL ST. J. (Sept. 26, 2021), www.wsj.com/articles/facebook-algorithm-change-zuckerberg-11631654215.

16 William J. Brady et al., *How Social Learning Amplifies Moral Outrage Expression in Online Social Networks*, 7 SCI. ADVANCES 1 (2021); Alexander Bor & Michael Bang Petersen, *The Psychology of Online Political Hostility: A Comprehensive, Cross-National Test of the Mismatch Hypothesis*, 116 AM. POL. SCI. REV. 1, 1–18

(2021); Kevin Roose, *The Making of a YouTube Radical*, N.Y TIMES (June 8, 2019), https://nyti.ms/2ZAuyxK.

17 SELECT COMM. ON INTEL., RUSSIAN ACTIVE MEASURES CAMPAIGNS AND INTERFERENCE IN THE 2016 U.S. ELECTION VOLUME 2: RUSSIA'S USE OF SOCIAL MEDIA WITH ADDITIONAL VIEWS, S. Rep. 116-XX, at 47 (1st Sess. 2019).

18 *Id.* at 64.

19 ERVING GOFFMAN, THE PRESENTATION OF THE SELF IN EVERYDAY LIFE 2 (1959).

20 FRANK PASQUALE, THE BLACK BOX SOCIETY: THE SECRET ALGO-RITHMS THAT CONTROL MONEY AND INFORMATION 54–65 (2015).

21 IMMANUEL KANT, GROUNDWORK OF THE METAPHYSICS OF MORALS 4:420–4:429 (18th ed. 2021).

22 GERALD DWORKIN, THEORY AND PRACTICE OF AUTONOMY 12–13 (1988).

23 Robert Post, *Meiklejohn's Mistake: Individual Autonomy and the Reform of Public Discourse*, 64 COLO. L. REV. 1109, 1115 (1993). *See also* Tom Christiano & Sameer Bajaj, *Democracy*, THE STANFORD ENCYCLOPEDIA OF PHILOSOPHY (Spring 2022 edition), Edward N. Zalta (ed.) (describing democracy as "a method of col-lective decision making characterized by a kind of equality among the partici-pants at an essential stage of the decision-making process"), https://plato.stanford.edu/archives/spr2022/entries/democracy.

24 *See* Maimon Schwarzschild, *Popular Initiatives and American Federalism, or Putting Direct Democracy in Its Place*, 13 J. CONTEMP. LEGAL ISSUES 531, 538 (2004).

25 Zechariah Chafee, Jr., *Freedom of Speech in War Time*, 32 HARV. L. REV. 932, 957 (1919).

26 *See* C. Edwin Baker, *Counting Preferences in Collective Choice Situations*, 25 UCLA L. REV. 381, 414 (1978).

27 Philip Pettit, *Democracy, Electoral and Contestatory*, in DESIGNING DEMO-CRATIC INSTITUTIONS 105, 106 (Ian Shapiro & Stephen Maedo eds., 2000).

28 John Christman, *Feminism and Autonomy*, in "NAGGING" QUESTIONS: FEMI-NIST ETHICS IN EVERYDAY LIFE 18 (Dana E. Bushnell et al. eds., 1995). *See also* Robert Post, *Participatory Democracy and Free Speech*, 97 VIRG. L. REV. 477, 487–88 (2011).

29 *See* JOHN RAWLS, A THEORY OF JUSTICE 81, 137–41(rev. ed. Harv. Univ. Press, 1999).

30 *Id.* at 453.

31 MICHAEL J. SANDEL, LIBERALISM AND THE LIMITS OF JUSTICE 179 (2nd ed. 1998).

32 KWAME ANTHONY APPIAH, THE ETHICS OF IDENTITY 37 (2005).

33 Thomas May, *The Concept of Autonomy*, 31 AM. PHIL. Q. 133, 141 (1994).

34 GERALD DWORKIN, THE THEORY AND PRACTICE OF AUTONOMY 12–13 (1988).

35 Marilyn Friedman, *Autonomy and Social Relationships: Rethinking the Feminist Critique, in* FEMINISTS RETHINK THE SELF 55–59(Diana Tietjens Myers ed., 1997).

36 AMARTYA SEN, THE IDEA OF JUSTICE 231 (2009).

37 *Id.* at 241.

38 *Id.*; AMARTYA SEN, DEVELOPMENT AS FREEDOM 17 (1999); *see also* JAMES S. FISHKIN, DEMOCRACY WHEN THE PEOPLE ARE THINKING: REVITALIZING OUR POLITICS THROUGH PUBLIC DELIBERATION (2018).

39 Amartya Sen, *Dialogue Capabilities, Lists, and Public Reason: Continuing the Conversation*, 10 FEMINIST ECON. 77, 80 (2004).

40 Albert Bandura, *Self-Efficacy Mechanism in Human Agency*, 37 AM. PSYCH. 122, 126, 137 (1982).

41 YUVAL NOAH HARARI, SAPIENS: A BRIEF HISTORY OF HUMANKIND 20–40 (2015); EMILE DURKHEIM, SOCIOLOGY AND PHILOSOPHY 37 (D. F. Pocock trans. 1974).

42 Daniel Philpott, *Self-Determination in Practice, in* NATIONAL SELF-DETERMINATION AND SECESSION 81–82 (Margaret Moore ed. 1998).

43 MARTHA C. NUSSBAUM, CREATIVE CAPABILITIES: THE HUMAN DEVELOPMENT APPROACH 33–34 (2011).

44 Pamela Oliver & Gerald Marwell, *Mobilizing Technologies for Collective Action, in* FRONTIERS IN SOCIAL MOVEMENT THEORY 252 (Aldon Morris & Carol McClurg Mueller eds. 1992); Verta Taylor & Nancy E. Whittier, *Collective Identity in Social Movement Communities: Lesbian Feminist Mobilization, in* FRONTIERS IN SOCIAL MOVEMENT THEORY 105 (Aldon Morris & Carol McClurg Mueller eds. 1992).

45 Taylor & Whittier, *supra* note 44, at 104.

46 Steven M. Buechler, *Beyond Resource Mobilization? Emerging Trends in Social Movement Theory*, 34 SOCIO Q. 217, 228 (1993).

47 Hank Johnston, Enrique Laraña, and Joseph R. Gusfield, *Identities, Grievances and New Social Movements, in* NEW SOCIAL MOVEMENTS: FROM IDEOLOGY TO IDENTITY 10 (Enrique Laraña, Henry Johnston & Joseph R. Gusfield eds. 1994).

48 Buechler, *supra* note 46, at 228.

49 Alberto Melucci, *Getting Involved: Identity and Mobilization in Social Movements, in* INTERNATIONAL SOCIAL MOVEMENT RESEARCH: ORGANIZING FOR CHANGE: SOCIAL MOVEMENT ORGANIZATIONS IN EUROPE AND THE UNITED STATES (Bert Klandermans ed., 343 1988).

50 *See* Taylor & Whittier, *supra* note 44, at 105.

51 Judith M. Gerson & Kathy Peiss, *Boundaries, Negotiations, Consciousness: Reconceptualizing Gender Relations*, 32 SOC. PROBLEMS 317 (1985).

52 Debra Friedman & Doug McAdam, *Collective Identity and Activism: Networks, Choices, and the Life of a Social Movement, in* FRONTIERS IN SOCIAL MOVEMENT THEORY 157 (Aldon Morris & Carol McClurg Mueller eds., 1992).

53 *Id.*

54 *Id.*

55 Steven M. Buechler, *Beyond Resource Mobilization? Emerging Trends in Social Movement Theory*, 34 SOCIO. Q. 217 (1993). This incorporation of identity into theory is similar to the approach toward identity found in Critical Race Theory and similar theories.

56 Bruce Fireman & William A. Gamson, *Utilitarian Logic in the Resource Mobilization Perspective*, in THE DYNAMICS OF SOCIAL MOVEMENTS: RESOURCE MOBILIZATION, SOCIAL CONTROL, AND TACTICS 21 (Mayer N. Zald & John D. McCarthy eds., 1979).

57 Taylor & Whittier, *supra* note 44, at 104–29.

58 SIDNEY G. TARROW, POWER IN MOVEMENT: SOCIAL MOVEMENTS AND CONTENTIOUS POLITICS 10 (Rev. and updated 3rd ed., 2011) (emphasis in original).

59 *Id.*

60 Alberto Melucci, *A Strange Kind of Newness: What's "New" in New Social Movements*, in NEW SOCIAL MOVEMENTS: FROM IDEOLOGY TO IDENTITY 117 (Enrique Laraña, Henry Johnston & Joseph R. Gusfield eds., 1994).

61 ALEXIS DE TOCQUEVILLE, DEMOCRACY IN AMERICA 180–85 (Harvey C. Mansfield & Delba Winthrop trans., 2000).

62 THEDA SKOCPOL, DIMINISHED DEMOCRACY: FROM MEMBERSHIP TO MANAGEMENT IN AMERICAN CIVIL LIFE (2003).

63 Arthur M. Schlesinger, *Biography of a Nation of Joiners* 50 AM. HISTORICAL REV. 1 (1944).

64 B. GUY PETERS, INSTITUTIONAL THEORY IN POLITICAL SCIENCE: THE NEW INSTITUTIONALISM 23 (4th ed., 2019).

65 Avner Grief, *Foreword: Institutions, Markets, and Games*, in THE ECONOMIC SOCIOLOGY OF CAPITALISM xiii (Victor Nee & Richard Swedberg eds., 2005)

66 Lynne G. Zucker, *The Role of Institutionalization in Cultural Persistence*, 42 Am. Sociological Rev. 726, 728 (1977).

67 *Id.* at 729

68 *See* WEBSTER'S ONLINE DICTIONARY, www.merriam-webster.com/dictionary/institution.

69 DOUGLASS C. NORTH, INSTITUTIONS, INSTITUTIONAL CHANGE, AND ECONOMIC PERFORMANCE 3 (1990).

70 *Id.* at 3–10.

71 *See* Part II., C., *infra*.

72 *See, e.g.*, NORTH, *supra* note 69; ELINOR OSTROM, GOVERNING THE COMMONS: THE EVOLUTION OF INSTITUTIONS FOR COLLECTIVE ACTION (1990); NEIL K. KOMESAR, IMPERFECT ALTERNATIVES: CHOOSING INSTITUTIONS IN LAW, ECONOMICS, AND PUBLIC POLICY 4–5 (1997).

73 Roger Friedland & Robert A. Alford, *Bringing Society Back in: Symbols, Practices, and Institutional Contradictions*, in THE NEW INSTITUTIONALISM IN ORGANIZATIONAL ANALYSIS 249 (Walter W. Powell & Paul J. DiMaggio eds., 1991) (citations omitted).

74 *Id.*

75 *Id.*

76 *Id.*

77 *Id.*

78 *Id.*

79 Sometimes the definition of "institution" simply collapses the concepts together. *See* MARY DOUGLAS, HOW INSTITUTIONS THINK 46 (1986) (defining institutions as "legitimized social grouping" and including "a family, a game, or a ceremony" as examples of institutions).

80 DARON ACEMOGLU & JAMES A. ROBINSON, WHY NATIONS FAIL: THE ORIGINS OF POWER, PROSPERITY, AND POVERTY 428–37 (2012); Daron Acemoglu & Simon Johnson, *Unbundling Institutions*, 113 J. POL. ECON. 949, 988 (2005); Frank B. Cross, *Law and Trust*, 93 GEO. L.J. 1457, 1525–27 (2005); Martin Leschke, *Constitutional Choice and Prosperity: A Factor Analysis*, 11 CONST. POL. ECON. 265 (2000).

81 ACEMOGLU & ROBINSON, *supra* note 80, at 74.

82 *Id.* at 75–76.

83 CASS R. SUNSTEIN, HOW CHANGE HAPPENS 35–37 (2019).

84 *Id.* at 4–10.

85 *Id.* at 20.

86 For a description of the American Suffrage Movement, see SUSAN WARE, WHY THEY MARCHED: UNTOLD STORIES OF THE WOMEN WHO FOUGHT FOR THE RIGHT TO VOTE (2019).

87 William N. Eskridge, *Channeling: Identity-Based Social Movements and Public Law*, 150 UNIV. PA. L. REV. 419, 425–26 (2001).

88 FRANCIS FUKUYAMA, IDENTITY: THE DEMAND FOR DIGNITY AND THE POLITICS OF RESENTMENT 158 (2018); MARK LILLA, THE ONCE AND FUTURE LIBERAL: AFTER IDENTITY POLITICS 58–59 (2017).

89 SKOCPOL, *supra* note 62, at 205.

90 MARSHALL GANZ, WHY DAVID SOMETIMES WINS: LEADERSHIP, STRATEGY, AND ORGANIZATION IN THE CALIFORNIA FARM WORKER MOVEMENT 193 (2009).

91 William A. Gamson, *The Social Psychology of Collective Action, in* FRONTIERS IN SOCIAL MOVEMENT THEORY 60 (Aldon Morris & Carol McClurg Mueller eds., 1992).

92 *Id.*

93 BERT KLANDERMANS, THE SOCIAL PSYCHOLOGY OF PROTEST 204–06 (1997).

94 Friedman & McAdam, *supra* note 52, at 157.

95 Mary L. Dudziak, *Desegregation as a Cold War Imperative*, 41 STANFORD L. REV. 61, 118–19 (1988).

96 Eskridge, *supra* note 87, at 419–59.

97 Riva B. Siegel, *Community in Conflict: Same-Sex Marriage and Backlash*, 64 UCLA L. REV. 1728, 1744–46 (2017).

98 Eskridge, *supra* note 87, at 425–26.

99 KLANDERMANS, *supra* note 93, at 204–06.

100 MANCUR OLSON, THE LOGIC OF COLLECTIVE ACTION: PUBLIC GOODS AND THE THEORY OF GROUPS (1965).

101 OLSON, *supra* note 100, at 1–28.

102 Robert Hockett, *Recursive Collective Action Problems: The Structure of Procyclicality in Financial and Monetary Markets, Macroeconomies and Formally Similar Contexts*, 3 J. OF FIN. PERSP. 1, 3 (2015).

103 OSTROM, *supra* note 72, at 90–102.

104 Olson described "federated" organizations as ones that were made up of small, local cells connected to a larger network. OLSON, *supra* note 99, at 61–63. Ostrom described these as "nested enterprises." Ostrom, *supra* note 72, at 101–2.

105 MARGARET WEIR & MARSHALL GANZ, RECONNECTING PEOPLE AND POLITICS IN THE NEW MAJORITY: TOWARD A POPULAR PROGRESSIVE POLITICS 160 (Stanley B. Greenburg & Theda Skocpol eds. 1997).

106 *See* Theda Skocpol, Ariane Liazos & Marshall Ganz, *The Achievements of African American Fraternalism, in* WHAT A MIGHTY POWER WE CAN BE: AFRICAN AMERICAN FRATERNAL GROUPS AND THE STRUGGLE FOR RACIAL EQUALITY, 214–28 (Theda Skocpol, Araine Liazos & Marshall Ganz eds., 2006).

107 On the role of local leaders in several place-based campaigns during the civil rights era, see J. MILLS THORNTON III, DIVIDING LINES, MUNICIPAL POLITICS AND THE STRUGGLE FOR CIVIL RIGHTS IN MONTGOMERY, BIRMINGHAM AND SELMA (2002).

108 John D. McCarthy & Mark Wolfson, *Resource Mobilization by Local Social Movement Organizations: Agency, Strategy, and Organization in the Movement against Drunk Driving*, 61 AM. SOCIO. REV. 1070 (1996).

109 Elisabeth S. Clemens & James M. Cook, *Politics and Institutionalism: Explaining Durability and Change*, 25 ANN. REV. OF SOCIOLOGY 441, 454 (1999) (citation omitted).

110 L. J. Hanifan, *The Rural School Community Center*, 67 ANNALS AM. ACAD. POL. & SOC. SCI. 130, 130–31 (1916).

111 ROBERT D. PUTNAM, BOWLING ALONE: THE COLLAPSE AND REVIVAL OF AMERICAN COMMUNITY (2001).

112 ROBERT D. PUTNAM, ROBERT LEONARDI & RAFFAELLA Y. NANETTI, MAKING DEMOCRACY WORK: CIVIC TRADITIONS IN MODERN ITALY 171 (1993).

113 Robert D. Putnam, *Bowling Alone: America's Declining Social Capital*, 6 J. DEMOCRACY 65, 66–67 (1995).

114 *Id.* at 67.

115 One might say, as Viljoen describes privacy, that social capital is relational. Salomé Viljoen, *A Relational Theory of Data Governance*, 131 Yale L. J. 573, 580 (2021).

116 Mario Diani, *Social Movements and Social Capital: A Network Perspective on Movement Outcomes*, 2 MOBILIZATION 129 (2006).

117 John D. McCarthy & Mark Wolfson, *Consensus Movements, Conflict Movements, and the Cooptation of Civic and State Infrastructures, in* FRONTIERS IN SOCIAL MOVEMENT THEORY 278–79 (Aldon Morris & Carol McClurg Mueller eds., 1992).

118 ALDON D. MORRIS, *The Origins of the* CIVIL RIGHTS *Movement: Black Communities Organizing for Change*, 35–38 (1986).

119 Jo Freeman, *The Origins of the Women's Liberation Movement*, 78 AM. J. SOCIO. 792 (1973); *see also* Suzanne Staggenborg, *The Consequences of Professionalization and Formalization in the Pro-Choice Movement*, 53 AM. SOCIO. REV. 585, 593–94 (1988).

120 ANTHONY OBERSCHALL, SOCIAL CONFLICT AND SOCIAL MOVEMENTS 125 (1973); Bert Klandermans & Dirk Oegema, *Potentials, Networks, Motivations, and Barriers: Steps Towards Participation in Social Movements*, 52 AM. SOCIO. REV. 519, 520 (1987) (and citations found therein).

121 Doug McAdam, *Recruitment to High-Risk Activism: The Case of Freedom Summer*, 92 AM. J. SOCIO. 64, 86–87 (1986).

122 David A. Snow, Louis A. Zurcher Jr. & Sheldon Ekland-Olson, *Social Networks and Social Movements: A Microstructural Approach to Differential Recruitment*, 45 AM. SOCIO. REV. 787, 798 (1980).

123 Elisabeth S. Clemens & James M. Cook, *Politics and Institutionalism: Explaining Durability and Change*, 25 ANN. REV. OF SOCIOLOGY 441, 444 (1999).

124 Danial J. Solove, *A Taxonomy of Privacy*, 154 U. PA. L. REV. 477, 487 (2006) (describing what is referred to as the "dignitary harm" associated with privacy violations).

125 Anita L. Allen, *Coercing Privacy*, 40 WILLIAM & MARY L. REV. 723, 738–40 (1999).

126 Joseph Turow, Yphtach Lelkes, Nora A. Draper, and Ari Ezra Waldman, *Americans Can't Consent to Companies' Use of Their Data*, Annenberg School for Communication, University of Pennsylvania (2023).

3. POLITICAL PRIVACY, TRUST, AND TECHNOLOGY

1 Donatella Della Porta and Mario Diani, SOCIAL MOVEMENTS: AN INTRODUCTION, 105–07 (2d ed. 2006).

2 Rosa Ehrenreich, *Privacy and Power*, 89 GEO. L. J. 2047, 2051 (2001).

3 *See* Allyson Haynes Stuart, *Social Media, Manipulation, and Violence*, 15 S. C. J. OF INT'L L. & BUS. 100, 104–18 (2019).

4 Wilkes v. Wood (1763) 98 E.R. 489.

5 John Adams, THE WORKS OF JOHN ADAMS, 248 (Charles Francis Adams ed., vol. 10 1856).

6 Akhil Reed Amar, *Fourth Amendment First Principles*, 107 HARV. L. REV. 757, 772–75 (1994).

7 Joseph A. Adelman, *A Constitutional Conveyance of Intelligence, Public and Private: The Post Office, the Business of Printing, and the American Revolution*, 11 ENTERPRISE & SOCIETY 709, 724 (2010).

8 Postal Act, 1 Stat. 232 (1792).

9 Andrew Jackson, "Seventh Annual Message to Congress," in *A Compilation of the Messages and Papers of the Presidents*, ed. James D. Richardson (1902; Project Gutenberg, 2004), 3:176, www.gutenberg.org/files/11202/11202-h/11202-h.htm.

10 Samuel D. Warren and Louis D. Brandeis, *The Right to Privacy*, 4 HARV. L. REV. 193, 193 (1890). The Supreme Court has referred to this work by Warren and Brandeis as the "root article" in the development of the right to privacy in the law. Cox Broadcasting Corp. v. Cohn, 420 U.S. 469, 487 (1975).

11 *Id.* at 195.

12 *Id.*

13 *Id.* at 196.

14 *Id.* at 215.

15 *Id.*, at 205.

16 William L. Prosser, *Privacy*, 48 CAL. L. REV. 383, 383 (1960).

17 *See* NAACP v. Alabama ex rel. Patterson, 357 U.S. 449 (1958).

18 *See* NAACP v. Button, 371 U.S. 415 (1963).

19 John D. Inazu, *The Strange Origins of the Constitutional Right to Association*, 77 TENN. L. REV. 485, 485 (2010).

20 *Patterson*, 357 U.S. at 460–61 (citations omitted).

21 *Id.*

22 *Button*, 371 U.S. at 430.

23 *Id.* (citing *Patterson*, 357 U.S. at 460).

24 *Button*, 371 U.S. at 430 (citation omitted).

25 *Id.* at 431 (citation omitted).

26 *Id.*

27 Martin v. City of Struthers, 319 U.S. 141, 146 (1943).

28 *See* Griswold v. Connecticut, 381 U.S. 479 (1965).

29 *Id.* at 483 (citation omitted).

30 *Id.*

31 *Id.*

32 *Id.* at 482.

33 *Id.* at 484.

34 *Id.*

35 *Id.* at 485.

36 Planned Parenthood of Southeastern Pennsylvania v. Casey, 505 U.S. 833 (1992).

37 *Id.* at 851.

38 *Id.*

39 *Id.*

40 *Id.* at 916 (Stevens, J., concurring in part and dissenting in part).

41 *Id.* at 926–27 (Blackmun, J., concurring in part, concurring in the judgment in part, and dissenting in part) (citations omitted).

42 Obergefell v. Hodges, 576 U.S. 644 (2015).

43 *Id.* at 651–52.

44 *Id.* at 652.

45 *Id.* at 675.

46 *See* Luke A. Boso, *Dignity, Inequality, and Stereotypes*, 92 WASHINGTON L. REV. 1119, 1137–38 (2017).

47 Kenneth L. Karst, *The Freedom of Intimate Association*, 89 YALE L. J. 624, 636–37 (1980) (footnotes omitted).

48 *See* Zachary A. Kramer, *The New Sex Discrimination*, 63 DUKE L. J. 891, 945–46 (2014).

49 *See* Griswold v. Connecticut, 381 U.S. 479, 485–86 (1965).

50 West Virginia State Bd. of Educ. v. Barnette, 319 U.S. 624, 641–42 (1943).

51 Loving v. Virginia, 388 U.S. 1, 12 (1967); *see also* Obergefell, 576 U.S. at 674.

52 *Griswold*, 381 U.S. at 482 (collecting cases).

53 Dobbs v. Jackson Women's Health Organization, 597 U.S. 215, 231 (2022).

54 *Id.*, at Concurring Opinion by Thomas, J.

55 *Button*, 371 U.S. 415, 430–31 (1963).

56 Anthony V. Alfieri *(Un)Covering Identity in Civil Rights and Poverty Law*, 121 HARV. L. REV. 805, 806 (2008).

57 MARTHA C. NUSSBAUM, CREATIVE CAPABILITIES: THE HUMAN DEVELOPMENT APPROACH 33–34 (2011).

58 LAURENCE H. TRIBE, AMERICAN CONSTITUTIONAL LAW 1453 (2d ed. 1988).

59 Carpenter v. U.S., 585 U.S. 296, 309–10 (2018).

60 47 U.S.C. §§ 151–609.

61 Now codified at 18 U.S.C. §§2510–2522 (2000).

62 Electronic Communications Privacy Act of 1986, 18 U.S.C. §§ 2510–2523.

63 Orin S. Kerr, *The Next Generation Communications Privacy Act*, 162 Univ. of Penn. L. Rev. 373, 378–79 (2014).

64 565 U.S. 400 (2012).

65 RAY BRESCIA, THE FUTURE OF CHANGE: HOW TECHNOLOGY SHAPES SOCIAL REVOLUTIONS 16 (2020).

66 Julie E. Cohen, *What Privacy Is For*, 126 Harv. L. Rev. 1904, 1913 (2013).

67 *See generally* Mancur Olson, THE LOGIC OF COLLECTIVE ACTION: PUBLIC GOODS AND THE THEORY OF GROUPS (1965) (outlining dilemmas inherent in group efforts).

68 Keith Dowding, POWER 31 (1996).

69 Olson, *supra* note 67, at 54–55.

70 Garrett Hardin, *The Tragedy of the Commons*, 162 SCIENCE 1243, 1244 (1968).

71 Dennis D. Hirsch, *Privacy, Public Goods, and the Tragedy of the Trust Commons: A Response to Professors Fairfield and Engel*, 65 DUKE L. J. ONLINE 67, 70–74 (2016).

72 Hardin, *supra* note 70, at 1244–45.

73 Robert Axelrod, THE EVOLUTION OF COOPERATION 7–11 (1984).

74 Bert Klandermans, *The Social Construction of Protest and Multiorganizational Fields, in* FRONTIERS OF SOCIAL MOVEMENT THEORY, 89–90 (Aldon D. Morris and Carol McClurg Mueller eds., Yale Univ. Press 1992).

75 James L. Loomis, *Communication, the Development of Trust, and Cooperative Behavior*, 12 HUMAN RELATIONS 305, 314–15 (1959).

76 Issue Brief, Council of Economic Advisors, The Digital Divide and Economic Benefits of Broadband Access at 1 (Mar. 2016), https://obamawhitehouse.archives. gov/sites/default/files/page/files/20160308_broadband_cea_issue_brief.pdf.

77 Nicole B. Ellison, Charles Steinfield & Cliff Lampe, *The Benefits of Facebook "Friends:" Social Capital and College Students' Use of Online Social Network Sites*, 12 J. OF COMPUTER-MEDIATED COMMC'N 1143, 1153–65 (2007).

78 Diane Leenheer Zimmerman, *The "New" Privacy and the "Old": Is Applying the Tort Law of Privacy Like Putting High-Button Shoes on the Internet?*, 17 COMMC'N L. AND POL'Y 107, 126 (2012).

4. COMPARING INSTITUTIONS

1 DARON ACEMOGLU & JAMES ROBINSON, HOW NATIONS FAIL: THE ORIGINS OF POWER, PROSPERITY, AND POVERTY 74 (2013).

2 NEIL K. KOMESAR, IMPERFECT ALTERNATIVES: CHOOSING INSTITUTIONS IN LAW, ECONOMICS, AND PUBLIC POLICY 4–5 (1997).

3 *Id.*, at 4–7.

4 JOSEPH SCHUMPETER, CAPITALISM, SOCIALISM, AND DEMOCRACY 83 (3d ed. 1962).

5 KOMESAR, IMPERFECT ALTERNATIVES, *supra* note 2, at 123–26.

6 For criticism of judges that promote their own values over more carefully circumscribed principles, see JOHN HART ELY, DEMOCRACY AND DISTRUST 43–71 (1980).

7 *See, e.g.*, Alexander M. Bickel, *Foreword: The Passive Virtues*, 75 Harv. L. Rev. 40, 51–71 (1961) (discussing institutional legitimacy achieved through conformity with institutional norms and expectations).

8 26 N.Y.2d 219 (1970).

9 KOMESAR, IMPERFECT ALTERNATIVES, *supra* note 2, at 14–17.

10 26 N.Y.2d at 223, 227–28.

11 KOMESAR, IMPERFECT ALTERNATIVES, *supra* note 2, at 15–16.

12 Neil Komesar, *The Logic of the Law and the Essence of Economics: Reflections on Forty Years in the Wilderness*, 2013 WIS. L. REV. 265, 299–301 (2013) (hereinafter Komesar, *The Logic of the Law*).

13 *See generally* KOMESAR, IMPERFECT ALTERNATIVES, *supra* note 2, at 177–95.

14 *See, e.g.*, Mancur Olson, THE LOGIC OF COLLECTIVE ACTION: PUBLIC GOODS AND THE THEORY OF GROUPS (1965).

15 KOMESAR, IMPERFECT ALTERNATIVES, supra note 2, at 177–95.

16 KOMESAR, IMPERFECT ALTERNATIVES, *supra* note 2, at 8.

17 Neil K. Komesar, *Perils of Pandora: Further Reflections on Institutional Choice*, 22 L. & Soc. Inq. 999, 1008 (1997).

18 Neil K. Komesar, Law's Limits: Rule of Law and the Supply and Demand of Rights 59–60 (2001).

19 *Id.* at 74–76.

20 *Id.* at 75–76.

21 *Id.* at 79–81.

22 *Id.* at 80–81.

23 *Id.* at 81.

24 Daron Acemoglu & James A. Robinson, The Narrow Corridor: States, Societies, and the Fate of Liberty xv (2019).

25 *Id.* at xv–xvi;

26 *Id.*, at 450–53.

27 *Id*, at 147–50.

28 Nancy S. Kim, Wrap Contracts: Foundations and Ramifications 48–49 (2013).

29 On asymmetry of information in these arrangements, see Margaret Jane Radin, Boilerplate: The Fine Print, Vanishing Rights, and the Rule of Law 7–16 (2013).

30 Brett Frischmann & Evan Selinger, Re-engineering Humanity 209–10 (2018). Indeed, when faced with terms of service agreements, acceptance of such terms is the norm. *Id.* at 210

31 Michael L. Rustad & Thomas H. Koenig, *Towards a Global Data Privacy Standard*, 71 Fla. L. Rev. 365, 371–80 (2019).

32 Communications Decency Act of 1996, Pub. L. No. 104–104, tit. V, 110 Stat. 56, 133–43 (codified in scattered sections of Titles 18 and 47 of the U.S.C.).

33 Reno v. Am. Civil Liberties Union, 521 U.S. 844 (1997).

34 47 U.S.C. § 230(c) (2018). Jeff Kossoff, The Twenty-Six Words That Created the Internet (2019).

35 Anupam Chander, *How Law Made Silicon Valley*, 63 Emory L.J. 639, 651–52 (2014).

36 *See* Twitter v. Taamneh, 598 U.S. 471 (2023), and Gonzalez v. Google, 598 U.S. 617 (2023).

37 *Taamneh*, 598 U.S. at 505 (finding that social media companies did not "consciously, voluntarily, and culpably participate in or support the relevant wrongdoing," but suggesting that, if they had, it might lead to liability).

38 Jeremy B. Merrill, *One-Third of Top Websites Restrict Customers' Right to Sue*, N.Y. Times (Oct. 23, 2014)

39 AT&T Mobility LLC v. Concepcion, 563 U.S. 333, 344–52 (2011); American Express Co. v. Italian Colors Restaurant, 570 U.S. 228, 235–36 (2013).

40 *See, e.g., AT&T Mobility LLC*, 563 U.S. at 344–52; Judith Resnik, *Fairness in Numbers: A Comment on* AT&T v. Concepcion, Wal-Mart v. Dukes, *and* Turner v. Rogers, 125 Harv. L. Rev. 78, 122 (2011).

41 RADIN, BOILERPLATE, *supra* note 29, at 133–34.

42 David Horton & Andrea Cann Chandrasekher, *After the Revolution: An Empirical Study of Consumer Arbitration*, 104 GEO. L.J. 57 (2015)

43 Ann C. Hodges, *Can Compulsory Arbitration Be Reconciled with Section 7 Rights?*, 38 WAKE FOREST L. REV. 173, 218 (2003); David Dayen, *Tech Companies' Big Reveal: Hardly Anyone Files Arbitration Claims*, AM. PROSPECT (Nov. 26, 2019).

44 *But see* FTC v. Wyndham Worldwide Corp., 799 F.3d 236, 243–49 (3d Cir. 2015) (upholding FTC authority to prosecute companies for data breaches).

45 *See, e.g.*, Kara Swisher, *Put Another Zero on Facebook's Fine. Then We Can Talk*, N.Y. TIMES (April 25, 2019).

46 Press Release, Letitia James, Attorney General, New York, AG James Sues Dunkin' Donuts for Glazing over Cyberattacks Targeting Thousands (Sep. 26, 2019), https://ag.ny.gov/press-release/2019/ag-james-sues-dunkin-donuts-glazing-over-cyberattacks-targeting-thousands

47 RADIN, BOILERPLATE, *supra* note 29, at 16.

48 *See, e.g.*, In re Google Inc. Cookie Placement Consumer Privacy Litigation, 806 F.3d 125 (3d Cir. 2015) (holding that technology company could face potential liability for breaches of its own end-user agreements).

5. BLENDED RULES, HYBRID INSTITUTIONS

1 Joel Thayer, *Privacy—a Big Tech Sleight of Hand*, THE HILL (May 27, 2022), https://thehill.com/opinion/cybersecurity/3503439-privacy-a-big-tech-sleight-of-hand.

2 NEIL K. KOMESAR, IMPERFECT ALTERNATIVES: CHOOSING INSTITUTIONS IN LAW, ECONOMICS, AND PUBLIC POLICY 6 (1997).

3 Nathan D. Harp, *Imperfect Immunity: How State Attorneys General Could Sue Firearm Manufacturers under the Predicate Exemption to the Protection of Lawful Commerce in Arms Act*, 30 CORNELL J. L. & PUB. POL'Y 797, 802–07 (2021) (describing federal and state statutory immunity afforded to gun manufacturers).

4 Pub. L. No. 104–99 (1996).

5 INSTITUTE FOR THE ADVANCEMENT OF THE LEGAL SYSTEM, FAQS: JUDGES IN THE UNITED STATES (June 2012), https://iaals.du.edu/sites/default/files/documents/publications/judge_faq.pdf.

6 *See, e.g.*, William J. Brennan, Jr., *State Constitutions and the Protection of Individual Rights*, 90 HARV. L. REV. 489 (1977) (describing state courts as a potential locus of advocacy when the Supreme Court appears hostile to certain claims).

7 FRANCES FOX PIVEN & RICHARD A. CLOWARD, POOR PEOPLE'S MOVEMENTS: WHY THEY SUCCEED, HOW THEY FAIL 24 (1977).

8 Civil Rights Act of 1964, § 701 et seq., 42 U.S.C.A. § 2000e et seq.

9 Pub. L. No. 89–110, 79 Stat. 437 (codified as amended at 52 U.S.C. §§ 10101–10702 [2018]).

10 42 U.S.C.A. §§ 3601 et seq. (1968).

11 NEIL K. KOMESAR, IMPERFECT ALTERNATIVES: CHOOSING INSTITUTIONS IN LAW, ECONOMICS, AND PUBLIC POLICY 6 (1997).

12 Guido Calabresi & A. Douglas Melamed, *Property Rules, Liability Rules, and Inalienability: One View of the Cathedral*, 85 HARV. L. REV. 1089, 1093 (1972).

13 *Id.*, at 1092

14 *Id.*

15 *Id.*

16 *Id.*

17 *Id.*, at 1107.

18 *See* Calabresi & Melamed, *supra* note 12, at 1106–15.

19 A body of scholarship, Critical Institutionalism, refers to this approach as "bricolage," the concept of constructing something new out of existing elements. *See* Frances Cleaver and Jessica de Koning, *Furthering Critical Institutionalism*, 9 INT'L J. OF THE COMMONS 1, 4–5 (2015). On the concept of bricolage, see CLAUDE LÉVI-STRAUSS, THE SAVAGE MIND 16–36 (University of Chicago Press 1966). For an application of bricolage to cultural theory and its effect on ideology, see generally JACK M. BALKIN, CULTURAL SOFTWARE: A THEORY OF IDEOLOGY (1988).

20 Garrett Hardin, *The Tragedy of the Commons*, 162 SCIENCE 1243, 1244 (1968).

21 Jeffrey Hiles, *The Implied Warranty of Habitability: A Dream Deferred*, 48 UMKC L. REV. 237 (1980). *See also* Francis S. L'Abbate, *Recovery Under the Implied Warranty of Habitability*, 10 Fordham URB. L.J. 285, 291–92 (1982); Javins v. First Nat'l Realty Corp., 428 F.2d 1071, 1072–73 (D.C. Cir. 1970).

22 *See, e.g.*, Lemle v. Breeden, 462 P.2d 470, 473–75 (Haw. 1969) (describing emergence of the warranty of habitability as a response to the needs of urban settings).

23 Jean C. Love, *Landlord's Liability for Defective Premises: Caveat Lessee, Negligence, or Strict Liability*, 1975 WIS. L. REV. 19, 99 (1975).

24 *Id.*

25 Hiles, *supra* note 21, at 241.

26 42 U.S.C.A. §§ 3601 et seq.

27 42 U.S.C.A. §§ 12101 et seq.

28 *See, e.g.*, Trentacost v. Brussel, 412 A.2d 436, 445 (1980).

29 U.S. Dep't of Housing & Urb. Dev't, Real Estate Settlement Procedures Act (RESPA): Rule to Simplify and Improve the Process of Obtaining Mortgages and Reduce Consumer Settlement Costs, 73 FED. REG. 68203, 68238 (2008).

30 Joseph M. Kolari & Jonathan D. Jerison, *The Home Mortgage Disclosure Act: Its History, Evolution, and Limitations*, 59 CONSUMER FIN. L. Q. REP. 189, 193–95 (2005).

31 42 U.S.C.A. 3601 *et seq.*

32 15 U.S.C.A. §§ 1691, *et seq.*

33 15 U.S.C.A. § 1601, *et seq.*

34 12 U.S.C.A. § 2601, *et seq.*

35 12 U.S.C.A. § 2801, *et seq.*

36 *See, e.g.*, 12 U.S.C. §2601(a).

37 12 U.S.C.A. §2601(a)

38 Richard D. Marsico, *Looking Back and Looking Ahead as the Home Mortgage Disclosure Act Turns Thirty-Five: The Role of Public Disclosure of Lending Data in a Time of Financial Crisis*, 29 REV. BANKING & FIN. L. 205 (2009).

39 Vincent Di Lorenzo, *Legislative Heart and Phase Transitions: An Exploratory Study of Congress and Minority Interests*, 38 WM. & MARY L. REV. 1729, 1766–67 (1997).

40 Handy v. Anchor Mortg. Corp, 464 F.3d 760, 765 (7th Cir. 2006) (citations omitted).

41 Rachel Godsil, *Viewing the Cathedral from Behind the Color Line: Property Rules, Liability Rules, and Environmental Racism*, 53 EMORY L. J. 1807, 1858 (2004) (citation omitted).

42 *See* Jerry Frug, *The Geography of Community*, 48 STAN. L. REV. 1047, 1081–89 (1996).

43 *See, e.g.,* DANIEL R. MANDELKER, LAND USE LAW ch. 5 (4th ed. 1997)

44 Andrea J. Boyack, *Limiting the Collective Right to Exclude*, 44 FORDHAM URB. L.J. 451, 486 (2017).

45 DOUGLAS S. MASSEY ET AL., CLIMBING MOUNT LAUREL: THE STRUGGLE FOR AFFORDABLE HOUSING AND SOCIAL MOBILITY IN AN AMERICAN SUBURB 121 (2013).

46 334 U.S. 1 (1948).

6. ZONING CYBERSPACE

1 ZAC GERSHBERG & SEAN ILLING, THE PARADOX OF DEMOCRACY: FREE SPEECH, OPEN MEDIA, AND PERILOUS PERSUASION 6 (2022).

2 *Id.*

3 *Id.* at 2–3.

4 ID., at 39.

5 *Id.* at 7.

6 *Id.* at 1.

7 *Id.* at 190.

8 *Id.* at 2.

9 *Id.*

10 *Id.* at 7.

11 *Id.*

12 *Id.*

13 *Id.*

14 *Id.* at 2.

15 What has come to be known as the Communications Decency Act appears as Section 230 of the Telecommunications Act of 1996. 47 U.S.C.A. §§ 151 et seq.

16 Guido Calabresi & A. Douglas Melamed, *Property Rules, Liability Rules, and Inalienability: One View of the Cathedral*, 85 HARV. L. REV. 1089, 1106–10 (1972).

17 *Id.* at 1124–27.

18 *Id.*

19 For a discussion of the Calabresi–Melamed analysis in light of the differences between *ex ante* and *ex post* approaches, see Lucian Arye Bebchuk, *Property Rights and Liability Rules: The Ex Ante View of the Cathedral*, 100 MICH. L. REV. 601 (2001).

20 Ian Ayres & Alan Schwartz, *The No-Reading Problem in Consumer Contract Law*, 66 STAN. L. REV. 545, 579–95 (2014).

21 *Id.*, at 580–87.

22 John Kozup, Charles R. Taylor, Michael L. Capella & Jeremy Kees, *Sound Disclosures: Assessing When a Disclosure is Worthwhile*, 31 J. PUB. POL'Y & MARKETING 313, 315–17 (2012); Vanessa G. Perry & Pamela M. Blumenthal, *Understanding the Fine Print: The Need for Effective Testing of Mandatory Mortgage Loan Disclosures*, 31 J. PUB. POL'Y & MARKETING 305, 307 (2012).

23 Omri Ben-Shahar & Carl E. Schneider, *The Failure of Mandated Disclosure*, U. PA. L. REV. 647, 665–71 (2011); on measures for overcoming disclosure's failures, see *id.* at 743–47.

24 LAWRENCE LESSIG, CODE AND OTHER LAWS OF CYBERSPACE 160 (1999); Michael J. Madison, *Legal-Ware: Contract and Copyright in the Digital Age*, 67 FORDHAM L. REV. 1025, 1135 n.444 (1998); David R. Johnson & David Post, *Law and Borders—The Rise of Law in Cyberspace*, 48 STAN. L. REV. 1367, 1379 (1996).

25 Lawrence Lessig, *The Zones of Cyberspace*, 48 STAN. L. REV. 1403, 1409 (1996).

26 Lawrence Lessig & Paul Resnick, *Zoning Speech on the Internet: A Legal and Technical Model*, 98 MICH. L. REV. (1999).

27 *Id.*

28 *See, e.g.*, DANIEL J. SOLOVE, THE DIGITAL PERSON: TECHNOLOGY AND PRIVACY IN THE INFORMATION AGE 103–04 (2004).

29 Chloe Aiello, *Tech Pioneer Jaron Lanier Says Companies Should Pay for Data: "Let's Get Out of the Manipulation Business,"* CNBC (June 21, 2018), www.cnbc.com/2018/06/21/tech-pioneer-jaron-lanier-says-companies-should-pay-for-data.html.

30 MARGARET JANE RADIN, CONTESTED COMMODITIES 79–84 (1996); Julie E. Cohen, *Examined Lives: Informational Privacy and the Subject as Object*, 52 STAN. L. REV. 1373, 1391 (2000); Jessica Litman, *Information Privacy/Information Property*, 52 STAN. L. REV. 1283, 1303 (2000).

31 Uri Gneezy & Aldo Rustichini, *A Fine Is a Price*, 29 J. OF LEG. STUD. 1 (2000).

32 Ayres & Schwartz, *supra* note 20, at 579–95 (2014); John Kozup, Charles R. Taylor, Michael L. Capella & Jeremy Kees, *Sound Disclosures: Assessing When a Disclosure is Worthwhile*, 31 J. PUB. POL'Y & MARKETING 313, 315–17 (2012); Vanessa G. Perry & Pamela M. Blumenthal, *Understanding the Fine Print: The Need for Effective Testing of Mandatory Mortgage Loan Disclosures*, 31 J. PUB. POL'Y & MARKETING 305, 307 (2012).

33 *See, e.g.*, Kashmir Hill, *How Target Figured Out A Teen Girl Was Pregnant Before Her Father Did*, FORBES (Feb. 16, 2012).

34 Mark Mazzetti, Nicole Perlroth & Ronen Bergman, *It Seemed Like a Popular Chat App. It's Secretly a Spy Tool*, N.Y. TIMES (Dec. 22, 2019).

35 Twitter v. Taamneh, 598 U.S. 471 (2023), and Gonzalez v. Google, 598 U.S. 617 (2023).

36 Carol M. Rose, *Trust in the Mirror of Betrayal*, 75 B.U. L. REV. 531, 531–32 (1995); ROBERT AXELROD, THE EVOLUTION OF COOPERATION 19–20 (1984); Dan M. Kahan, *The Logic of Reciprocity: Trust, Collective Action, and Law*, 102 MICH. L. REV. 71, 71–72 (2003).

37 PAUL M. SCHWARTZ & JOEL R. REIDENBERG, DATA PRIVACY LAW: A STUDY OF UNITED STATES DATA PROTECTION, §§ 5-1-5-5 (1996).

38 In re: Nickelodeon Consumer Privacy Litigation, 827 F.3d 262, 293–95 (Cir. 2015) *cert. denied sub nom.* C.A.F. v. Viacom Inc., 137 S.Ct. 624 (2017).

39 Cass R. Sunstein, *Empirically Informed Regulation*, 78 U. CHI. L. REV. 1349, 1369–70 (2011).

40 Jerry L. Mashaw & David L. Harfst, *From Command and Control to Collaboration and Deference: The Transformation of Auto Safety Regulation*, 34 YALE J. ON REG. 167, 258–60 (2017).

41 For a description—and critique—of the restaurant grading system, see Daniel E. Ho, *Fudging the Nudge: Information Disclosure and Restaurant Grading*, 122 YALE L. J. 574 (2012).

42 WOODROW HARTZOG, PRIVACY'S BLUEPRINT: THE BATTLE TO CONTROL THE DESIGN OF NEW TECHNOLOGIES 176–77 (2018).

43 S. Hatfield, *Google's "Google's Use" Is Your Illusion: Proposing an Agency Analysis to Trademark Infringement Lawsuits AgainstOnline Advertising Service Providers*, 25 TEMP. INT'L & COMP. L. J. 423, 426–28 (2011).

44 Ayres & Schwartz, *supra* note 20, at 552–54.

45 *See, e.g.*, IAN AYRES & JOHN BRAITHWAITE, RESPONSIVE REGULATION: TRANSCENDING THE DEREGULATION DEBATE 105–08 (1992).

46 42 U.S.C.A. § 2000e-3(a).

47 14 CFR § 121.317

48 Arnold W. Reitze, Jr., *The Volkswagen Air Pollution Emissions Litigation*, 46 ENVTL. L. REP. NEWS & ANALYSIS 10564 (July 2016).

7. INSTITUTIONAL CONVERGENCE

1 Paul Brest, *The Power of Theories of Change*, STAN. SOC. INNOV. REV. 46, 49 (Spring 2010)

2 347 U.S. 483 (1954).

3 Herbert Wechsler, *Toward Neutral Principles of Constitutional Law*, 73 HARV. L. REV. 1, 15 (1959).

4 *Id.* at 34.

5 *Id.* (footnote omitted).

6 Derrick A. Bell, Jr., Brown v. Board of Education *and the Interest-Convergence Dilemma*, 93 HARV. L. REV. 518, 523 (1980).

7 *Id.* at 524–25.

8 Bell, *supra* note 6, at 522–28.

9 *See generally* David A. Singleton, *Interest Convergence and the Education of African-American Boys in Cincinnati: Motivating Suburban Whites to Embrace Interdistrict Education Reform*, 34 N. KY. L. REV. 663 (2007).

10 For a collection of scholarship applying the Interest-Convergence Thesis to other contexts, see Justin Driver, *Rethinking the Interest-Convergence Thesis*, 105 NW. U. L. REV. 149, 154–55, nn.25–28 (2011).

11 *See* Mary L. Dudziak, *Desegregation as a Cold War Imperative*, 41 STAN. L. REV. 61, 118–19 (1988) (providing historical support for Bell's theory regarding elite interests related to the Court's decision in *Brown v. Board of Education*).

12 On the relationship between public opinion and the Supreme Court's Second Amendment jurisprudence, see Kristin A. Goss & Matthew J. Lacombe, *Do Courts Change Politics? Heller and the Limits of Policy Feedback Effects*, 69 EMORY L.J. 881, 892–98 (2020).

13 Bell, *supra* note 6.

14 *See* Dudziak, *supra* note 11 (detailing convergence of interests behind the *Brown* decision).

15 Dudziak, *supra* note 11.

16 For a description of the work of some of the judges who helped advance civil rights in the legal campaign against the Jim Crow system, see JACK BASS, UNLIKELY HEROES (1981).

17 Brad Snyder, *Frankfurter and Popular Constitutionalism*, 47 U.C. DAVIS L. REV. 343, 390–93 (2013).

18 *See* Brown v. Board of Education, 349 U.S. 294, 301 (1955) ("*Brown II*") (directing governments to end school segregation with "all deliberate speed").

19 See Michael Schwarz & Shuva Paul, *Resource Mobilization versus Mobilization of People: Why Consensus Movements Cannot Be Instruments of Change*, in FRONTIERS IN SOCIAL MOVEMENT THEORY 206 (Aldon D. Morris & Carol McClurg Mueller eds. 1992).

20 Mark Tushnet, *What Really Happened in* Brown v. Board of Education, 91 COLUM. L. REV. 1867, 1867 (1991) (arguing "gradual segregation . . . provided the opportunity for massive resistance in the Deep South and for token desegregation elsewhere").

21 According to legal scholar Cheryl Harris, that minimal antidiscrimination mandate "engendered increasingly protracted battles with social and political forces that defiantly resisted court-ordered integration." Cheryl Harris, *Whiteness As Property*, 106 HARV. L. REV. 1709, 1755 (1993) (arguing weak enforcement mandate led to protracted legal battles over desegregation).

22 Sweatt v. Painter, 339 U.S. 629 (1950); Plessy v. Ferguson, 163 U.S. 537 (1896).

23 Snyder, *supra* note 17, at 390–91.

24 *Id.*

25 For the litigation in the trial courts that led to the Supreme Court's ultimate ruling in *Brown*, see RICHARD KLUGER, SIMPLE JUSTICE: THE HISTORY OF *Brown v. Board of Education* AND BLACK AMERICA'S STRUGGLE FOR EQUALITY 481–554 (1975).

26 *Id.*

27 *Id.*

28 *See* Driver, *supra* note 10, at 156–57.

29 On the importance of a social movement organization's belief in its own efficacy, see SAUL ALINSKY, RULES FOR RADICALS: A PRAGMATIC PRIMER FOR REALISTIC RADICALS 20 (1971).

30 Dudziak, *supra* note 11.

31 As mentioned above, the Court issued two decisions in the *Brown* litigation, with the second addressing enforcement of the prior order. I will refer simply to "the decision" in *Brown* here for the sake of simplicity.

32 GERALD N. ROSENBERG, THE HOLLOW HOPE: CAN COURTS BRING ABOUT SOCIAL CHANGE? (3d ed. 2023).

33 For a critique of Rosenberg's assessment that the decision in *Brown* did not help catalyze change, see David Schultz & Stephen E. Gottlieb, *Legal Functionalism and Social Change: A Reassessment of Rosenberg's* The Hollow Hope: Can Courts Bring About Social Change?, 12 J. L. & POL'Y 63 (1996).

34 John D. McCarthy & Mayer N. Zald, *Resource Mobilization and Social Movements: A Partial Theory*, 82 AM. J. OF SOC. 1212, 1216 (1977).

35 DOUGLASS C. NORTH, INSTITUTIONS, INSTITUTIONAL CHANGE, AND ECONOMIC PERFORMANCE 7 (1990).

36 *Id.*

37 Cass R. Sunstein, *On the Expressive Function of Law*, 144 U. PA. L. REV. 2030–31 (1996) (describing norm entrepreneurship).

38 John D. McCarthy & Mark Wolfson, *Resource Mobilization by Local Social Movement Organizations: Agency, Strategy, and Organization in the Movement against Drunk Driving*, 61 AM. SOC. REV. 1070 (1996).

39 Memorandum from Lewis F. Powell, Jr., to Eugene B. Syndor, Jr., U.S. Chamber of Commerce, Washington, D.C., Attack on American Free Enterprise System 1 (Aug. 23, 1971).

40 *Id.* at 1.

41 *Id.* at 2.

42 *Id.* at 2–3.

43 *Id.* at 3.

44 *Id.*

45 *Id.* at 6.

46 *Id.* at 8.

47 *Id.*

48 *Id.*

49 *Id.* at 9.

50 *Id.* at 11.

51 *Id.*, at 15–16.

52 *Id.* at 16–17.

53 *Id.* at 17.

54 *Id.*

55 *Id.*

56 *Id.*

57 *Id.*

58 *Id.* at 21.

59 *Id.* (emphasis in original).

60 *Id.*

61 *Id.* at 25–26.

62 *Id.* at 26.

63 *See, e.g.*, Mark Schmitt, *The Legend of the Powell Memo*, THE AM. PROSPECT (Apr. 27, 2005) (describing debate over the impact of Powell's recommendations).

64 ERICA CHENOWETH, CIVIL RESISTANCE: WHAT EVERYONE NEEDS TO KNOW (2021). This work builds on prior work by Chenoweth with co-author Maria Stephan: ERICA CHENOWETH & MARIA STEPHAN, WHY CIVIL RESISTANCE WORKS: THE STRATEGIC LOGIC OF NONVIOLENT CONFLICT (Kindle ed. 2012).

65 CHENOWETH, *supra* note 64, at 113.

66 *Id.* at 102.

67 *Id.*

68 *Id.*

69 *Id.* at 103.

70 *Id.*

71 *Id.*

72 CHENOWETH & STEPHAN, *supra* note 64, at Loc. 969.

73 *Id.*, at Loc. 969.

74 GENE SHARP, FROM DICTATORSHIP TO DEMOCRACY: A CONCEPTUAL FRAMEWORK FOR LIBERATION 32 (2012).

75 Winston S. Churchill, Speech at the Lord Mayor's Day Luncheon at the Mansion House, The Bright Gleam of Victory (Nov. 10, 1942).

76 NATHANIEL FRANK, AWAKENING: HOW GAYS AND LESBIANS BROUGHT MARRIAGE EQUALITY TO AMERICA 169 (2017).

77 *Id.* at 165.

78 Defense of Marriage Act, Pub. L. No. 104–99 (1996).

79 FRANK, *supra* note 76, at 164.

80 *Id.*

81 *Id.* at 177.

82 *Id.* at 186–87.

83 Molly Ball, *The Marriage Plot: Inside This Year's Epic Campaign for Gay Equality*, ATLANTIC (Dec. 11, 2012), www.theatlantic.com/politics/archive/2012/12/the-marriage-plot-inside-this-years-epic-campaign-for-gay-equality/265865.

84 *Id.*

85 *Id.*

86 ARLIE RUSSELL HOCHSCHILD, STRANGERS IN THEIR OWN LAND: AN-
    GER AND MOURNING ON THE AMERICAN RIGHT 137–38 (2016).

87 FRANK, *supra* note 76, at 96, 162–63.

88 Richard Socarides, *Fighting, and Winning, Against Prop 8*, THE NEW YORKER
    (Apr. 19, 2014) (describing team of David Boies and Ted Olson who joined forces
    to challenge Proposition 8 in the courts).

89 For a description of the grassroots effort around the Maine ballot initiative in
    2012, see RAY BRESCIA, THE FUTURE OF CHANGE: HOW TECHNOLOGY
    SHAPES SOCIAL REVOLUTIONS 129–45 (2020).

90 Ball, *supra* note 83.

91 FRANK, *supra* note 76, at 285–87.

92 Rev. Dr. Nancy Wilson, *SCOTUS and Marriage Equality—The Sky Is Not Falling*,
    HUFF. POST (Apr 28, 2015, 03:59 PM EDT, updated Dec. 6, 2017), www.huffpost.
    com/entry/scotus-and-marriage-equal_b_7154012.

93 On images of gay and lesbian characters in popular culture, see FRANK, *supra*
    note 76, at 123–24.

94 United States. v. Windsor, 570 U.S. 744, 774 (2013).

95 570 U.S. at 799–802 (Scalia, J., dissenting).

96 *See, e.g.*, Jack M. Balkin, Brown, *Social Movements, and Social Change*, in
    CHOOSING EQUALITY: ESSAYS AND NARRATIVES ON THE DESEGREGA-
    TION EXPERIENCE 246 (Robert L. Hayman Jr. & Leland Ware eds., 2009).

97 Obergefell v. Hodges, 577 U.S. 644 (2015).

98 *Id.*, at 670

99 *Id.*

100 *Id.* at 646–47.

101 517 U.S. 620 (1996).

102 539 U.S. 558 (2003).

103 James G. Ennis & Richard Schreuer, *Mobilizing Weak Support for Social Move-
    ments: The Role of Grievance, Efficacy, and Cost*, 66 SOCIAL FORCES 390 (1987).
    According to Bandura, individual efficacy is a critical element of an individual's
    willingness to attempt to accomplish a specific goal. Albert Bandura, *Self-Efficacy
    Mechanism in Human Agency*, 37 AM. PSYCHOLOGIST 122 (1982).

104 For a description of this "new localism" in labor advocacy, see Andrew Elmore,
    Labor's New Localism, 95 S. CAL. L. REV. 253 (2021).

105 For an overview of recent efforts to secure a right to counsel in eviction cases for
    low-income tenants in various localities across the United States, see Natalie D.
    Fulk, *The Rising Popularity of the Right to Counsel in Eviction Cases*, 35 NOTRE
    DAME J. L. ETHICS & PUB. POL'Y 325 (2021).

106 Elisabeth S. Clemens & James M. Cook, *Politics and Institutionalism: Explaining
    Durability and Change*, 25 ANN. REV. OF SOCIOLOGY 441, 457 (1999).

107 SUNSTEIN, HOW CHANGE HAPPENS, ix (2019).

108 MALCOLM GLADWELL, THE TIPPING POINT: HOW LITTLE THINGS CAN
    MAKE A BIG DIFFERENCE 9 (2000).

109 ERNEST HEMINGWAY, THE SUN ALSO RISES 141 (1926).

110 On state governments banning TikTok on government-issued devices, see Brian Fung & Christopher Hickey, *TikTok Access from Government Devices Now Restricted in More than Half of US States*, CNN (Jan. 6, 2023), www.cnn.com/2023/01/16/tech/tiktok-state-restrictions/index.html. On colleges and universities prohibiting their students from using TikTok on school devices and wifi networks, see Mariah Espada, *Universities Are Banning TikTok on Their Campuses. Here's Why*, TIME (Jan. 23, 2023), https://time.com/6249522/public-universities-banning-tiktok.

111 *See State Laws Related to Digital Privacy*, NAT'L CONF. STATE LEGISLATURES (June 7, 2022) (noting California, Virginia, and Utah are among the states adopting privacy legislation).

112 For an overview of California's privacy bill and the European General Data Protection Regulation (GDPR), see Navdeep K. Singh, *What You Need to Know About the CCPA and the European Union's GDPR*, AM. BAR ASS'N (Feb 26, 2020), www.americanbar.org/groups/litigation/resources/newsletters/minority-trial/what-you-need-know-about-ccpa-european-unions-gdpr.

113 Alice Miranda Ollstein, Megan Messerly & Jessica Piper, *The Supreme Court Dismantled Roe. States Are Restoring It One by One*, POLITICO (Nov. 9, 2023) (noting success of abortion-access referenda, even in traditionally conservative states) www.politico.com/news/2023/11/09/abortion-rights-elections-red-states-00126225

114 Daniel Kahneman & Amos Tversky, *Prospect Theory: An Analysis of Decision Under Risk*, 47 ECONOMETRICA 263, 277–80 (1979) (describing prospect theory).

115 *See* American Privacy Rights Act of 2024, S. ____, 118th. Cong. (2024) ("discussion draft"), https://d1dth6e84htgma.cloudfront.net/American_Privacy_Rights_Act_of_2024_Discussion_Draft_0ec8168a66.pdf.

116 For an overview of the kosher system's evolution in the United States, see TIMOTHY D. LYTTON, KOSHER: PRIVATE REGULATION IN THE AGE OF INDUSTRIAL FOOD (2013).

117 For a description of this type of private certification, see Suntae Kim et al., *Why Companies Are Becoming B Corporations*, HARV. BUS. REV. (Jun. 17, 2016).

INDEX

Abolitionist Movement, 10–11, 14, 53
academic institutions, 5, 156–57, 170, 172, 202n110. See also *Brown v. Board of Education*
accountability, 123, 134; digital zoning and, 132, 138–41
Acemoglu, Daron, 22, 39–40, 69, 74–75, 81
activism, 4–5, 27–28, 45, 149–52, 158; change and, 160–62; social capital and, 47. *See also* local activism
Adams, John, 52
adjudicative immunity, extractive institutions and, 79–80
advertising, 17, 137, 139; identity and, 5–6, 178n23
advocacy, 6, 12–13, 88–90, 94, 149, 166; change and, 83–85, 102, 142, 160–64; community, 5, 11, 26–27, 36, 40, 43, 47, 72, 156–57, 161–65; elites and, 143, 145–46; federal government and, 171–72; property law and, 167–68; reforms and, 102–3, 111; state government and, 167–70
affiliation, identity and, 7, 34–35, 59
Alford, Robert, 39
algorithms, 18, 79, 136–37; digital zoning and, 131–32; transparency of, 125
Amar, Akhil Reed, 52
American Privacy Rights Act of 2024, 172
anonymity, of data, 137
Appiah, Kwame Anthony, 33
artificial intelligence, 1–2, 12, 30, 38, 113
associations, 8–10, 153; attachments and, 47, 49; freedom of, 13, 54–56, 144;

identity and, 29–30, 34, 41–42, 47–48, 58–59; as institutions, 37
asymmetry, 122; collective action problems and, 103; of information, 105–7, 120, 138; in relations, 77–78
attachments: associational, 47, 49; autonomy and, 32–34
"Attack on American Free Enterprise System," 154–57
authoritarianism, social movements and, 158–59
autonomy, 31, 36–37, 50, 59, 138; attachments and, 32–34; collective identity and, 35; democracy and, 117. *See also* self-determination

Bandura, Albert, 33–34, 201n103
Beecher, Lyman, 14
Bell, Derrick, 24, 142–46. *See also* Interest-Convergence Thesis
Berlin, Isaiah, 9
Beuchler, Steven, 34
Biden, Joe, 95
biometric data, 2, 128–29
Blackmun, Harry, 57
Boomer v. Atlantic Cement Co., 72–73, 119
Brandeis, Louis, 53–54, 118
breaches, 77–83, 132, 172; digital zoning and, 133–34, 136–37
Brest, Paul, 142
Brown v. Board of Education, 96–97, 144–52, 160–61, 199n31; marriage equality and, 164. *See also* Civil Rights Movement

Reagan, Ronald, 154

Real Estate Settlement Procedures Act (RESPA), 107–8

reforms, 20, 23, 99–100; advocacy and, 102–3, 111; policy, 24, 71–72, 89–92, 102, 104; political privacy and, 48–49, 89–90; property law, 107–8; rules and, 102; social change and, 87–88, 96–97

regulation, 19, 26–27, 99, 106–7; enforcement and, 140; of guns, 4–5, 90, 146; by institutions, 67–68; laws and, 71–73; private entities and, 17–18, 111; protections in, 105; punishment and, 119–20

relations, 11, 39, 45–47, 89; asymmetry in, 77–78; laws and, 105–7, 110

RESPA. See Real Estate Settlement Procedures Act

restrictive covenants, 109–10

Richards, Neil, 1

rights: discrimination and, 144–45; identity and, 16–17, 57–58; negative, 49, 59; positive, 9, 59, 77; to privacy, 8, 53–54

risks, 5–6, 23, 128, 147–48; of freedom, 113–14; of policy change, 89–90, 92

Robinson, James, 22, 39–40, 69, 74–75, 81

Rodgers, Cathy McMorris, 171–72

Rolling Stones, 5–6, 178n23

Romer, Paul, 16

Roosevelt, Franklin D., 96

Rosenberg, Gerald, 150–51, 160

rules: for collective action problems, 99–102; enforcement of, 110–11, 122–23; inalienability, 100–101, 105, 109–10; institutional settings and, 101–2; as institutions, 100, 104; property, 100–101, 105, 109, 118–19, 121–22; for protection of privacy, 87, 118–26; typology of, 100–103, 105, 108–9, 112, 115–16, 118

sale, of personal information, 27, 29–30, 76–77, 128–31

Sandel, Michael, 32

Sandy Hook school shooting, 4–5

Scalia, Antonin, 164

Schlesinger, Arthur, 36

search. See internet search

self-determination, 5–8, 36, 49, 61–62, 117; democracy and, 31–32; limits on, 127; political privacy and, 24–25, 127; technology and, 113–14

Selinger, Evan, 77

Sen, Amartya, 33, 34, 36

Sharp, Gene, 159

Shelley v. Kraemer, 110

simplicity, in contracts, 120–21, 123, 138–39

Smith, Brad, 26

social capital, 45–47, 187n115

social change, 11, 69, 157; identity and, 127, 163; institutional change and, 46, 48–49; institutional convergence and, 151–52, 173–74; institutional perspective and, 24–25, 40–49; institutional spillover and, 91–92; Interest-Convergence Thesis and, 142–43, 145; laws and, 54–55; reforms and, 87–88, 96–97; success and, 168–69; Supreme Court and, 150–51; tipping point of, 148–49, 164, 168–69

social media, 1, 18–19, 170; digital zoning and, 126; Facebook, 26–29, 80; liability and, 192n37; manipulation and, 86–87, 130–31; statutory immunity and, 78–79; TikTok, 14; Twitter, 139

social movements, 4–5, 7, 40, 49; Abolitionist Movement, 10–11, 14, 53; authoritarianism and, 158–59; collective identity and, 35; identity and, 31, 35–36, 41–42; influence of, 153–54; institutional change and, 30–31, 46–48, 152–53; institutions and, 20–21; labor, 15, 42, 55, 156–57; leaders of, 152–53; manipulation of, 28–30; marriage equality, 43, 57–58, 90–91, 97, 154, 160–66, 170; protests and, 1, 13, 27–28, 158–59; success of, 42–47; technology and, 10–13, 61. See also Civil Rights Movement

ABOUT THE AUTHOR

RAY BRESCIA is the Associate Dean for Research and Intellectual Life and the Hon. Harold R. Tyler Professor in Law & Technology at Albany Law School. He is the author or editor of *The Future of Change: How Technology Shapes Social Revolutions, Crisis Lawyering: Effective Legal Advocacy in Emergency Situations, How Cities Will Save the World: Urban Innovation in the Face of Population Flows, Climate Change, and Economic Inequality,* and *Lawyer Nation: The Past, Present, and Future of the American Legal Profession.*